Sacred Players

Sacred Players

The Politics of Response in the
Middle English Religious Drama

Heather Hill-Vásquez

The Catholic University of America Press
Washington, D.C.

Library of Congress Cataloging-in-Publication Data
Hill-Vásquez, Heather.
  Sacred players : the politics of response in the Middle English religious
drama / Heather Hill-Vásquez.
    p. cm.
  Includes bibliographical references and index.
  ISBN-13: 978-0-8132-1497-9 (cloth : alk. paper)
  ISBN-10: 0-8132-1497-1 (cloth : alk. paper)   1. Mysteries and
miracle-plays, English—History and criticism.   2. English drama—to
1500—History and criticism.   3. Christianity and literature—England—
History—to 1500.   4. Christian drama, English (Middle)—History
and criticism.   5. Theater—England—History—Medieval, 500–1500.
6. Civilization, Medieval, in literature.   7. Cycles (Literature)   I. Title.
  PR643.M5H55 2007
    822'.05160901—dc22   2006030541

Contents

Acknowledgments

THE COMPLETION OF THIS BOOK is due, in large part, to two Mellon Grants awarded to me by the University of Detroit Mercy. In addition, I owe a special debt of gratitude to John Staudenmaier, S.J., and his ongoing enthusiasm for and support of this project. Special thanks are also due to Michael Barry, Claire Crabtree, John Freeman, Marcel O'Gorman, Nicholas Rombes, and Rosemary Weatherston— my colleagues in the English Department at the University of Detroit Mercy—who advised me regarding various parts of the manuscript. I must also happily acknowledge the importance of John Coldewey's mentorship throughout the initial stages of this project—his scholarly work was and is an inspirational force for its inception and completion. I would also like to thank David McGonagle and Theresa Walker of the Catholic University of America Press for shepherding me through the various stages of publication.

Acknowledgment is also due to the *Records of Early English Drama Newsletter*, to *Early Theatre*, and to *Publications of the Medieval Association of the Midwest*, which originally published parts of three of the following chapters in different forms.

Finally, and most importantly, I cannot adequately express my thanks to Mark Vásquez and Olivia Hill Vásquez. They have lived with this book more than they should have, and it is as much theirs as mine.

Sacred Players

Introduction

CHRIST IN HIS ADDRESS from the cross near the end of the York cycle's *Crucifixion* pageant calls out to "Al men that walkis by waye or strete . . . ," thereby making contemporary the events of salvation history enacted throughout the pageant and implicating its audience as participants in those events. "Byholdes," Christ says, "myn heede, myn handis, and my feete,"

> And fully feele now, or ye fyne,
> If any mournyng may be meete,
> Or myscheve mesured unto myne.[1]

Connecting the space of his body to city and audience, Christ indicates the presence of the sacred in the streets of York and reminds his spectators of their role in enacting that presence. Directed to contemplate—indeed to "measure"—the very parts of Christ's body that the soldiers have just labored to nail to the cross, the audience are invoked as workers in their own right, enabling the significance and power of the Crucifixion to span a time and space that includes their own streets, homes, and storefronts. Past and present, divine and human meet as all actors of the drama are expected to participate in a merger of the mundane and sacred labor necessary for spiritual enlightenment and salvation.

1. Beadle (1982), 321, ll. 253, 255–58.

Yet in the Chester cycle, whose pageants cover a similar range of sacred history, expectations for audience involvement can seem quite different. In contrast to the temporal and spatial continuity encouraged by Christ and other audience-attentive figures like him in the York cycle, Chester offers a different model of response. A designated "Expositor" figure, acting as a readerly interpreter, sets himself and his audience apart from the time and space of sacred history:

> Lordinges, what may this signifye
> I will expound it appertly
> the [that] unlearned standinge herebye
> maye knowe what this may bee.
> This present, I saye veramente,
> signifieth the new testamente
> that nowe is used with good intente
> throughout all Christianitye.[2]

Whereas the worshipful work invoked and modeled by the York Christ assumes an audience's devotional response that includes participating in a fusion of sacred past with mundane present, the response activity modeled by Expositor textualizes the performance as past event requiring contemporary explication. Rather than physical participation and emotional immediacy, Expositor stresses interpretation and edification as devotional responsibility and sacred necessity.

While at least one hundred years and England's break with Rome separate the surviving text of the York cycle from the extant Chester cycle manuscripts (the York text dates from 1463–1477; the earliest of the Chester manuscripts dates to the late sixteenth century), the Chester cycle has often been treated as a medieval text preserved in Renaissance manuscripts. Yet in steering his audience to a reception role markedly different from that urged upon the audience by York's Christ, Expositor reveals sensibilities more aligned with Protestant than with Catholic belief. He demonstrates, in fact, an ideological shift regarding the role of devotional response and re-

---

2. Lumiansky and Mills (1974), 62, ll. 113–20.

sponsibility that more rightly corresponds with the Elizabethan date of the extant manuscripts of the cycle than with the worship practices of late medieval Catholicism.

Indeed, the different treatments of audience and performance that the York and Chester cycles communicate confirm that the performance life of the Chester cycle may have continued into the Reformation and Renaissance eras and thus well beyond its traditional placement in "medieval" history. Such a possibility has significant implications for how we might approach other religious drama also traditionally relegated to England's medieval period. This historically expansive notion of the drama's performance capabilities—that it could serve, and help to determine, Protestant as well as Catholic notions of devotional experience—reveals the drama as a shaping force of religious culture beyond its supposedly medieval boundaries: a consistently popular form of decidedly lay worship powerful enough to craft and define, as well as reflect, the nature of religious discourse well into, and beyond, the Reformation.[3]

Thus the following study of the Middle English religious drama begins in the time period usually associated with its demise—the time period of the Chester manuscripts. The intention, however, in beginning "at the end" is not to document that demise but to investigate how Protestant forces, rather than wholly eradicating the drama of the earlier faith, may have found the Catholic drama a useful means for crafting and communicating what distinguished the new, "true" faith from the old. Expositor thus becomes an example of a "reforming" figure whose attention to how an instance of religious performance ought to be used demonstrates an important second life for the religious drama in England. This second life requires that at least some of the dramatic texts previously labeled "medieval" be reexam-

3. Cf. the response of Clopper (2001, 20, n. 53) to what Cox and Kastan say in *A New History of the Early English Drama* (1998): "Despite saying that its 'primary aim is to provide the most comprehensive account yet available of early English drama' (1) and 'to erase the sharp distinction between *Medieval* and *Renaissance* that has traditionally been used to mark the period boundary' (3), the *History* primarily concerns sixteenth-century drama."

ined and understood in light of emerging Protestant beliefs. Possibly, a conscious program for reseeing and reworking Catholic plays to suit Protestant sensibilities existed in late-sixteenth-century England. Moreover, such a program would demonstrate the historical culmination of ongoing struggles regarding a use of religious plays that can be traced throughout the life of the early English drama. Rather than documents that preserve a fixed religious meaning, therefore, the existing manuscripts present instead texts closely wed to the inherent fluidity of performance and performance history, and to the possibility of alternative forms of production and religious sensibilities.[4] These alternative forms and their theological connections are often fundamentally linked to different expectations regarding the appropriate role of an audience in response to a religious performance.[5]

Mindful, therefore, of the fact that an important portion of the extant body of dramatic texts we call "medieval"—and the Chester cycle is a major example—date in manuscript and/or performance record to the Reformation and Renaissance periods in England, a re-

4. Cf. Clopper (2001): "It has been the practice to treat medieval and early modern dramatic texts as if they were fixed at the time of their writing and that the meaning we attach to them remained with them through their performance histories. These assumptions are simplistic in several ways. First, we know that some of the oldest texts were periodically revised. Equally important, however, is that even if the texts were not revised, their reception might change, especially as England moved through the Reformation period" (23).

5. Cf. Clark (1999): "[T]he most obvious tools of interpretation that we do possess may be of only limited value. For example, interpreting the reversal of social statuses so often included in confraternity ritual, we are of course reminded of standard Christian teaching: 'The last shall be first,' etc. But to interpret the ritual in terms of Church doctrine leaves us in the same position as the anthropologist who would accept at face value the account of a ritual participant: standing outside the ritual looking in. The traditional Christian interpretation may serve as a point of departure . . . but it does not explain to us the particular efficacy of the ritual as it may have been experienced by the participants. Nor can it explain why certain ritual actions or mechanisms were used instead of others" (44). Emmerson (1999) also discusses "the tendency of even the best scholars to remove the text from history" (94). Coletti (1990) imparts a similar concern regarding the interpretive implications surrounding the use of records associated with the early English drama: "REED's positivism results in a social and historical decontextualizing of the drama that is in its own way as radical as anything accomplished by the formalist readings it was originally intended to oppose" (271).

cursive approach to the drama directs Parts I and II of this study. Beginning with the Chester cycle, this book traces how the religious drama may have been used to shape, communicate, and distinguish different roles for its audiences in order to suit (as well as, in some cases, to define) alternative religious sensibilities. Thus, in keeping with this focus on audience roles, my examination of the religious drama maintains an ongoing attention to alternative forms of audience attentive figures—those who, like the Chester Expositor or the York Christ, address, direct, or otherwise involve the audience in the performances of which they are a part. While in a position of empowering religious ideology, these figures, because of their mediatory capabilities, can also voice cultural reactions to that ideology, disclosing the changing dynamics of response processes that develop that ideology in cultural practice and belief. Shaping dramatic response thus becomes a means of shaping faith.

As, then, an examination of response—and, perhaps, as a construction of a history of response—this book implements the theories of Hans Robert Jauss and his *Rezeptionsästhetik*, or "reception aesthetics." While Jauss's theories are most explicitly applied in Part I (through direct attention to alternative forms of response and the embodiment of these forms in various audience-attentive figures), Jauss's form of reader response criticism influences this study throughout. The discussions that follow also have been informed by new historicism, in their investigations of a range of textual documents and devotional customs, as well as their focus on audience roles and audience attentive figures as a means for understanding the ability of the sacred to manifest and enable ideological shifts in religious belief and discursive practice. Finally, Part III of this study turns to feminist criticism and its attention to ideological forces, extending the examination of the potential of the drama for shaping religious discourse and worship practice to explore issues of gender, including gender itself as a means for characterizing, distinguishing, and critiquing response. Yet Jauss's theories permeate this book. My explicit use of Jaussian attentions to audience and reception aesthetics in my first chapter provides a foundation and model for the analyses of response, performance, and texts that follow, even as these analyses incorporate other forms of interpretive praxes that scholars of the drama have found useful and enlightening.

Beginning with an investigation of a possible second life for the Chester cycle, I advocate in Part I (Chapters 1–2) a reexamination of other examples of the early English drama (previously labeled "medieval" despite the Renaissance date of their extant manuscripts) in light of potential Reformation and Renaissance revisions focused primarily on characterizing, distinguishing, and shaping audience response and devotional behaviors. Yet Protestant revisers could not hope to shape audience response without identifying Catholic behaviors in order to distinguish them from Protestant ones. This revisionist history—the purposeful looking back at the Catholic drama, its performances, and its audiences in order to craft new devotional responses and behaviors—strongly suggests that the role of response in connection with the religious drama, rather than a Renaissance invention, had accompanied the drama as a prominent aspect for shaping devotional practice throughout its lifetime. Thus, working recursively in Part II (Chapters 3–4), I turn to two examples of the late medieval drama that exemplify this attention to and conflict over the role of response. While tensions over and explorations of audience roles and accompanying devotional behaviors engage sacramental issues applicable to the late Middle Ages, they also reveal a fundamental attention to the role of audience response that indicates a powerful precedent for Protestant attentions to the potential for audience response to shape devotional practices. Moving in Part III (Chapters 5–6) to the role of gender in shaping response, I identify a more specific aspect of this attention to audience response—an aspect shared, again, in medieval and Renaissance contexts for the drama yet taken, again, in different directions. Attending first to a play that partakes of the late medieval devotional climate for audience roles and belief practices explored in Part II, I examine how the Digby *Candlemas Day and the Killing of the Children of Israel* extends the meaning of that devotional climate to an exploration of the potential of gendered behaviors for audiences in understanding and enacting the miracle of Christ's birth and life. I then select explicitly Protestant versions of the religious drama in order to examine how associations between Catholic audience behaviors and fluid gender roles may have been seized upon by Protestant authorities as another means for critiquing the earlier faith. Part III thus analyzes the gendering of response as but a further development of the history of response for the early English drama throughout the Middle Ages and into the Renaissance.

Part I (Chapters 1 and 2) asserts that defining an appropriate response role for an audience attending a religious performance often proves a central concern for, and focus of, Reformation efforts to reclaim, remake, and recycle the drama of the earlier faith. The opening chapter begins with an explicit analysis of audience-address figures in the Chester cycle, demonstrating how potentially Protestant changes to a play cycle, whose religious affiliations would ostensibly offend adherents of the country's new faith, uncover alternative theological beliefs regarding the role of audience response. This chapter also examines documents and texts whose voicing of Protestant sentiments regarding reception roles and religious discourse complements the shifting of response that Expositor's presence in the manuscripts seems to indicate. A similar shifting of response appears at work in the Digby *Conversion of Saint Paul,* discussed in the following chapter. Investigating the implications of a likely staging of the play in 1560s Chelmsford and focusing on the audience-attentive figures present in the text, this chapter argues that the *Saint Paul* manuscript provides ample evidence of a Protestant reshaping of reception roles that resembles the "reforming" of response attempted in the Chester cycle. Paul's conversion may have become a useful model for Protestant forces seeking likewise to convert resistant Catholics to the new faith. Thus the Digby *Saint Paul* play elucidates a larger ideological paradigm of "reform" that effectively likened Catholicism to the faith of the Old Testament and Protestantism to the faith of the New Testament. Within the play, this paradigm is also applied to the issue of appropriate response roles. Moreover, Old Testament and diabolical figures—including Paul before his conversion—prompt the audience's physical, emotional, and sense-driven involvement with the performance in order to characterize and demonize a Catholic audience's response. Meanwhile, New Testament figures and the converted, Christian Paul urge their audiences toward a different reception role, one stressing the clarity of Scripture and characterized by the control of speech, senses, and body in order to distinguish and celebrate the correct response of a Protestant. Like the Expositor of the Chester cycle, Paul thus becomes a figure who reforms response.

Rather than a victim of wholesale eradication, then, the Middle English religious drama, at least in part, seems to have been subjected to a kind of "reforming" process as Protestant forces, ostensibly dedicated to righting the wrongs of the earlier faith, produced a kind of revisionist history of the religious drama in the Reformation and early Renaissance era. Yet the offering in England's early Protestant period of a new definition of appropriate Christian behavior for the audience of a religious play suggests that concerns over the place of the drama in religious worship and ritual may have also accompanied the drama throughout the later Middle Ages in England and thus prior to the Reformation and Renaissance. Moreover, the efforts of those engaged in the "reforming" process to distinguish Catholic participants' earlier use of the drama as misuse also point to the strong possibility that how the drama was performed, received, and understood in relation to belief practices emerged as a topic of discussion, concern, and struggle prior to the Reformation. Working recursively, then, in Part II (Chapters 3 and 4), I explore the role and use of the religious drama in the late medieval period in England, focusing primarily on the century or so preceding the break with Rome. As it would prove later for the Church of England, the drama was a problematic phenomenon for Catholic authorities, but with a fundamental difference: while Protestant forces focused on appropriate and inappropriate uses of the drama and sought, in part, to assign that responsibility to individual audience members, the Catholic Church worried instead about the potential of the drama—as a form of worship accessible to the lay population—to usurp the unique position of its priestly classes. Chapter 3 asserts that the Croxton *Play of the Sacrament* and the *Tretise of Mira-*

clis Pleyinge, studied together, reveal a fundamental link between the religious drama and the transformative power of the Eucharist. Both texts are concerned with establishing who has a right of access to that power, and thus in turn with defining the role of an audience member in relation to the presence of that power. Strengthened by Eucharistic devotional practices in the later Middle Ages, the use of the religious drama by late medieval audiences was thus intricately linked to lay beliefs in a transformative power that might extend beyond the grasp of priest and Church. Chapter 4 investigates an instance of sacred performance in which that belief, rather than proving centrally problematic, fully infuses the mundane and the everyday with sacramental potential. York, its cycle play, and its audience-attentive figures urge their audiences to participate in a convergence of sacred past and mundane present. Focusing on the exceptionally fluid aesthetics of performance that accompanied York's staging of its "miracle" play, this chapter describes and analyzes the dynamics of spirituality, devotion, and entertainment that converge in the York cycle. In a large-scale celebration of Incarnation belief and the transformative powers of Eucharistic piety, the physical and temporal spaces of the city of York and its citizens are exuberantly mingled with the space, time, and bodies of sacred history. Based so holistically upon an audience's direct emotional and physical involvement in the religious drama, the reception role expected of a York audience could permeate an entire community both within and beyond the annual performance, extending even to include a sanctifying of the commercial and economic aspects of the city. Offering audience address figures and expectations for audience response that differ significantly from those presented in the Chester cycle, the York cycle reveals a full-scale example of late medieval associations between the drama and the transformative powers of the Eucharist that influenced audience response roles and devotional practices (as well as civic and commercial life). The considerable difference of these roles and practices from Renaissance expectations demonstrates a useful prehistory for a Protestant polemic eager to malign the earlier faith.

Part II, then, illustrates an attention to audience response as a constant and consistent aspect of the early English drama. This attention was employed, as I argue in Part I, in the Renaissance to reshape devotional practice because it was already an issue with which medieval Catholic audiences and authorities were familiar (and an issue with which they had to grapple). Moreover, the attention to the role of audience response found in the Croxton *Play of the Sacrament,* the *Tretise of Miraclis Pleyinge,* and the York cycle suggests how the Protestant revisers of the Chester cycle and the *The Conversion of Saint Paul* could readily rely upon audiences to be aware of their roles as audience members, as well as aware of how these roles could indicate and influence Christian belief and behavior.

Maintaining a focus on how audience response could demonstrate and shape belief practice, I move in Part III (Chapters 5 and 6) to the significant place of gender in the history of response for the early English drama. I first investigate the role of gender in a late medieval devotional climate by building upon the influence of Eucharistic piety and Incarnational faith on the types of audience roles and belief practices presented in the York cycle, the Croxton play, and the *Tretise.* Centering on the Digby *Candlemas Day and the Killing of the Children of Israel,* Chapter 5 details the late medieval emphasis upon the humanity and physicality of Christ, a characterization that accompanied devotion to the Eucharist and the doctrine of the real presence, and that may have encouraged a fluid approach to gender and its role in devotional experiences and rituals. The same "transubstantiating" potential that may have inspired participants in the religious drama to see the boundaries between past and present, sacred and mundane, divine and human as imminently permeable may have provoked similar attitudes toward the boundaries that distinguished masculine from feminine behavior. The Candlemas play constructs alternative representations of gender through, in part, its unique pairing of Herod's tyranny and the innocents' massacre with Mary's purification and presentation of Christ. Consequently, the audience is guided toward a response role that breaks down rigid definitions of masculinity and femininity, and for which Christ himself is a model in the later Middle Ages. Gender may have provided for the drama and its late medieval audiences a further means for experiencing and enabling the transformative and sanctifying power of the drama—a power linked to the fluidity of Christ's body and anchored by transubstantiation doctrine.

My final chapter returns to Protestant reactions and remakings of that drama in order to demonstrate how gender plays a fundamental role in reforming response in the late life of the Middle English religious drama. I explore how, in keeping with Renaissance attempts to reinvent audience behaviors and religious practice, Protestant audiences were encouraged to think of Catholic audiences as effeminate, exhibitionist, and fundamentally anti-Christian. The consideration of gender illustrated in the preferred response role communicated in the Candlemas play—despite that role's association with masculine as well as feminine forms of devotional response—may have become, in the hands of Protestant forces, another means for characterizing Catholic audiences' misuse of the religious drama. If late medieval Eucharistic piety, accentuated by an emphasis on Christ's humanity, valorized a use of the drama (and other devotional rituals) that included expansive definitions of gender, such a use—likewise linked firmly to transubstantiation doctrine—may account for the strongly gendered language charging negative portrayals of Catholic forms of worship, including responses to the religious drama. The attention to gender that informs Lewis Wager's Protestant saint play *The Life and Repentaunce of Marie Magdalene* shows that a part of the adaptation and reforming process that Reformation and Protestant forces applied to the religious drama of the earlier faith included a distinctly gendered characterization of Catholic audiences. This portrayal described and denigrated those audiences as (like the preconverted Magdalene) overly emotional, weak-minded, and dangerously prone to spectacle and physicality: in short, as "feminine." Mary Magdalene, like Paul, provided for Protestant thinkers another useful example of a conversion experience that could be aligned with the national change in faith.

This phenomenon provides a plausible explanation for the fact that the Digby *Mary Magdalene* and the Digby *Saint Paul* survived the Reformation. In Wager's adaptation, Mary becomes a more overt model for the reforming of response promoted by both the Expositor of the Chester cycle and the converted Paul. If Expositor and Paul are exemplars of appropriate response whose reforming presence is intended to demonstrate the superiority of Protestant reception roles, Wager's Mary may be seen as the direct subject of that reform process. She is an example of an audience member whose inappropriate "feminine" response to sacred truths has led her in a sinful direction that can be corrected only through the truth and light of Protestantism. Wager therefore seizes upon a potentially Protestant interpretation and use of a Catholic saint play—the Digby *Mary Magdalene*—but makes such an interpretation and use more explicit in his version through a gendering of response that provides yet another means for celebrating and sustaining the predominance of the country's new faith: the convention of male superiority. Not only, then, are Catholic audiences criticized as spectacle-seekers who wish merely to indulge their senses—a characterization communicated in the Chester cycle and the Digby *Conversion of Saint Paul*—they are also portrayed as womanly and overly emotional, and consequently lacking in restraint, reason, and the desire for mindful understanding.

Gender, as a result, becomes a powerful, defining force in the Protestant recycling of the drama of the earlier faith, distinguishing inappropriate from appropriate response as Protestant writers and thinkers craft an aesthetics of reception (and a form of religious discourse) that they portray as more fully masculine, and therefore more "true," "right," and "rational" than the fickle, emotional, and consequently "feminine" form of worship they assign to the Catholic form of worship and its "popery." Part III addresses in the late history of the Middle English religious drama a politics of gender operating through the alternative response roles that the drama was capable of encouraging, creating, and sustaining. Indeed, the gendering of response is but one part of a larger politicizing of audience reception styles and devotional practices that establishes the role of the drama in shaping religious ideology from the early Middle Ages into the Renaissance. Offering a unique interpretive approach to the drama—one inspired by a recursive attention to historical and cultural forces whose impact on our own understandings of the drama have not been examined—the following study details and evaluates a previously unacknowledged politicizing of response accompanying the early religious drama in England throughout much of its lifetime.[6]

6. In this study, I have of course not been able to address all of the Middle English religious drama. The Chester and York cycles, however, can work as registers that compose the chronological edges of the performance history of the cycle drama, and as such they may frame future work with the other extant cycles. The Towneley cycle, for instance, contains a variety of performance styles and mediating figures (ranging from the audience-attentive torturers of Christ to the didactic figures of *The Play of the Prophets*), and a number of iconic audiences addresses, all of which deserve close examination. This is especially the case in relation to the borrowings of the Towneley plays from the York cycle, the contributions of the Wakefield Master, and the apparent lack of craft guild influence upon the pageants. Such a detailed examination, however, would require more than the space available here. Intriguingly, the rather didactic, preacherly tone that characterizes a number of Towneley's individual plays suggests an influence reminiscent of the Poeta in the Digby *Conversion of Saint Paul* or the Chester Expositor, perhaps revealing the potential that some of the plays of the cycle may have held for Protestant use. And, of course, the two versions of the Norwich Grocers' Play (1533 and 1565) merit mention for the evidence that the latter contains of revisions clearly intended to adapt the story of Adam and Eve to align with Protestant ideology.

In addition, the morality plays, while including many themes and qualities of the audience-attentive figures and forms of response I examine throughout this study, seem more self-consciously devoted to exploring response practices for their audiences. The moralities, in their emphasis on the personified Christian's actions and roles in the world, seem to consider a direct object of study response itself—a process of spiritual enlightenment represented on stage through personifications of human and sacred qualities. The audience is thus asked to identify with one character (e.g., "mankind" or "everyman") in accessing the divine, in bringing spiritual and worldly processes to meeting and fruition. The moralities divulge an apparent self-consciousness about the the role of response in worship and sacred performance, marking the development of a dramatic tradition that examines issues and meanings regarding response and self-performance within the orbit of the drama. In taking religious concerns into the emphatically lay (even low country) world of "everyman," the devotional potential and quality of the drama seems somewhat removed from the audience as the role of response becomes a more explicit topic connected to dramatic self-exploration. The moralities seriously question whether drama can, in fact, be religious if it is so keenly tied to worldly concerns. They voice openly a conflict between expressing reality and demonstrating moral conduct which, while entertainingly familiar, leaves the role of audience response in a spiritual vacuum, incapable of overcoming a protracted distance between earthly and heavenly life.

Part I

Reforming Response

Protestant Adaptations

Chapter One

Modeling Response in the Chester Cycle

"What may this signifye"[1]

SINCE THE 1950s, scholars and critics of the medieval drama have considered the unique position of the Chester cycle in the history of Middle English religious theater.[2] The thorough reexamination of manuscripts and documents, including the pre- and post-Reformation Banns of the cycle, indicate that in its present form the Chester cycle is a product of the sixteenth century, and that elements previously and misleadingly termed "primitive," "unsophisticated," and "didactic" do not indicate an early composition date.[3]

1. The quotation is from Lumiansky and Mills (1974), 62, l.113. All future references are from this edition and will be cited parenthetically by pageant and line number.

2. See Salter (1955); Prosser (1961), esp. 6–11; Richard Axton (1974), 185ff.; Clopper (1978), esp. 41ff.; Lumiansky and Mills (1983); Stevens (1987); and Diller (1992).

3. See R. M. Lumiansky and David Mills's Introduction (1974) to their edition, ix–xxvii, and Mills (1994). Indeed, the omission from the late Banns and from the extant cycle versions of a play of "the Assumption of Our Lady" (originally noted in the early Banns) suggests Reformation activity, placing the cycle in the late sixteenth century (at the earliest). In a recent essay, Happé (2004) provides a useful overview of potential Protestant reactions to and revisions of the cycle plays.

Dating from late Elizabethan and Jacobean times, the extant manuscripts of the Chester cycle are late entries in the history of Middle English religious drama—perhaps even products of a time when, as the later Banns (extant manuscripts 1600–1609) indicate, the civic sponsors of the plays hoped to align their popular performance text with Protestant sensibilities. Ascribing (without support) the authorship of the cycle to the fourteenth-century monk Ranulph Higden, these Banns describe Higden as a proto-reformer who, responding to the fact that "[t]hese storyes of the testamente at this tyme . . . / in a common Englishe tonge never reade nor harde" (21–22), was "nothinge affrayde"

> with feare of borninge, hangeinge, or cuttinge of heade
> to sett out that all maye deserne and see,
> and parte of good belefe, beleve ye mee.
>
> (24–27)[4]

The Chester cycle is thus characterized as a prophetic vehicle for the reformed religion, working to bring the message of the Bible directly to the lay population.[5] As David Mills notes, portraying the cycle

4. All citations are from Lumiansky and Mills (1983, 285–95). All future references are from this edition and will be cited parenthetically by line number.
5. In his "Epistle to the Reader" (1848a, 390), included at the end of his first version of the New Testament, William Tyndale expresses comparable sentiments about the previously unprecedented use of the vernacular. He also asserts that in his text "many things are lacking which necessarily are required. Count it as a thing not having his full shape, but as it were born before his time, even as a thing begun rather than finished." In addition, his attention to a future version in which he will "seek in certain places more proper English, and with a table to expound the words which are not commonly used, and shew how the scripture useth many words which are otherwise understood of the common people, and to help with a declaration where one tongue taketh not another" (390) also resounds, to some extent, in the later Banns:

> Condemne not oure matter where groose wordes you heare
> which importe at this daye smale sence or understandinge
> —as sometymes "postie," "bewtye," "in good manner," or "in feare"—
> with such-like wilbe uttered in theare speaches speakeinge,
> At this tyme those speches caried good lykinge;
> thoe if at this tyme you take them spoken at that tyme—
> as well matter as words—then all is well fyne.
> (49–55)

"as inspired by Protestant evangelizing zeal rather than a Catholic sacramental concern was an ingenious attempt" to ensure its survival (1992, xviii), yet the late Banns demonstrate that the plan for preservation extended beyond claiming Higden as author.[6] In fact, much of the defense of the cycle focuses on the role of the audience, on the responsibility of current Christians for recognizing the true meaning of the plays. Contemporary audiences of the cycle are prompted to distinguish themselves, their comprehension of, and their responses to the plays from an earlier time of religious darkness and "ignorance":

> As all that shall see them [the plays] shall moste welcome bee,
> so all that doe heare them we moste humblye praye
> not to compare this matter or storye
> with the age or tyme wherein we presentlye staye—
> but to the tyme of ignorance whearein we doe [did] straye.[7]
>
> (35–39)

Encouraged to acknowledge a spiritual perspective and accompanying viewing abilities as superior to those of previous audiences—"better men and finer heades now come" (205)—contemporary witnesses to the plays are identified as beneficiaries of a more enlightened age, and are entreated to approach the plays with a different, more informed understanding, underwritten by the clarifying power of the reformed faith.[8]

Concurrently, rather than eliminating elements of the plays that adherents of the true faith might find objectionable, the late Banns build upon this more enlightened perspective, empowered by that faith, in order to account for aspects of the cycle lacking scriptural authorization. "[T]hinges not warranted by anye wrytte" are described as "[i]nterminglinge therewithe onely to make sporte . . ." (11–12), and are portrayed as harmless remnants of the old faith.

---

6. See also Mills's brief discussion of the late Banns (1985, 5–7).

7. Mills translates "doe" as "did" (1992, 40).

8. Cf. Tyndale: "now the gospel all the world in as much as it crieth openly" (1848d, A Pathway, 10).

Consequently, appealing (and theologically suspect) throwbacks to the outdated faith, such as the shepherds' feasting and wrestling (96–102), the Harrowing of Hell (146–52), and the midwives at the Nativity (89–95), remain intact in the current performance, ostensibly for comic and/or antiquarian effect. Thus assisting the survival of a text and performance that would ordinarily have troubled Protestant adherents, the Banns cleverly divert attention and theological responsibility from the cycle itself to those who choose to view it. Whereas past audiences were unable to see the beliefs that inspired the cycle, contemporary audiences (it is implied) are capable of recognizing the true religious allegiance of the plays. This difference in perspective and insight occurs, for example, in the description of the pageant dedicated to Christ's trial and flagellation, highlighted by a reference to the older faith's misconception of Eucharist doctrine:

> Yow Fletchares, Boyeres, Cowpers, Stringers, and Irnemongers,
> see soberlye ye make oute Cristes dolefull deathe:
> his scourginge, his shippinge, his bludshede and passion,
> and all the paynes he suffred till the laste of his breathe.
> Lordinges, in this storye consistethe our chefe faithe,
> The ignorance wherein hathe us manye yeares soe blinded
> as though now all see the pathe playne . . . .
>
> (138–44)

Applying the Reformation emphasis on the responsibility of individual Christians to read and interpret the Bible for themselves to audiences of the Chester plays, the authors of the late Banns place the cycle firmly within the auspices of the new faith while simultaneously constructing a situation (based upon the responsibility of the audience to view the plays properly) that preserves textual and performance elements associated with the older faith. Holding the audience responsible for deriving the meaning of that text, the late Banns permit potentially divergent reception styles within the same performance text. The theological revisions and recharacterization required by late-sixteenth-century performances of the Chester cycle responded in part to the strength and popularity of the vernacular religious drama, and to the role its reception style expected of its audiences. Therefore, different reception styles necessitated by the staging of a Catholic play in a Protestant context suggest that shifting religious ideologies in Reformation England may have included the development of a communication and reception aesthetic that Reformers sought to distinguish from that of the earlier faith—even as, in shaping that aesthetic, they adapted the texts, worship practices, and performance styles of the condemned faith.

A "Change of Horizons": Shaping a Protestant Response

If, as reader response critics have argued, the reader or audience assumes primary responsibility for constructing the meaning of a text, then the divergent reception styles that the late Banns subtly ascribe to the Chester cycle may provide an avenue for understanding the different meanings and uses that audiences, influenced by their theological leanings, might assign to a performance text. Departing from the majority of reader response criticism in his belief that the experiences of readers and audiences can be understood and realized, Hans Robert Jauss, in his theory of *Rezeptionsästhetik* (or "reception aesthetics") argues that examining the shifting history of the reception of a text can disclose, rather than obscure, those experiences:

[T]he horizon of expectations of a work allows one to determine its artistic character by the kind and the degree of its influence on a presupposed audience. If one characterizes as aesthetic distance the disparity between the given horizon of expectations and the appearance of a new work, whose reception can result in a "change of horizons" through negation of familiar experiences or through raising newly articulated experiences to the level of consciousness, then this aesthetic distance can be objectified historically along the spectrum of the audience's reactions and criticism's judgment. (1982, 25)

In an attempt to reshape theologically the meaning and message of the Chester cycle, the late Banns appear to participate in such a "change of horizons": to characterize an ostensibly Catholic text as, really, a Protestant one in disguise, the Banns rely upon audience response, articulating an experience for reformed viewers that differs from (but also reveals) the experiences of earlier viewers. Importantly, the late performance history of the cycle also intimates a strong context for the articulation of shifting reception aesthetics.[9] Given that the last two performances of the Chester cycle occurred in 1572 and 1575, each under the authority of a Protestant mayor, attention to the objectionable experiences of past audiences may have been especially keen. While the 1572 staging proceeded, it did so only "againste ye willes of ye Bishops of Canterbury[,] York and Chester" (REED, 96).[10] This conflict, along with the attempt of the archbishop to halt the performance through "an Inhibition" which "Came too late" (97), suggests that the plays inspired doctrinal controversies. Yet, since the late Banns placed emphasis on distinguishing audience roles and experiences, the staging of the cycle may have also involved objections to a performance and reception style still used by the cycle and associated with the old faith. Although doctrinal changes undoubtedly accounted for many of the modifications required by Chester's aldermen prior to the 1575 performance, the authorities may have been concerned with performance technique, as well as appropriate audience response. The files of the assembly that detail the proceedings of Chester council meetings note that in 1575 it was "agreid" that the cycle "shall be seet furth in the best fayssion with such reformacion as mr maior with his advice shall think meet and convenient." Moreover, the official council record contained in the Assembly Book documenting the events of the same

9. For a discussion of manuscript dates and history, see Lumiansky and Mills (1974), 1–86. Lumiansky and Mills argue for a single precursor document (the "Reginall") for all five manuscripts maintained in Chester, which underwent revision and editing over several decades (1983, 186–88); and see Mills (1992), xvi–xvii. Mills also claims that "by the late sixteenth century [the Reginall] was a record of repeated revision and selection, with words, phrases, long sections, and even whole plays, obscured, emended, or offered in alternative forms—in effect, 'a cycle of cycles'" (1994, 111). See also the important work of Clopper (1978).

10. All citations are from Clopper (1979) (hereafter REED) and will henceforth be cited parenthetically by page number within the text.

date asserts that the plays "shalbe sett furth and plaied in such orderly maner and sorte as the same haue ben Accostomed with such correction and amendement as shalbe thaught Convenient by the said
Maior" (104). The fact, however, that both John Hanky (mayor in
1572) and Sir John Savage (1575) were called before the Privy Council regarding their role in promoting the respective stagings (109–10,
113–17) indicates that any changes made were likely found insufficient. Perhaps, as the preservation attempts of the late Banns suggest, the content of the plays was less at issue than the style of production. At the very least, the late performance dates of the cycle
attest to its ongoing popularity and to the desire, also illustrated in
the late Banns, to maintain some of the plays' original (if theologically suspect) elements while repositioning the text to suit Protestant
sensibilities. The sentiments expressed in the Banns may thus reflect
the desires and methods of those who wished to preserve the cycle
and continue its performances in the late sixteenth century through
an emphasis on the role of the audience.

Expositor as Protestant Role Model

As Mills, Peter Travis, Martin Stevens, and others have remarked,
the Chester cycle maintains an ongoing awareness of its audience
(1985, 10–13; 1987, 1982; 1987, 266–70). Throughout the cycle, the
role of the audience is highlighted: they aid in the progression of
scenes; they participate in transforming present-day Chester into lo-
cations from sacred history; they confirm doctrine and help communicate sacramental meaning; and, as the late Banns also show, they
readily accept a combination of comic elements and religious topics.[11] More fundamentally, the audience is addressed by several figures who provoke them to participate actively and communally
in the action and meaning of the scenes enacted both before and

---

11. As Eamon Duffy (1992) has asserted, we must guard "against underestimat-
ing the links between liturgical observance and the 'secular' celebratory and ludic
dimensions of lay culture at the end of the Middle Ages" (22).

among them. The most consistent of these figures in the Chester cycle is Nuntius, a messenger appearing in numerous plays. When, for example, Nuntius refers to the pageant of *Noah's Flood* in his opening to the play that follows, he notes the physical presence of the audience, and mentions their imminent contact with the events concluded and those about to unfold:

> All peace, lordinges that bine presente
> and herken mee with good intente,
> howe Noe awaye from us hee went
> and all his companye;
> and Abraham through Godes grace,
> he is commen into this place,
> and yee will geeve us rowme and space
> to tell yow thys storye.
>
> (4.1–8)

Encouraging a temporal as well as a spatial continuity, Nuntius acknowledges the presence and power of the audience. His invocation to those "that bine presente" is inclusive; and his declaration clearly implicates this audience in the process by which historical events are recreated and reexperienced.[12]

12. Invocations present in early fourteenth-century sermons, such as that contained in Sloane Ms. 2478, suggest a similar attention to establishing the spatial and temporal continuum between sacred past and audience present, as found throughout the Chester cycle. In the sermon, part of a Palm Sunday celebration, the speaker/performer addresses his audience as Caiphas and proceeds to describe his role in Christian history, while explaining the past and contemporary significance of Palm Sunday. Speaking to a contemporary audience about the meaning and necessity of the Palm Sunday observance, Caiphas connects his past weariness with that of his audience and will later maintain this continuum in order to demonstrate that present-day palms are as significant to the original event as the original event is to the present-day palms (see Brown, 1913, 105–17, for text). The Caiphas-Palm Sunday sermon is an example of the *sermone semidrammatico,* a genre that played a large role in Franciscan evangelicalism throughout the early and high Middle Ages (see Jeffrey, 1975). It connects the aesthetics of a dramatic sermon to the early career of religious vernacular drama, suggesting that in Franciscan theology may be found more specific ideological precedents for the participatory and inclusive response style undertaken by Moses and his audience-attentive counterparts in the Chester cycle.

The Chester cycle, however, also contains another principal audience-address figure who introduces a reception style different from the experience that Nuntius promotes for his audience. Appearing as a readerly guide figure for the audience, a character designated as "Expositor" also makes significant (if limited) appearances throughout the cycle.[13] In contrast to the communal participatory experience Nuntius expects of characters, actors, and audience, Expositor adopts an interpretive stance. For instance, Nuntius announces the pageant that contains the episode of Balaak and Balaam, and constructs a physical closeness among audience, performers, and the events to come: "Make rowme, lordinges, and give us way, / and lett Balack come in and playe" (4.484–85).[14] On the other hand, Expositor entreats his audience to a more direct interpretation of the episode. This interpretation, rather than emphasizing audience participation, privileges clear and immediate understanding:

> Lordinges, what may this signifye
> I will expound it appertly
> the [that] unlearned standinge herebye
> maye knowe what this may bee.
> This present, I saye veramente,
> signifieth the new testamente
> that nowe is used with good intente
> throughout all Christianitye.
>
> (4.113–20)

13. Expositor delivers three addresses in pageant 4, concludes pageants 5 and 6 with lengthy speeches, delivers two addresses in pageant 12 and four in pageant 22; Nuntius appears twice in pageant 4—announcing the end of pageant 3 and the beginning of pageant 4, and then concluding pageant 4 with a speech declaring the opening of pageant 5—and appears once in the middle of pageant 6. Emmerson (1999) explores alternative audience responses to the Chester Antichrist.

14. Richard Axton (1974) describes the "exhortation" speeches of the "Cambridge Prologue" and "Rickinghall Fragment" (dating from the late thirteenth or early fourteenth century) in terms that seemingly describe Nuntius's audience addresses: "[T]he whole dramatic function of the conventional exhortation to silence and good order seems to be a positive invitation to frolic—a challenge to a 'game' in which actors and audience provoke one another . . . a 'game' drama in which both actors and audience have a physical part" (166). See also Kolve (1966), 8–32.

Differing substantially from Nuntius as well as from Chester's other audience attentive figures, Expositor articulates a reception style for his audience more self-conscious in its deliberate attention to expose and deliver clearly ("appertly") the meaning of the theological texts and events enacted before them.[15] Moreover, by indicating that the New Testament "nowe is used with good intente," Expositor echoes the sentiments of the late Banns regarding the superior comprehension abilities of contemporary, reformed Christians—of all those who "now . . . see the pathe playne" (144). Similarly, in the pageant of the *Prophets of Antichrist*, Expositor offers a "plain" interpretation of Zacharias's prophecy while calling upon his audience to respond appropriately:

> Nowe for to moralyze aright
> which this prophett sawe in sight,
> I shall found through my might
> to you in meeke mannere,
> and declare that soone in height
> more playnlye, as I have teight.
> Lystens nowe with hartes light
> this lesson for to learne.
>
> (22.73–80)

Seemingly more preoccupied than is Nuntius with his audience's reception role and with their ability to understand the meaning of what the play brings to them, Expositor anticipates the emphasis of the late Banns on audience responsibility for disclosing the true

15. Hans-Jürgen Diller (1992), drawing upon Dilthey's distinction between the world of the play and the world of the audience, has described Expositor as an "edificational" audience-address figure, one who "inform[s] and edif[ies] the audience while at the same time keeping the play-sphere closed" to the audience (114). For Diller, though, Nuntius also qualifies as an edificational figure, one who also maintains a closed play-sphere (114–15). This characterization, however, does not account for the significant differences between these two figures and their contrasting treatments of performance and audience. More recently, Karen Sawyer Marsalek's examination of the character "Appendix" in *The Resurrection of Our Lord* reveals an audience-address figure comparable to Expositor in his capacity as a mouthpiece for Protestant doctrine and performance aesthetics.

meaning and value of text and performance. As William Tyndale, whose complete works were republished in 1573 (one year after the earliest of the extant manuscripts of the Chester cycle), entreated his readers: "Cleave unto the text and plain storye and endeavour thyself to search out the meaning of all that is described therein" (1848f, *Prologue*, 411). More specifically, Tyndale stressed the importance of appropriate perception; the proper interpretive approach remains an important theme throughout his writings. Explaining, for instance, that Christ's blood assists right thinking, Tyndale declares the need to "have eyes of God to see the right meaning of the text" and claims that "except a man cast away his own imagination and reason, he cannot perceive God" (1848d, *Pathway*, 18; 1848b, *Obedience*, 310; 1848d, *Pathway*, 16).[16] Expositor's appearance in the text may therefore occasion the kind of "shifting of horizons" that Jauss describes in his attention to revealing divergent aesthetics of reception. When Expositor appears, the audience is called upon to approach the plays differently, to view them as opportunities for uncovering sacred truths through attentive interpretation rather than participatory engagement. Expositor thus serves as a model for the proper approach to the plays that will, as the late Banns insist, illustrate how the plays align with Protestant thought.

Given Expositor's divergent style, the possibility exists that he was a conscious Reformation addition, intended to convince authorities of the Protestant capacity of the cycle in order to preserve it. Yet, would this addition have guaranteed, ironically, the survival of much of the earlier character and reception style of the Chester cycle? The late Banns seem to detail such a process, and Expositor's attitude toward text, performance, and audience seems poised to con-

---

16. Cf. also, e.g., the following: "if the Spirit be not in a man, he worketh not the will of God, neither understandeth it, thou he babble never so much of the scriptures. Nevertheless such a man may work after his own imagination, but God's will can be not work" (1848c, *Parable*, 78); "where he [the Spirit of God] is not, there is not the understanding of the scripture, but unfruitful disputing and brawling about words" (88); and "let every man pray to God to send him his Spirit, to loose him from his natural blindness and ignorance, and to give him understanding and feeling of the things of God" (88–89).

vince a theologically suspicious viewer that the cycle has a religious merit that supersedes its connections to the older faith. Perhaps the revisions required by authorities before the last performance of the cycle in 1575 prompted the addition of the Expositor figure who, despite his impressively distinctive demeanor, may necessarily have been limited in his theologically transformative influences. His appearance, ultimately, in only five pageants may account somewhat for the continued objections to the 1575 performance, even after apparent changes had been made (REED, 104, 109–10, 113–17).[17]

Certainly, there is no definitive way to know when Expositor may have been added to the cycle. As scholars of the plays well know, the figure was likely added to the text along with interpolated sections from the *Stanzaic Life of Christ,* itself a text with strong Chester connections, yet whose date and manner of compilation remain unclear. Moreover, despite Peter Travis's contention that the *Stanzaic Life* and related Expositor additions probably correspond with the moving of the performance of the cycle from Corpus Christi Day to Whitsun-

17. Expositor, moreover, despite his authoritative stance, occasionally betrays an uncertainty about his actual role. He emphatically asserts his and his audience's temporal and spatial distance from the play and the events it portrays, but he vacillates between interpretations and summary while providing direct references to authoritative citations. His indeterminate role suggests that he is a recently employed figure, not as clearly defined as the theatrical aesthetic and tradition to which he is a controlling response. Nuntius, by contrast, seems to belong to a previously established tradition, signaled by two separate speeches in two different pageants in which he repeats a similar parting invocation to his audience:

> That lord that dyed one Good Frydaye,
> all, both night and daye,
> Farewell, my lordinges, I goe my waye;
> I may noe lenger abyde.
>> (4.488–91)

> That lord that dyed on Good Frydaye
> hee have you all both night and daye.
> Farewell, lordinges. I goe my waye;
> I may noe lenger abyde.
>> (6.181–84)

Nuntius uses an invocation reminiscent of folk play traditions that seem to predate the origin of vernacular religious drama in the fourteenth century (see Axton 184ff.).

tide in the 1520s or 1530s (1982, 44–61), David Mills has asserted that that "[n]either the date" of the "composition" of the *Stanzaic Life,* "nor the date and circumstances of the incorporation of its material into the cycle can be determined" (1994, 114). Mindful of the rather didactic and moralistic character of the *Stanzaic Life,* several critics have noted a feature of the text that provides a sometimes startlingly contrast to the appealing style of the Chester drama (Mills, 1994, 114; E. Salter, 1974, 96). Perhaps advocates of the cycle seized an opportunity to incorporate a text that, while sounding old, might likewise (and prophetically) appeal to reform thought. This strategy would concur with the Banns' proto-Protestant description of both the Chester cycle and the author claimed for it, Ranulph Higden. Indeed, as the *Stanzaic Life* itself was compiled, in large part, from Hidgen's *Polychronicon,* naming Higden as author hints at another, more concrete, connection between the *Stanzaic Life* and the Banns' defense of the cycle. Even if Travis rightly associates the *Stanzaic Life* revision with the shift in the play's performance to Whitsuntide, the move away from medieval Catholicism's premier religious observance, the feast of Corpus Christi, provides the appropriate context for a revision that might transform the cycle into a performance text appropriate for the new faith's emphasis on individual authority and scriptural access.[18] Perhaps a test case for changing the means by which sacred topics are communicated to and received by an audience, the Chester cycle, as an essentially medieval and Catholic play still in active production in the early modern period, thus emerges as a pivotal text for voicing the shifting ideologies of spirituality, worship, language, text, and authority that accompanied the widespread change instigated by the religious reformers of the period.

"Horizon[s] of Expectation": The Audience-Address Figure

The possible result of a limited attempt to convince doctrinally attentive authorities that the Chester cycle was redeemable and

---

18. Travis's work builds, in part, upon that of Clopper (1978).

even valuable to the goals of the reformed religion, Expositor demonstrates a reception aesthetic that differs markedly from much of the cycle's emphasis on communal audience participation. In calling upon his apparently more informed (and reformed) viewers as fellow seekers of scriptural truth, as self-consciously attentive readers of texts brought to life for the edification of all Christians, Expositor models an experience of the play and a form of response that boldly contrasts with that of Nuntius, whose audience addresses include audience members in the action of individual scenes, creating an almost festive atemporality that connects sacred history to present-day Christians. Yet, more than merely contrasting this alternative style of performance, response, and worship, Expositor may also have articulated it both for early modern Christians (who, perhaps despite their Protestant allegiances, wished to preserve it), and for reformers (who, in their desire to forge a reception style more attuned to Protestant theology, necessarily characterized earlier belief practices in order to critique them and distinguish them from their own). Paul White (1993) describes how, in the minds of many early reformers, ideas and "images" associated with Catholicism "need[ed] to be presented in order to be literally or ritualistically destroyed" so that playwrights such as John Bale often "use[d] an image to make a point about the *abuse* of images" (15; 2). This process is reminiscent of Jauss's claim that shifts in a work's "horizon of expectations" may be revealed "through negation of familiar experiences or through raising newly articulated experiences to the level of consciousness" (1982, 26). Moreover, as I have argued, the audience attentive figure of the drama emerges as a particularly valuable means for demonstrating this process. For although this figure deals primarily with processes of communication and response, by his very nature as a mediating figure he also discounts no perspective of history. He, as well as the drama in which he operates, exposes the struggles between all voices of culture: ideology is consistently invoked, tested, and rewritten within the working space of the dramatic performance.[19]

19. My work here is influenced by Jauss's theory of conceptualizing history through reconstructing the readers and audiences of literature and their shifting

Spanning the different regions of past and present, sacred and mundane, the audience-address figure brings about meaning even as he discloses the changing dynamics of how it can be displayed and understood.[20] In many ways, he resembles the translator in the late Middle Ages, the figure upon whom Michel de Certeau (1992) has interestingly seized as an aid to understanding his own study of shifting aesthetics and "'ways of speaking'": "Like the ethnologist," de Certeau says, the translator

> presented a foreign region, even though he did so to give an adaptation of it by allowing it to disturb his own native language. He produced otherness, but within a field that didn't belong to him any more than that other language did, a field in which he had no right of authorship. He produced, but without any place of his own, in that no-man's land, on that meeting of the waters where the waves of language roll back upon themselves. . . . The translator [was] caught up in the other's language and creating possibility, by means of it while at the same time losing himself in the crowd. (119)

The audience-address figure, then, remains a supremely fluid character, at work in a kind of "no-man's-land" that is the dramatic performance, experiencing and divulging the passages of ideology and culture that reverberate in those instances of enactment, on the borders of, yet centrally located in, the struggles of a society to understand itself in relation to the divine.

Thus the attempt in the late Banns both to preserve much of the original character of the Chester cycle and to associate it with Protestant thinking may also indicate a tendency in the early modern period to probe the remnants of the old faith, if only to set about tearing them down. Ironically (and thankfully), this tendency may have permitted the survival of texts that might otherwise have been destroyed. Expositor may not participate directly in this destructive

---

responses through time—"the dialectical character of historical praxis for art and literature" (1982, 14–15).

20. The very nature of the audience-address figure and the drama itself, therefore, requires that, in addition to reception aesthetics, my work attends to a theoretical approach that, while "decentering systems of authority and dismantling hierarchies leads not merely to eclecticism but to new, more egalitarian structures of relationship" and "dispenses with historiographic *grands recits* not in order to escape from historicity but to recover it in its local, concrete form" (Patterson, 1990, 90).

process. But, given the distinctiveness of his approach to text, performance, and audience within the Chester cycle, he does articulate a reception aesthetic that may have encouraged reformers such as Bale and Tyndale to characterize much of the older faith's worship practices as mere entertainments, indulging human senses and desires rather than the truth and clarity of God's Word. In Bale's accounting, for example, "In the place of Christe [they] have sett up supersticyons; / For preachynges, ceremonyes, for Gods wurde, mennys tradicyons" (1985, *King Johan,* 76). Similarly, Tyndale termed the practices of the old faith "persuasions of worldly wisdom" and "blind ceremonies [and] superstitiousness of disguised hypocrisy," and claimed that its beliefs encouraged "the people [to] think that they have done abundantly enough for God . . . if they be present once in a day at such mumming" (1848b, *Obedience,* 220, 226–27). Viewed as an aid to a textual interpolation process, as an insertion into a performance that probably reflected a long-standing religious tradition of audience reception, Expositor imposes one style of response that discloses another, clarifying what Bale and Tyndale defined and described when they critiqued the methods and practices of the "popish" faith.

Crafting an Alternative Style of Reception

Chester's fifth pageant (dedicated to the stories of *Moses and the Law* and to *Balaak and Balaam*) distinctly shows how Expositor's particular treatment of text, performance, and audience might bring "to the level of consciousness" a complex tradition of worship practices and religious theater likely not articulated until the Reformation. In addition to Expositor in this pageant, several other figures address the audience; yet, unlike Expositor, these other figures identify the audience as "Godes folke of Israel," making them participants and coproducers in the re-creation of sacred events. Before Expositor's first speech in the play, Deus and Moses, namely, each have speeches in which they invoke the present audience, partaking of the same continuum employed by Nuntius in the previous pageant. Opening the play, Deus (with a seemingly overt reference to the audience) casts them as physical and temporal contemporaries: "Moyses, my servant leeffe and dere, / and all my people that bine here . . ." (5.1–2). Moses, too, includes the audience directly in the scene when, following Deus's lead, he begins his speech with the words "Good folke, dread yee nought." Even the stage directions that precede this speech note that "Tunc Moyses in monte dicat populo" (sd. ff. 5.32) and the audience become those people, direct recipients of Moses' message.

Describing what she saw as indicative of the typical experience of a medieval audience, Anne Righter (1962) long ago pointed specifically to this Chester pageant: "There is much to be said for the subtlety of a theatre in which Moses can enjoin obedience to the commandments of God upon an audience of Israelites who lived before the birth of Christ and, at the same time, with all the force and directness of the original incident, upon medieval people who, at the conclusion of a day of pageants and processions, will make their way home through the streets of an English town."[21] This style of performance and worship displays a principal concern with establishing and maintaining a coalescence between the sacred events portrayed and the lives of the audience assembled at performance time. It also requires participants to contribute to this coalescence, drawing upon a view of history for which David Jeffrey (1973) provides historical and religious precedent:

The view of history as an artificial frame for the recurrence of divine pattern had been common to several centuries of European culture. . . . This view saw men of every generation participating in one great *historia*— in the *speculum humanae salvationis*. In this view nothing happens for the first time. . . . The theme is recurrence. Christ lives and dies and is born again daily in the sacrament and in the hearts of men. There is no "pretense" as such even in a crucifixion play, for the actor, like his audience, is participating in a divine pattern. . . . [T]hey try to come to grips in a powerful way with what it means to be crucified with Christ. (72)[22]

21. Interestingly, Mills (1993) resurrected Righter's concept in his essay on the *Balaak and Balaam* episode in the Chester cycle.
22. This view of history is also, as I discuss in Parts II and III of this study,

Illustrating this idea of "recurrence" in portraying sacred history, actors and audiences attempt a temporal and spatial continuum between re-created past and performative present. As with other examples of Middle English religious drama (a number of which I examine in Parts II–III of this study), the Chester cycle contains figures who can facilitate and maintain this continuum, infusing past events with present meaning, connecting sacred deeds with mundane experience, and involving all participants in the "one great *historia*" of the *"speculum humanae salvationis."*[23]

Yet the Chester cycle also shows how an audience attentive figure can present to his audience an alternative style of reception, one meant to participate in a shifting perspective on the proper use of religious texts and an emphasis on the interpretive responsibility of the individual Christian. Such a shifting perspective may be detected in a 1539 royal proclamation that focuses on the "right use" of religious ceremonies:

[C]eremonies should be observed and used in their right use (all ignorance and superstition clearly taken away) . . . that in such places, and all such days as the said ceremonies shall be chiefly celebrated, the bishop, dean, curate,

---

related to the impact of beliefs associated with the Incarnation and the Eucharist, to the meeting of divine and physical bodies that these doctrines detailed. Perhaps influenced by the late medieval emphasis upon Christ's worldly and physical presences, those who participated in the religious drama may have sought a tactile, emotional immediacy connected to Jeffrey's idea of "recurrence." See Rubin (1986, 1991, 1992); Gibson (1989), esp. 1–18; Beckwith (1986, 1993); Zita (1988); Robinson (1965); and Aulén (1960).

23. What occurs in these moments of communication and reception in the early drama is perhaps different from what Anthony Gash (1986) has called a tension between the "'abstract'" and "'monolithic'" language of the official ecclesiastical hierarchy and the "'materialist'" and "'ambivalent'" of "the carnivalesque idiom." Instead, the audience experiences a cocreation of meaning and consequence that melds the monolithic and abstract with the carnivalesque (or celebratory) and the materialistic. Compare also Hubert and Mauss's assertion regarding [worship] ceremonies that "with no intermediary there is no sacrifice. Because the victim [or intermediary] is distinct from the sacrifices and the god, it separates them while uniting them: they draw close to each other, without giving themselves to each other entirely" (1964, 100). In the case of this earlier aesthetic that I examine, the mediating goal seems an overt attempt at a complete "giving [of the audience's] selves" to the creation and meaning of the events presented.

or parish priest, for that time the minister, shall truly and plainly instruct the people [in] the good and right use and effects of such ceremony as is used that day, by which knowledge the people so using and observing the same ceremony may be fruitfully edified in . . . godly thoughts of such things as those ceremonies, well understood, were ordained to preach unto us. (Hughes and Larkin, 1964, 278)

Although a number of the proclamations concerning religious issues respond to disruptions caused by overly zealous religious reformers, others demonstrate a desire to curb the influence of the older faith's traditions and worship practices.[24] Attentive to the means by which meaning is made and communicated, as well as to the appropriate role of the Christian worshipper, the 1539 proclamation (contemporary with the moving of the Chester cycle from Corpus Christi Day to Whitsuntide) suggests a shift in the reception aesthetics of religious ceremony and belief practice with which the sponsors, audiences, and critics of the cycle may have been grappling throughout the sixteenth century and later. Through his treatment of audience and performance in Chester's fifth pageant, similarly, Expositor illustrates fundamental differences between what the old and the new faiths expected from their followers in terms of belief and worship. Expositor offers an alternative process of response that interrupts the participatory atmosphere created by Deus and Moses for the audience, as he allows Moses only a single eight-line stanza (5.33–40). Furthermore, Expositor draws attention to the kind of reception experience in which the audience has been suspended.[25] As Jauss (1982) contends, an emphasis on the *pro-*

24. "The early Tudor royal proclamation can be defined as: a public ordinance issued by the King, in virtue of his royal prerogative, with the advice of his council, under the Great Seal, and by royal writ" (Hughes and Larkin, 1964, xxiii). Furthermore, "the general protocol of the document thus reveals it as a public ordinance having its origin in the King's prerogative" (xxiv).

25. Indeed, Diller (1992) has suggested that "the plays [of Chester] as we have them constitute a sixteenth-century reaction to earlier popular forms of dramatic activity" (74). Yet while Diller distinguishes between edificational figures (such as Expositor) who "sall[y] forth from the 'World' of the play, keeping it thus open to the First World of the audience," and "histrionic" figures (113) who "break . . . the play sphere" (117), he also assumes that a space exists between play and audience

cess of the drama itself, based as it is on the dialogic *work* of communication and reception, reveals the true nature of a past literary and historical creation: "The work lives to the extent that it has influence. Included within the influence of a work is that which is accomplished in the consumption of the work as well as in the work itself. That which happens with the work is an expression of what the work is. . . . The work is a work and lives as a work for the reason that it *demands* an interpretation and 'works' [influences, *wirkt*] in many meanings" (15).[26] Expositor measures and interprets an earlier process of consumption and "work" and posits a different process, and we, in turn, measure his attempted "work" of the text as a way to uncover its "many meanings." Perhaps responding to the passage of time and the strengthening of Protestant religious ideology, the latest manuscript version of the Chester cycle, the H manuscript (Harley 2124), increases the number of Expositor's appearances in the play, while decreasing those of Nuntius. If we assume that the H manuscript was a presentation copy and not intended for performance (all of the extant complete manuscripts, of course, postdate Chester's last production),[27] we can detect a more extensive attempt in this latest version of the cycle to represent a reception style more acceptable to Protestant thought than the one associated with the religious drama of the old faith.

(what he terms the "two worlds") for both figure types. This gap over which Diller's histrionic figures reach seemingly contradicts his own description of the Middle English cycle plays' original aesthetic: unlike liturgical drama, he asserts that the "play-sphere and audience sphere" of the cycle plays did not face "each other, but the play-sphere arose from the world in which the audience lived" (75).

26. Travis (1987) has also usefully described this distinction: "[U]nlike reader-response criticism, *Rezeptionsästhetik* emphasizes the historicity and alterity of literary works from the past." Travis also argues that both reader response criticism and *Rezeptionsästhetik* "are . . . explicitly inscribed in the strategies of various kinds of medieval literature. Reader-response criticism naturally suits the more bookish and self-reflexive literary forms, and *Rezeptionsästhetik* more appropriately pertains to oral and dramatic forms addressed to a large public audience" (202).

27. See Lumiansky and Mills (1974), xxiii–xxviii.

Examples from the Past: A Different Devotional Response

Exhibiting a changing view of the reception process and what should be accomplished by that process, Expositor, in the first lines he speaks in pageant five, disregards the apparent atemporality of the Deus-Moses scene and treats it as an event from the past: "Lordings, this commandement / was the first lawe that ever God sent" (5.41–42). Expositor presents an alternative view of time and history, one that differs from the inclusive stance that figures such as Deus and Moses assume for their audience. Expositor locates the scene in history and makes it an object of study, communicating an alternative to, in Stanley Fish's terms, the current "system of intelligibility" (1986, 524–33) in the play—the process by which meaning is made and communicated. Yet Expositor also necessarily draws attention to that current "system." Comparing the play and its subject to a written text—he insists that "wee reden of this storye" (5.49)—Expositor seemingly diminishes the performative and active quality of the play. His treatment of audience and performance exemplify what Jeffrey (1973) describes as the new faith's changing view of history and its "rising opposition" in the early years of the Reformation to an "open-ended" view of biblical history. "This criticism," Jeffrey notes, "would come particularly from those new churchmen whose use of the Scriptures was based upon a reverence for literal historical accuracy" (47). Expositor's assertions, coupled with his swift rendering of the scenes to the past, require the audience to think in linear terms, establishing an atmosphere that differs from the "view of history as an artificial frame for the recurrence of divine pattern" (72). Treating events from sacred history as events firmly located in a time and place different from those of the present audience, Expositor attempts instead to extract meaning, truth, and usefulness, rather than to bring his audience to that meaning through their joint "participat[ion] in a divine pattern" (72).

These different perspectives on time, sacred history, and reception roles continue to emerge in Chester's fifth pageant. When Balaak enters, apparently at the level of the audience, declaring his identity and describing his power and greatness, his speech is punctuated with three stage directions: "Florish," "Caste up," and "Sworde" (sds. ff. 5.111, 115, 143).[28] Describing physically vigorous actions, the directions amplify the intended immediacy of his entrance as he makes his way through the crowd, who themselves are playing the role, designated by Moses, as "Godes folke of Israell." Quite possibly, then, Balaak "flourishes" and "casts up" directly at the audience, since in his tirade against Moses and the Israelites he orders one of his knights to go "fetche" Balaam "that he may curse *these people heare*" (5.164–65; my emphasis).[29] As with Nuntius's physical interactions with the audience in Chester's fourth pageant, Balaak here assumes and maintains a physical, spatial intimacy with the audience, subjecting them to his tirades and anger. The present and personal history of the audience mingles with that of a sacred history whose meaning and significance are clarified through audience participation. Yet, in a move that diverges from (and therefore helps to articulate more fully) the participatory atmosphere that has dominated much of the pageant, Balaam's curse, noticeably, is not reenacted. Instead, it is described to the audience by Expositor, who instigates a devotional experience in contrast to the interactive flourishings of Balaak. In fact, in the Harley manuscript version of the cycle, in which Expositor's appearances are more frequent, Balaak's dynamic swordplay does not appear (neither does Nuntius). In all manuscripts, furthermore, Expositor asserts the position of audience as viewers—"Lordes and ladyes tha here bine lente" (5.388)—while describing the Israelites as a distant people located in the distant past, historical persons whose story is communicated to the audience in a style requiring a new devotional response:

---

28. See also Peter Meredith's speculations about these stage directions and Chester's tyrants (1985, 58).

29. Interestingly, the Nuncius of *The Pride of Life* describes the King of Life as one who "florresschist with thi brigt bronde" (Davis, 1970, 98, l. 277). Both Nuncius and the King of Life are audience attentive figures, interacting with them physically and spatially.

and to Godes people hee hath them brought—
God knoweth, a perlouse thinge.

For when *they* had of *them* a sight,
manye of *them* agaynste right
gave *themselfe* with all *theyre* might
those women for to please.
And then soone to *them they* went;
to have *theyre* [love] was *there* intent,
desyringe those women of *theyr* consent
and soe to live in pease.

(5.394–403; my emphasis)

Referring to "all saints whose lives thou readest in the scriptures,"
as well as other figures from biblical history, Tyndale urged "all that
are present and gone before are but ensamples, to strength our faith
and trust in the word of God" (1848c, *Parable*, 110). Expositor also
seems to expect this approach of his audience. Although not all of
the third-person plural pronouns in his description refer to the Israelites, the repetition emphatically stresses "Godes people" (originally identified so closely with the audience throughout much of
the previous play) as examples from the past for understanding and
revelation. In fact, in the Harley manuscript this process of exem-
plification and revelation is expanded through the addition to the
end of the pageant of a procession of prophets which includes in-
tervening explanations from Expositor. Otherwise engaging figures
who step into the time and place of the contemporary audience to
impart information to a contemporary congregation, become, once
interpreted by Expositor, the conveyers of sacred utterances from
the past whose words now require explanation.[30]

---

30. Prophet processions are not an uncommon feature of medieval religious
drama. Without Expositor's intercessory explanations, perhaps Chester's prophet
procession would resemble a form of the *sermone semidrammatico*. See above, n. 12.

A Pre-Reformation Aesthetic: Re-Creating Sacred History

Expositor's presence in the Chester cycle works to distinguish proper from improper response and to present an alternative means for interacting with the plays. This alternative requires his audience to see a difference—in essence, to view the errors of past audiences in order to overcome those errors with a reformed sensibility. Hence, the style of performance and reception adopted by Nuntius and figures like him remains intriguingly intact—a convention strongly bound to pre-Reformation notions of time, history, and worship practice. Having elucidated his position on the proper role of response, the figure of Expositor thus helps to reveal a pre-Reformation reception aesthetic that might otherwise remain hidden. This aesthetic, as we have seen, embraces contemporaneity, immediacy, and a notion of time that makes the re-creation of sacred history a highly participatory and salvific activity for all those involved. When, in the fifth pageant, Moses, Balaak, and Balaam each address the audience, they assume between the audience and "the people of Israel" a contemporaneity that acknowledges and invokes the audience's expected role in the successful restaging of sacred events. The stage directions, too, evince this audience engagement: "Tunc Moyses faciet signum quasi effoderet tabulas de monte et, super ipsas scribens *dicat populo*" (s.d. ff. 5.80; my emphasis). The assertion in the stage directions that Moses will speak to the people anticipates that his declaration will include the audience:

> Godes folke of Israell,
> herkens you all to my spell.
> God bade ye should keep well
> this that I shall saye.
>
> (5.81–84)

Following this short speech, another stage direction indicates Moses' position on the mountain, designated as a location on the pageant wagon (or on a hill if part of a stationary performance), which places him in an opportune location for addressing the audience and including them in the sacred enactment. Later intermingling with the crowd that is both ancient people and contemporary audience, Balaak commands his knight:

> Yea, looke thou hett him gould great one
> and landes for to live upon
> to destroye them as hee cann,
> *these freekes* that bine soe fell.
>
> (5.172–75; my emphasis)

Balaak's plans "to destroye" the crowd may have elicited an animated response from them. And less than one hundred lines later, he has occasion to refer to them again in enlisting Balaam's aid. Balaam here sees the very audience to whom he refers in lines 280–82 ("How may I curse here in this place / that people that God blessed hasse?") and whom he directly invokes a few lines later: "Now on thinge I will tell you all, / hereafter what shall befall" (320–21ff.).[31]

Likewise invoking a temporal and spatial proximity between audience members and figures from sacred history, Nuntius at the beginning of Chester's sixth pageant *(The Annunciation and the Nativity)* requests that the audience:

> Make rowme, lordinges, and give us waye
> and lett Octavian come and playe,
> and Sybell the sage, that well fayre maye,
> to tell you of prophecye.
>
> (6.177–80)

In contrast to Expositor's insistence on immediate interpretation and understanding for his audience, Nuntius's declaration is a necessary, immediate address to a contemporary crowd, an acknowledgment of their commanding presence as both past and present participants. In addition, the duality of performance space and medieval audience mirrors the messenger's double identity: his role as both

---

31. See Powlick (1993) for a convincing argument for stationary performance. For recent work in support of pageant wagon production, see Davis (1993).

Nuntius, audience-address figure, and Preco, Octavian's messenger, contributes to a conflation of time and space that permits the recreation of sacred history.[32]

The conflation of past and present people, time, and space similarly informs the response of one of the Angels in the pageant to the expectant Mary. This response also provides a particularly descriptive example of the reception style this conflation inspires. Seeking to explain the significance of Mary's journey to Bethlehem with Joseph (to pay the tax), the Angel includes a convincing reference to the contemporary audience, providing another example of Jeffrey's "recurrence history":

> Marye, Godes mothere dere,
> the tokeninge I shall thee lere.
> The commen people, as thos seest here,
> are glad—as they well maye—
> that they shall see of Abrahams seede
> Christe come to helpe them in there neede.
>
> (6.437–42)[33]

Cast in an interesting dual role, the audience must see themselves as contemporaries not only to Mary and the virgin birth, but also to the performance of the current play. In fact, the two situations neatly connect in the Angel's smooth reckoning, and Mary herself is implicated as the past, present, and eternal mother of God. "Christe come to helpe them in there neede" transcends his original birth; he

---

32. A boastful speech from Octavian directed at the audience and contemporary crowd immediately follows Nuntius's declaration. Octavian begins his speech in garbled French, directly appealing to the audience: "Segneurs, tous si assembles a mes probes estates!" Mills, in his modern language edition, renders this in English as "Lords, all assembled here at my noble council" (1992, 108). With members of his court assembled around him, Octavian clearly aims his speech at more than just this limited audience. In fact, the audience easily assumes the role of the taxed people, and in ll. 373–88, the declaration by Nuntius/Preco of the taxation mandate further solidifies the role of the audience as people under Octavian's rule.

33. Cf., as well, the inclusive audience address style of the Angel audience-address figure (who also resembles Nuntius) at the end of pageant 11, ll. 327–34.

is humankind's salvation then, now, and always. The timelessness is constructed and celebrated in an inclusive, participatory process based on a view of "history as an artifical frame for the recurrence of divine pattern" and a view of "men of every generation [as participants] in one great *historia*—in the *speculum humanae salvationis*" (Jeffrey, 1973, 72).[34] The Angel in Chester's sixth pageant explains to Mary the purpose of Mary and Joseph's journey, conveying information and meaning to the audience not as outside viewers of history (a stance modeled, in part, by Expositor), but through their inclusiveness and participation in the sacred scenes. The journey, as the Angel explains it, actually motivates the communication continuum between the past event of the Nativity and the present-day audience. The Angel's explanation demonstrates that the synchronic nature of the performative process involves the prophetic perspective of figures from the sacred past as well as the nostalgic contemplation of the participants from the contemporary play. The actions of Mary and Joseph as they occurred, and now occur, are always and ever meant to convey meaning and significance to those who work to re-create them.

Similarly, in the twelfth pageant of the Chester cycle *(The Temptation of Christ),* the character of Diabolus creates a unique connection with the contemporary audience, ascribing his reasons for his temptation of Christ to emotions that could be shared by many audience members. The Devil opens the play with a speech of more than fifty lines delivered in soliloquy, describing and explaining his reasons for the temptation. Declaring his wonder and amazement at the nearly unbelievable state and attributes of the God-become-man, the Devil implicates the attendant audience. He asks, "What maister mon ever be this / that nowe in world commen is?" (12.9–10), engaging the audience's own questions and curiosity, their own

---

34. Cf. the participatory process in Caiphas's treatment of his audience in the dramatic sermon from the Sloane Ms. (see n. 12 above). There, audience members are present-day pilgrims bearing palms and, simultaneously, contemporaries of Caiphas and Christ; both of these roles meld in the necessity for re-creating and communicating the significance of the original event (see ll. 133–38).

"mervayle" (21) about Jesus. The Devil makes the audience his cohorts, informants who will understand and follow the reasoning behind his plan for the temptation. Indeed, once the actual temptation begins, Diabolus, while he speaks directly to Christ, also maintains an ongoing commentary upon his and Christ's actions, keeping the audience informed by consistently referring to Christ in the
third person, even though Christ is present before him and the audience:

> Owt, alas! What is this?
> This matter fares all amysse;
> hongree I see wel *hee* is,
> as man should kindlye.
>
> But through no craft ne no coyntyse
> I cannot torne *his* will, iwys;
> that neede of any bodely blys
> in *him* nothinge hasse hee.
>
> For *hee* may suffer all maner of noye
> as man should, well and stifflye;
> but aye *hee* winneth the victorye
> as godhead in *him* weare.
> Some other sleight I mott espye
> this disobedient for to destroye;
> for of mee *hee* hasse the maistrie
> unhappingely *nowe here.*
>
> (12.81–96; my emphasis)

Whereas in other circumstances the participatory aesthetic has often been most perceptively identifiable through the physical and
spatial continuum assumed by its mediating figures, here the Devil
establishes an emotional and intellectual continuum, employing the
audience's feelings of curiosity and wonder about Christ's nature
and his own diabolical reasons for the temptation.[35] This continu-

---

35. The Devil may have certainly aided this continuum by delivering his addresses while circulating through, looking at, and gesturing toward the audience.

um extends the temporal and spatial continuum (of which Christ "hasse the maistrie / unhappingely nowe here"), so that Diabolus can suggest that the curiosity and wonder behind his temptation has actually resurfaced in the minds of the contemporary audience. Just as they are implicated by him in the temptation process, so too are the audience members implicated by their own inevitable questioning of God's nature both within and without the play. From within the process of the dramatic performance, audience engagement and identification with the Devil's own perceptions encourage personal and present understanding; meaning unfolds in the "work" of the play.[36]

Correcting Audience Error: A Shifting Ideology of Response

In keeping with his reforming role, Expositor asserts a different method of deriving meaning in Chester's twelfth pageant, one which, again, presents the audience with a different, and potentially corrective, experience of the enacted scene. Exhibiting an alternative reception style, Expositor interprets the meaning of the *The Temptation of Christ* as a comment on the three sins of gluttony, vainglory, and pride (12.169ff.). He relegates the scene to the past, treating its significance as that which must be understood and explained from a distance:

> This overcome thrise in this case
> the devill, as playd was in this place,
> of the three sinnes that Adam was
> of wayle into woe weaved.
> But Adam fell through his trespas,
> and Jhesu withstoode him through his grace;
> for of his godhead soothnes
> that tyme was cleane disceived.
>
> (12.209–16)

---

36. See above, p. 36, for Jauss's comments on the process of "work."

Whereas in the temptation scene, as we have seen, meaning is communicated through a style of reception that invokes the present, active feelings of audience members, for Expositor the episode requires a clearer, more direct statement of understanding. The importance of Expositor's particular approach to events from sacred history presented by the play becomes clearer in his reference to the performance of *The Woman Taken in Adultery,* also staged in Chester's twelfth pageant:

> Nowe lordes, I pray you marke here
> the great goodnes of Godes deede.
> I will declare as *hit is neede*
> these thinges that playd were.
>
> (12.281–84; my emphasis)

In addition, the transition in pageant 12 to a thematically different episode in the life of Christ suggests that the addition of Expositor to the play may have been accompanied by additional emendations, including the curious pairing of the *The Temptation* with the *The Woman Taken in Adultery.* Christ's writing in the dirt in response to the Pharisees' accusations of the Adulteress implies a rather distant interpretation and commentary on the scene. This creates a potentially useful precedent for Reformation methodologies that Expositor has adopted in his own commentaries throughout the cycle. By extension, what also links the enigmatically paired *The Temptation* and *The Woman Taken in Adultery* is a sense of subverting the inconsistent and misleading perceptions of both the Devil and the Pharisees and, perhaps, the Devil's involvement of the audience in a participatory aesthetic. Expositor portrays the Devil, the Pharisees, and "these things that playd were" as confused and confusing figures from the past. They are archaisms that the audience must recognize as dangerous and misleading—along with the reception aesthetic they encourage.

In contrast, Expositor espouses a different type of accessibility to the past, one portrayed as a more direct textual understanding, perhaps similar to what Tyndale intended when he enjoined his read-

ers to "Cleve unto the text and playne storye" (1848f, *Prologue,* 411).
Similarly, in *The Prophets of Antichrist* (pageant 22, in which Expositor makes his last appearance), despite each prophet's explanation
of his respective vision, Expositor contributes yet another layer of
interpretation, stressing the need for an even clearer understanding.
Despite Ezechiel's assertion—

> This sawe I right in my sight
> to knowe that he was God almight
> that heaven and yearth should deale and dight
> and never shall ended bee
>
> (22.21–24)

—Expositor continues the revelatory process, highlighting the need
for the audience to "expresselye knowe":

> Nowe that you shall expresselye knowe
> these prophettes wordes upon a rowe,
> what the doe signifie I will shewe
> that mych may doe you good.
>
> (22.25–28)

Furthermore, after Zechariah's address, the explanation and meaning communicated by the prophet is simply insufficient:

> Nowe for to moralyze aright
> which this prophet sawe in sight,
> I shall found through my might
> to you in meeke mannere
> and declare that soone in height
> more playnle, as I have teight.
>
> (22.73–78)

Perhaps reminiscent of Tyndale's assertion that "a prophet signifi-
eth him that interpreteth the hard places of scripture, as him that
prophesieth things to come," (1848c, *Parable,* 80), Expositor demonstrates an apparent need to make further sense for the audience of

a past that needs careful and "plain" interpretation. A comparable insistence is communicated in the late Banns, where the victory of sight, assisted "now [by] the pathe playne," overcomes "[t]he ignorance wherein hathe us manye yeares soe blinded" (143–44).[37] Privileging explicative discourse, Expositor's addresses resemble a Protestant sermon whose goals and methods—focused on explication, clarity, and the revelation of previous misuses of religious ritual and ceremony—are outlined in a 1538 royal proclamation:

[G]reat and manifold superstitions and abuses . . . have crept into the hearts and stomachs of many of his [the King's] true, simple, and unlearned loving subjects for lack of the sincere and true explication, and the declaring of the true meaning and understanding of Holy Scripture, sacramentals, rites and ceremonies, as also the sundry strifes and contentions which have and may grow among many of his said loving subjects for lack of the very perfect knowledge of the true intent and meaning of the same, hath divers times most straightly commanded all and singular his archbishops, bishops, and other ministers of the clergy of this his most noble realm, in their sermons and preachings, plainly, purely, sincerely, and with all their possible diligence, to set forth first the glory of God and truth of his most blessed word, and after, the true meaning and end of the said sacramentals and ceremonies, to the intent that, all superstitious abuses and idolatries being avoided, the same sacramentals, rites, and ceremonies might be quietly used. (Hughes and Larkin, 1964, 274–75)

Expositor's speeches appear to fulfill the requirements decreed for religious authorities who "plainly, purely, sincerely, and with all their possible diligence . . . set forth first the glory of God and truth of his most blessed word, and after, the true meaning and end of the said sacramentals and ceremonies." Expositor embodies the growing emergence of a reception style created to expose the failings of the past religion as well as to sustain the true faith and its deliverance of God's Word.[38] Simultaneously, as noted in the proclamation,

37. See also Tyndale's explanation of what first encouraged him to translate the New Testament: "Because I had perceived by experience how that it was impossible to establish the lay-people in any truth, except the scripture wer plainly laid before their eyes in their mother-tongue, that they might see the process, order, and meaning of the text" (1848e, *Preface*, 394).
    38. Expositor's emphasis on explication, not surprisingly, resembles the formal practice of Protestant prophesying. Originally meetings of preachers for the

that reception style likely depended upon a shifting ideology of response for audiences and worshippers: the hope that "sacramentals, rites, and ceremonies might be quietly used" is also invoked in the concluding verse of the late Banns, which ends with an emphasis on the role and responsibility of future audiences:

> All that with quiett mynde
> can be contented to tarye
> be heere on Whitson-Mondaye;
> then begineth the storye.
>
> (210–13)

Distinguishable from the interactive aesthetic of communication and response espoused by the more audience interactive mediating figures of the Chester cycle, Expositor's seemingly self-imposed liminality and emphasis on interpretive understanding suggest a shift in spiritual discourse that breaks with the communal ethos of devotion from which the vernacular religious theater probably emerged. Indeed, the very "unease about the immediacy and openness of drama itself" which Mills has detected in the Chester cycle, as well as "the desire that audiences should be led to contemplate the action as a whole rather than identify with individuals within it closely" (1992, xxii),[39] can perhaps be explained by a reformist attention to the text and to its revelation of a style of production and reception that like-

---

purpose of explicating the Bible and theology, prophesyings gained popularity from the 1560s on in England and, as Collinson (1967) points out, grew to include sermons and "systematic Biblical exposition[s]" (51). Collinson also asserts that "by the public interest which they attracted and the indoctrination and homiletical training which they offered to the more ignorant clergy, the prophesyings did more than any other agency to propagate and establish the new religion in Elizabethan England" (51). Emphasizing the audience's auditory faculties rather than their visual and physical involvement, such prophesyings find echoes in Chester's pageant of *The Prophets of Antichrist,* as well as in the H manuscript's pageant of *Balaak and Balaam.* In "The Last Rise and Final Demise of Essex Town Drama," John Coldewey also suggests that the popularity of public prophesyings and sermons demonstrates a change in taste, a substitution for the "old religious plays" no longer in style (259ff.).

39. See also Mills (1985), 10–13. White (1999) has also commented upon this "guard[ing] against too much immediacy and openness of meaning" in the cycle (134).

ly troubled Protestant sensibilities. Believing that it was the improper *use* of sacred texts that mired the old faith in heresy, the overseers of the new faith often focused on distinguishing proper worship *practice* from such improper use. As Sir Richard Morison conceded in 1542 in "A Discourse Touching the Reformation of the Lawes of England," "those plaies" associated with the old faith should be made public because they "declare lyvely before the peoples eies the abhomynation and wickedness of the bisshop of Rome, monkes, freers, nonnes, and suche like" (qtd. in Anglo, 1957, 179). Given the late date of its manuscripts and of its last performances, the Chester cycle certainly seems a text that the forces of the Reformation were more at pains to modify and learn from than to destroy. Despite a Reformation dislike of the earlier faith's disorderly devotional practices, then, we ultimately may have that religious upheaval to thank for the survival of those practices and the texts that invoke them. The potentially reformist Expositor therefore may disclose not only the guiding principles of his sponsors but also the aesthetic of the older faith that necessitated for the new religion a reformulation of language, communication, and reception: in essence, the means by which one seeks the divine.

Chapter Two

Correcting Response in the Digby
Conversion of Saint Paul

"Stabyll your syghtys" and "Spare your speche"[1]

IN RECASTING THE CHESTER CYCLE as a proto-Protestant text, the writers of the post-Reformation Banns attempted to ensure the survival of the cycle, given the change in England's religious climate and accompanying reform efforts to rid the land of the errors of the earlier faith. Yet the inventive claim put forth in the Banns— that the cycle had in the past simply been misappropriated and misused by Catholic sponsors and audiences, and that this misuse could now be examined and overcome through the proper mechanisms of the true faith—may reflect other reform efforts to purge through a process other than overt destruction. As with the Chester cycle and its Expositor, the Digby *Conversion of Saint Paul* offers its audiences an address figure whose emphasis on scriptural authority asserts a

1. The quotation is from Baker, Murphy, and Hall (1982), 20, ll. 568 and 559. All future references are from this edition and will be cited parenthetically by line number. I have modernized some spellings throughout.

reception role that potentially conflicts with the one promoted by other elements of the performance that assume, for example, a spatial and physical immediacy with audience members. Reinterpreted as a play that has been misused by the earlier faith, *The Conversion of Saint Paul* becomes, like the Chester cycle, an arena for exposing the errors of the old religion and replacing them with the truths of the new religion. While, unlike the Chester cycle, this reinterpretation process is not directly attested to (as it is in the late Banns), *The Conversion of Saint Paul* contains several clues that indicate its immediate usefulness for a reformist program seeking to reveal the errors of one style of faith in order to replace them with the truths of the new style of faith.

Although the main text of the manuscript of the *Saint Paul* dates approximately to 1500, the condition of the manuscript and a number of scribal tinkerings with the main text suggest that the play enjoyed continued attention and use throughout the sixteenth century. Not only is the cover sheet of the manuscript (f. 37) rather worn and dirty, but two distinct creases or folds in the manuscript indicate that it was carried around, perhaps folded into pockets.[2] For Donald Baker, these manuscript details demonstrate a highly versatile play with a long performance life, adaptable to different performance situations (1989, 20–25). These details also point to the possibility that the play could suit alternative religious sensibilities, a flexibility supported by the probable performance of the *Saint Paul* (along with the Digby *Mary Magdalene*) in Chelmsford in 1562 (Coldewey, 1975). While the manuscript of the Digby *Saint Paul* predates the Reformation and must have been initially composed and produced to suit Catholic sensibilities, it was perhaps also later performed to suit an alternative theology. As records have demonstrated, saint plays seem to have been highly popular, possibly accounting for the most com-

---

2. See Baker, Murphy, and Hall (1982) for manuscript information and for a discussion of staging (xv–xviii and xxv–xxx). See as well the Introduction to Baker and Murphy (1976, vii–xii). Baker (1989) also explores the possible performance history of the plays (21–25). Coldewey (1975) provides a strong case for the 1562 staging. See also Baker and Murphy (1967, 162–63).

mon and numerous of all of the vernacular religious plays in medieval England.[3] In the wake of the Reformation's wholesale destruction of the genre,[4] the sole survival of the Digby *Saint Paul* and its companion saint play, the Digby *Mary Magdalene* suggests that these two plays may well have been deemed salvageable, if not remarkably useful, to the new religion.

The thematic foundation of the *Conversion of Saint Paul* is, of course, the act of conversion: of Paul's recognition of his spiritual ignorance and his transformation from persecutor to disciple. As a fawning and eager agent of the evil temple priests, Caiphas and Anna, Paul undergoes his change while journeying to Damascus to root out the followers of Christ. Gaining a new spiritual understanding, he converts from the old faith (of the Old Testament) to the new faith (of the New Testament). In his 1527–1528 *The Obedience of a Christian Man,* William Tyndale points specifically to Paul's conversion: "[I]f any may have resisted ignorantly, as Paul did, let him look on the truth which Paul wrote after he came to knowledge" (1848b, 143). Echoing Tyndale's admiration, John Bale identified his own cause and troubles with those of Paul.[5] Viewed, then, with the right proclivities, Paul's conversion, along with the struggles between the old and the new faiths portrayed in the *Saint Paul,* could become for some reformists divinely sanctioned prefigurations of their own activities and beliefs. Similarly, the play contains an audience guide figure, Poeta, whose conflicting treatments of play, performance, and audience (especially seen in relation to the play's enigmatic audience processional), may be interpreted as demonstrating different theological attitudes regarding the proper use of the play and the proper role of its audience. Reseen as a play whose true religious allegiances have been obscured by the incorrect theology and performance mishandling of the old, corrupt faith (a revisionist approach

3. See Grantley's accounting of the extensive number of references to these plays (1994, 266–67). See also Davidson (1986).

4. Discounting the Cornish *Life of Meriasek.*

5. See Happé (1986), 238, n. 5, as well as his discussion of Bale's identification with Paul (1985, 6–7).

that foreshadows the sentiment expressed in the post-Reformation Banns of the Chester cycle), *The Conversion of Saint Paul* in effect could endorse the Reformation and the new faith.

Late in its performance history, through a reinterpretation of its meaning, message, and production style that required little direct textual revision, the play may have admitted performances that could support alternative theologies. In the hands of a shrewd Protestant sponsor, the *Saint Paul* can become an effective proto-reformist play, undergoing and demonstrating a process of change from the old to the new faith, and capable of steering spectators sympathetic to Catholicism from their own familiar tradition of the religious drama toward a different theological use of that drama. Undergoing more than a thematic reconsideration, such a reformist use of the play would include critiquing a performance situation aligned with the earlier faith and its dramatic tradition, and replacing it with a style more consistent with Protestant notions of divine revelation and scriptural authority.

The Diabolical Catholic Clergy: Secondhand Vestments and Spiritually Deceptive Devils

Specifically, the interpolated devil scene of the play serves to connect its message of religious conversion to contemporary reformist ideas and activities. Added twenty to thirty (or possibly even fifty) years after the main text of the play was composed,[6] and therefore corresponding roughly to the date of Tyndale's *Obedience,* the scene seems to have been carefully crafted and deliberately added.

---

6. See Baker, Murphy, and Hall (1982), xvi–xvii, and Baker and Murphy (1976). See also Baker (1989): "To this manuscript about thirty or forty years later, a gathering of four leaves (only three leaves bear writing; the fourth is cut to a stub) was added, in which a second hand has marked out St. Paul's sermon after his conversion (f. 44v) and has inserted an interesting scene in which Belial receives news from Mercury about the conversion of St. Paul, their special agent. After this scene (ff. 45–47, ll. 412–515), the new scribe, or more probably the author of the scene, has carefully again written St. Paul's sermon on the Seven Deadly Sins; then the play continues as before."

As Baker asserts, "[T]he Belial scene is not a mere thoughtless attachment to tart up the play; it takes its cue from the prayers of the two priests, Caiphas and Anna, to their pagan gods. It . . . make[s] a good addition to the new play, attributing further motives to the scheming of the priests . . . and illustrating the sins against which the converted Paul is to preach" (1989, 23). In addition, to a reformist eager to reveal and revise the "real" theological meaning of the *Saint Paul*, the added devil scene cements the associations between the endeavors of Caiphas and Anna and those of Satan's ranks; just as the temple priests lament the loss of Paul to the new faith, so do Belial and Mercury. When Belial names them "my prelayts, Cayphas and Anna" (419), he draws a parallel between Catholic religious authorities and diabolical forces that characterized the thinking of a number of Reformation advocates and Protestants who connected the overturning of Old Testament religion with the subversion of Catholicism. Sir Richard Morison, for example (as we have seen), in "A Discourse Touching the Reformation of the Lawes of England," a text dating from around 1542 but possibly earlier, aligns the Catholic clergy with Old Testament religious figures, paralleling the pope and Pharaoh, Henry and Moses. He declares the necessity of a programmatic thematic attack upon "the bysshop of Rome, who provoked and forced us to commytt such Idolatrie and impiete as thother pharao did never more to the Hebreys" (Anglo, 1957, 177).[7] Likewise, in Lewis Wager's *The Life and Repentance of Marie Magdalene*—a Protestant rendition of the only other extant Middle English saint play, the Digby *Mary Magdalene*—the allegorical figure Infidelitie informs both players and audience that:

7. Anglo (1957), speculating on the date of Morison's text, comments that "all the suggestions for anti-papal propaganda, apart from the annual celebration, appear to have been put into practice long before 1542, so that the original date of composition might well have been some four, or more, years earlier, that is before such ideas had been applied throughout the country, and when they would still have had the force of an original theory" (177).

Infidelitie for divers respectes hath names divers,
Of the which some of them to you I propose to reherse.
With bishops, priests, scribes, seniors and pharisies.

(1992, 15, ll.469–71)[8]

And, in John Bale's *King Johan,* Treason, a representative of the Catholic clergy, directly associates his religious treachery with the very temple priests portrayed in the *Saint Paul:*

We selle our maker so sone as we have hym made,
And as for preachynge we meddle not with that trade
Least Annas, Cayphas, and the lawers shulde us blame.

(1985, 1853–55)

The interpolated devil scene, then, induces a thematic reinterpretation of the *Saint Paul* play that conceives of it and the Saint Paul story as symbolic foreshadowing of the new faith's superiority to, and triumph over, the old faith.[9]

The connection between the diabolical machinations of the Old Testament religious authorities in the *Saint Paul* and the contemporary Catholic clergy, moreover, becomes especially pronounced if the former were clad in the leftover vestments of the latter. Bale and other authors of Reformation polemic seem to have added a visual edge to their critique and ridicule of the Catholic clergy by using such vestments as costumes in their plays. As Peter Happé has noted, in *King Johan* "[t]here is extensive use of clerical and monastic garb, most of it with polemical intent. Possibly in the years of the Dissolution it was relatively easy to find unwanted ecclesiastical clothing, and Bale is adept at suggesting the tawdriness and staginess of Catholic rituals by employing it" (1985, 23). Despite Elizabeth's mid-sixteenth century Act of Uniformity, which required clergy to use and wear the "outward and visible remnants of the

8. In addition, Infidelitie asserts that "[t]he bishops, priests and pharisies do me so retayne, / That the true sense of the lawe they do disdayne" (12, ll. 349–50).
9. See Happé (1985), for a discussion of reformation adaptations and versions of the saint play genre.

old religion" (Coldewey, 1975, "Last Rise," 253), clergymen often refused. Churches sold off their garments, and playing companies benefited from a windfall of costume materials. (Even before Elizabeth's reign, in 1536, Cromwell took possession of certain monastic goods that seem to have fallen into the hands of Bale and his players.)[10] If the *Saint Paul* was one of the plays staged in 1562, as John Coldewey's scrutiny of the dramatic records shows, certainly the playing wardrobe, made from discarded clerical garments as described in the records, was used in its production.[11] The symbolic usefulness of such garments as costumes for Caiphas and Anna, and for the devils in the added scene, may have lent itself to a Protestant production, enhancing the damning associations between Catholic clergy and corrupt Old Testament figures. Perhaps Paul, too, in the "preconversion" scenes of the play, wore similar attire; the stage direction immediately preceding the converted Paul's sermon, *"Here aperyth Saul in hys dyscyplys wede . . ."* (s.d. before l. 502), communicates a decided change of costume that would indicate visually his literal and spiritual shedding of Old Testament and "popish" garb for his true "dyscyplys wede."

One small interpolated scene, therefore, encourages interpretive alterations to the play that extend beyond the boundaries of the scene. Although the contents of the play are not textually altered, dressing certain performers in vestments connects diabolical forces with Catholic clergy while endorsing religious reform. The religion of Caiphas and Anna, of the Old Testament (and, as the added scene makes clear, of the Devil) is that from which Paul tellingly converts. Moreover, the dramatic use of Catholic vestments may represent what reformists considered the overly elaborate, spectacularly indulgent, and ultimately dangerous nature of Catholic belief and ritual. More than a stylistic concern for Protestant advocates, the adornment of the Catholic clergy's attire exemplifies a larger

10. See Happé (1980).
11. See Coldewey (1975), "The Digby Plays" and (1975), "The Last Rise" (255, n. 33).

process of spiritual beguilement. In his 1527 *Parable of the Wicked Mammon*, Tyndale asserts the following:

> Though seest how Christ rebuketh the scribe and Pharisees in the gospel, (which were very Antichrists,) saying: "Woe be to you, Pharisees! . . . ye pray long prayers under a colour; ye shut up the kingdom of heaven, and suffer not them that would to enter in; ye have taken away the key of knowledge; ye have made men break God's commandments with your traditions": ye beguile the people with hypocrisy and such like; which things all our prelates do, but have yet gotten them new names, and other garments and weeds, and are other wise disguised. There is difference in the names between a pope, a cardinal, a bishop, and so forth, and to say a scribe, a Pharisee, a senior, and so forth; but the thing is all one. (1848c, 42–43)

As Tyndale describes, the corrupt faith's clergy not only disguise themselves by their use of "new names, garments, and weeds" though they are really only contemporary versions of Old Testament religious figures, but they also actively mislead people from spiritual truth through "long prayers with a colour": they keep people from heaven by concealing knowledge. Catholicism obscures and misleads with its elaborate, unnecessary, and dangerous trappings—its "traditions" and ceremonies both visual and verbal. As Paul White has commented, the reformists used Catholic clerical attire, "stunning visual pun[s]," and other spectacular scenes not only to "evoke laughter" but also to "satiriz[e] the tropological significance which Catholicism ascribes to visual images" (1993, 2, 1). Indeed, in the minds of many reformers, "the images need[ed] to be presented in order to be literally or ritualistically destroyed" so playwrights such as Bale often "use[d] an image to make a point about the *abuse* of images" (White, 1993, 15, 2). Hence, in the interpolated scene of the *Saint Paul*, it is appropriate that Belyall, the diabolical agent of Satan and the overseer of Paul's original superiors, Caiphas and Anna, declares his own machinations and beguilements of "Mans mynd":

> Ho! Thus as a god most hye in magestye
> I rayne and I rule over creaturys humayne.
> Wyth soverayne sewte sowte to ys my deyte;
> Mans mynd ys applicant as I lyst to ordeyne.
>
> (433–36)

A vestment-clad Belyall and his assertions, contained in the only major textual revision to the *Saint Paul,* unite extravagant garments, spectacles, and images with the faith of the Old Testament and Catholicism, while implying that these diabolical religions pursue a program of intentional spiritual deception.[12]

Viewed in this way, then, the spectacular nature of the interpolated scene, with its possibly vestment-adorned devils, provides a negative example of what the converted Paul (and the remainder of the play itself) rejects: uncontrolled, irreverent horseplay that encourages an audience role and spiritual stance unsuitable to the reformed faith. Like the corrupt Caiphas and Anna and their reincarnations in the present-day Catholic clergy, Belyall and Mercury deceive the audience spiritually, making a game of religion.[13] The added devil is a beguiling trap that must be scrutinized and conquered in the *Saint Paul* by the reasonable logic of the converted Paul and the Holy Scriptures. From this perspective, the *Saint Paul* becomes an iconoclastic play, reforming its audience's style of response, faith, and worship. The addition of the devil scene may certainly have been a response to an actor or actors' particularly strong "deviling" abilities (Baker, 1989, 23), yet it could also have been a useful scene for reformists, allowing them to convert a formerly Catholic play into one of "those plaies" that Morison in his "Discourse" asserts to be necessary because they "declare lyvely before the peoples eies the abhomynation and wickednes of the bisshop of Rome, monkes, freers, nonnes, and such like" (Anglo, 1957, 179).

12. Cox (1994–1995, 407–38) has argued that in the mystery plays courtier's garments were often worn by devils to suggest a connection between diabolical actions and contemporary social ills. Depending upon his attire, then, Belyall's intentions to beguile man's "applicant" mind could be performed as an indictment of wealth and extravagance. Dress Belyall and his cohorts in discarded vestments (which could also be linked to wealth and extravagance), however, and the attire links Catholicism with diabolical forces and the spiritual beguilement of souls.

13. Interestingly, before his conversion, Paul also seems to have been involved in similarly diabolical activities, as he swears "by the god Bellyall" in his opening line (29). Furthermore, the passage in the manuscript that contains this line (ll. 27–350) is in a different style from the rest of the text, although the date of the passage is indeterminate. See Baker, Murphy, and Hall (1982), 1, n. 2, and Baker and Murphy (1976).

Much of the dramatic tradition of the condemned faith was destroyed or lost during the Reformation, and the genre that probably suffered most was the saint play.[14] Yet, as ecclesiastical garments were occasionally used for polemical purposes, so too did Reformation advocates occasionally find it useful to revise a drama. Reworking visual spectacles and dramatic forms already familiar to the country's faithful, reformists attempted to convert people by convincing them that the true faith, once delivered from the evil, deceptive trappings of Catholicism, was imminent, ironically present, and ready to be disclosed in the very religious drama associated with the "popist" faith. Grounded in notions of revelation and reform, such a program of reinterpretation could transform the *Saint Paul* into a proto-reformist play (a process likewise revealed in the late Banns of the Chester cycle). This alternative theological interpretation of the play, aided by the symbolic use of Catholic vestments, asserts that the true meaning and message of Paul's conversion have been obscured by the practices of the older faith as enacted by the play's earlier, misleading performance style. As the play undergoes thematic reinterpretation, then, so too does it undergo a stylistic critique in which an alternative performance is publicized and dismissed in order to assert the correct form for communicating and receiving religious truths. Indeed, the reinterpretation of the Paul story provides precedent and support for the process: as Paul converted to the new faith by realizing and rejecting the excesses and ills of his previous religion, so too must the adherents of the new faith discover and discard the present ills and excesses of Catholicism found in the *Saint Paul* (and in other remnants of the earlier faith) to demonstrate the proper form and worship practices of the true faith.

The devil scene amended to the *Saint Paul* therefore indicates that the play can be performed to suit both a thematic reinterpretation and a stylistic reinterpretation of the Saint Paul story. Not only can Paul's religious awakening be interpreted as a proto-conversion from Catholicism to Protestantism, but the play detailing this change also undergoes a stylistic conversion that permits a different perfor-

14. See Tydeman (1994), Davidson (1986), and Grantley (1994).

mance style and a different spiritual stance for its audience. A highly demonstrative, physical, and noisy display that would draw upon all of the human senses, the additional devil scene demonstrates what for Protestant sensibilities was the earlier faith's use of the drama at its worst: a loose, uncontrolled event whose method and meaning remain open, allowing diabolic forces to determine the outcome. Similarly, in *King Johan*, Bale portrays Catholic rituals as mere appealing entertainments, resulting in a disorderly confusion: "To wynne the peple," Dissymulacyon says, "I appoynt yche man his place":

> Sum to syng Latyn, and sum to ducke at grace;
> Sum to go mummyng, and sume to beare the cross;
> Sum to stowpe downeward, as ther heades ware stopt with mosse;
> Sume rede the epystle and gospell at hygh masse;
> Sume syng at the lectorne with long eares lyke an asse.
> The pawment of the Chyrche the aunchent faders tredes,
> Sumtyme with a portas, sumtyme with a payre of bedes;
> And this exedyngly drawth peple to devoycyone,
> Specyally what they do se so good relygeon.
> Than have we imagys of Saynt Spryte and Seynt Savyer:
> Moche is the sekynge of them to gett ther faver;
> Yong whomen berfote and olde men seke them brecheles.

> (1985, 698–710)

In Bale's accounts, such a confusion of worship, entertainment, spectacle, and devotion precluded true spiritual experience founded on direct reception of truth. This reception he saw the Catholic clergy as forever corrupting: "the clergy wrowght by practyse / and left the scriptur for menny ymagynacyons" (1985, 38).[15] Consistently remarking on the misuse of human capacities and the danger of un-

---

15. See also Tyndale in *The Obedience of a Christian Man:* "Christ saith, that there shall come false prophets in his name, and say that they themselves are Christ; that is, they shall so preach Christ that men must believe in them, in their holiness, and things of their imagination, without God's word: yea, and that Against-Christ, or Antichrist, that shall come, is nothing but such false prophets, that shall juggle with the Scripture, and beguile the people with false interpretations, as all the false prophets, scribes, and pharisees did in the old testament" (1848b, 147).

defined involvement in ritual, Bale described and critiqued the impetus behind the participatory style of the earlier religious drama, one that conflicted with the reformists' emphasis upon scriptural authority, fixity, and clarity in the dissemination of information.

Dangerous Sight, Dangerous Speech: Correcting Audience Response

While the interpolated devil scene connects the evil temple priests to diabolical forces, the devils themselves illustrate the very sins that are the topic of the converted Paul's sermon; moreover, these sins characterize a style of performance and audience response that, once identified, could help Protestants distinguish, critique, and ultimately replace Catholic practice and worship. Again, the added scene can be viewed as extending beyond its boundaries, influencing the message and effect of Paul's sermon; indeed, the scene can serve as an admonishment with literal examples that purges the audience of the production style and sensibility in which they have just participated, one related to what Tyndale called "persuasions of worldly wisdom," "blind ceremonies [and] superstitiousness of disguised hypocrisy" (1848b, *Obedience,* 220). Bale, furthermore, hinted that the "papist" religion promoted practices that hindered and obscured truth: "In the place of Christe [they] have sett up supersticyons; / For preachynges, ceremonyes, for Gods wurde, mennys / tradicyons" (1985, *King Johan,* 1822–24). And, according to Tyndale, the converted Paul himself knew the dangers of "worldly wisdom" and "blind ceremonies":

[C]rieth he [Paul] to God to augment their knowledge; that they should be no more children, wavering with every wind of doctrine; but would vouchsafe to make them full men in Christ, and in the understanding of the mysteries or secrets of Christ, so that it would not be possible for any man to deceive them with any enticing reasons of worldly wisdom, or to beguile them with blind ceremonies, or to lead them out of the way with superstitiousness. (1848b, *Obedience,* 220)

Many of Tyndale's references to Paul, including this one, could describe Paul's specific actions and attitudes in the *Saint Paul*. In fact, Tyndale's description of Paul's battle against "worldly wisdom" provides a foundation for Paul's attack in his sermon upon the dangers of the human senses.

Paul's sermon, then, delivers a strong corrective regarding proper and improper styles of communication and reception. This lesson easily complements a reformist reading of the play that emphasizes textuality as a warning regarding the dangers of the drama itself as a source and means of spiritual understanding. The audience, having watched Paul's rather dramatic conversion, become the inadvertent congregation for a sermon on appropriate spiritual behavior. Such appropriate behavior requires careful control over the primary means by which humans receive information and by which they would participate in a religious drama:

> Stabyll your syghtys, and look ye not stunt,
> For of a sertaynte I know at a brunt,
> *"Oculus est nuncius peccati—"*
> That the Iey ys ever the messenger of foly.
>
> (568–71)

Paul's aural message here, as well as the insertion of a sermon in the middle of a performance, suppresses the audience's visual participation, reinforcing the reformists' dislike of visual spectacle. Taking a cue from the interpolated devil scene that "illustrat[es] the sins against which the converted Paul is to preach" (Baker, 1989, 23), both the presence of the sermon and its theme warn the audience to modify their behavior and style of response. Morison comments on this theological conflict for the reformists between visual and aural capabilities: "Into the common people," he concedes, "thynges sooner enter by the eies, then by the eares: remembryng more better that they see then that they heere" (Anglo, 1957, 179). The loss of sight that accompanies Paul's conversion, moreover, serves as a reminder of the dangers of this human faculty. Tyndale, in fact, specifically quotes Paul on this conflict of ear versus eye: "'Faith,' saith he [Paul], Rom x., 'cometh by hearing, and hearing cometh by the word of God'" (1848b, *Obedience,* 223).[16] The nine direct scriptural references in Paul's sermon, and his emphasis upon the role of the Word and its textual authority in and over the spiritual life, also suggest an alternative reception role for the audience of the play. Paul requests God to "gyf us grace to understand and persever, / Thys wurd, as thou bydyst, to fulfyll ever" and also "assent[s] and fully certyfy[s] / *In text*" to tell "the trw entencyon" (521–22, 525–26; my emphasis).[17] Paul guides the audience away from what the reformists portrayed as the confused, deceptive, and diabolical rituals of the earlier faith. Ironically, Paul himself participates in the very practice for which, before his conversion, he critiqued the disciples: "For they go aboute to preche and gyff exemplis" (27).[18] Now, however, he can be viewed as having taken up a practice that will be condoned and celebrated by the new English church.[19]

Having condemned the dangers of human sight, Paul then may lead the audience away from reciprocal involvement in the performance with his description of the lasciviousness that accompanies human speech:

> But spare your speche, and spek nott theron:
> *"Ex habundancia cordis os loquitur."*
> Who movyth yt oft, chastyte lovyth non;
> Of the hartys habundans, the tunge makyth locucyon.

16. And compare 268: "'Faith' (saith Paul . . .) 'cometh by hearing,' that is to say, by hearing the preacher that is sent from God. . . .'"

17. In addition, Protestant prophesyings were originally derived, as Collinson (1967) comments, "from a text of St. Paul: 'Let the prophets speak two or three, and let the other judge. . . . For ye may all prophesy one by one, that all may learn and be comforted'" (169). See Chapter One above, n. 38.

18. Like the lines that include Paul's swearing "by the God Bellyall," the passage that contains this condemnation of "preaching" and "giving examples"—what were privileged activities of Protestantism—is in a different style from the rest of the text. See n. 13 above.

19. Similarly, in Bale's *King Johan,* Treason, a Catholic figure, belittles and distances himself from the activity of preaching: "And as for preachynge we meddle not with that trade / Least Annas, Cayphas, and the lawes shulde us blame" (1985).

What manys mynde ys laboryd, therof yt spekyth—
That ys of suernes, as Holy Scryptur tretyth.

(559–64)

To "stabyll" (568), or to control, sight and to spare speech, in short, relate directly to the role of the audience. Paul cautions against the misuse of both faculties (the very tools used by humans to communicate and respond), and therefore apparently endorses a less active reception role that privileges silent listening. Having shed the extravagant garb and the evil disguising and excesses of the old faith, the converted Paul embodies the new faith, appearing "in hys dyscyples wede" (s.d. before l. 502). A Catholic audience might have seen themselves as active participants in Paul's conversion, engaged in revealing its meaning for past and present Christians; in a reformist reinterpretation, however, Paul's conversion and his garment change echo Tyndale's association of Catholic clerical attire with the evils and beguilements of that faith. Paul's change of clothes and his sermon therefore indicate a decided shift in religious faith and spiritual attitude. When Tyndale says that Paul "commandeth to labour for knowledge, understanding, and feeling; and to beware of superstition, and persuasions of worldly wisedom, philosophy, and of hypocrisy and ceremonies, and of all manner disguising, and to walk in the plain and open truth" (1848b, *Obedience*, 219–20), he almost directly describes the message and form of Paul's sermon in *The Conversion of Saint Paul*.

Open to Correction: Poeta, Audience Response, and the Processional

Paul, moreover, is not alone in addressing the audience regarding appropriate spiritual behavior. The Poeta figure of the play also seems aware of a need to change or correct the performance and meaning of the play, and to guide the audience to its proper role in response to these. He delivers self-conscious, almost hesitant, audience addresses that imply that the play can proceed only cautiously

and under careful, authoritative supervision. In two of his addresses, he refers specifically to a process of "correccyon" to which he, his
players, and all those involved with the performance are being subjected, although who is in charge of this process remains unclear:

> Honorable frendys, besechyng yow of lycens
> To procede owur processe, we may under your correccyon
> The conversyon of Seynt Paule, as the Bible gyf experyens.
> Whoo lyst to rede the booke *Actum Appostolorum,*
> Ther shall he have the very notycyon;
> But, as we can, we shall us redres,
> Brefly, wyth yowr favour, begynynge owur proces.
>
> (7–13)

> Thus we comyte yow all to the Trynyte,
> Conkludying this stacyon as we can or may,
> Under the correccyon of them that letteryd be;
> Howbeyt unable as I dare speke or say,
> The compyler hereof should translat veray
> So holy a story, but wyth favorable correccyon
> Of my honorable masters, of ther benygne supplexion.
>
> (353–59)

Illustrating the confusion both about who controls this "correccyon" and about what such an act entails, Poeta refers alternately to
two different types of "correccyon." In his first speech, he grants the
honor of correction to the audience as a whole—those "[h]onorable
frendys" gathered for the performance. Yet by the middle of the
play the epithet and the authority to correct, as well as ownership of
the performance, have shifted to "them that letteryd be"—the "honorable masters" without whose aid the current "compyler" of the
Saint Paul would not have been able to "translat veray / So holy a
story." These two speeches thus display conflicting attitudes regarding not only the locus of authority, interpretation, and meaning of
the play, but also the process and progress of its performance. Poeta
and his play seem torn between (or, alternatively, in a transition be-

tween) two different approaches to and uses of the drama. On the one hand, Poeta may be simply involving his audience in the intricacies of the story and its enactment: referring to the difficulty of the "compeyler" in bringing past events into the present-day experiences of his audience and therefore calling upon them as necessary participants in the process. On the other hand, his emphasis on scriptural authority, his references to a perhaps distinct group of elite overseers (or revisers) separate from the enactment of performance, and his own distanced stance from the audience suggest an alternative use of the play, one that might be more preferable to a reformed audience.

A comparable conflict emerges between Poeta's authorization of the audience and the "processe" itself, and his ongoing concession to the authority of specific passages from the Bible. As his opening address concludes, the *Saint Paul* becomes only a fair substitute for the "very notycyon" found in the *"Actum Appostolorum,"* and Poeta's tone becomes strikingly less confident: "But, *as we can,* we shall us redres" (my emphasis). Later, he will refer to the performance— "[t]hus Saul ys convertyed, as ye se expres" (346)—only to assert the preeminence of Holy Scripture:

> After his conversyon never mutable, but styll insue
> The lawys of God to teche ever more and more,
> As Holy Scrypture tellyth whoso lyst to loke therfore.
>
> (350–52)

The authoritative presence of the Bible, coupled with a "correccyon," or revision, process overseen by a few choice "masters" (who, it seems, follow in the converted Paul's path and have received his endorsement as the "never mutable" teachers of "the lawys of God") signifies an alternative performance style, one that conflicts with Poeta's earlier reference to a more performance-based process of production, more reliant upon its actors and audience. Making explicit the conflicts between two styles that require different roles for their respective audiences, Poeta evokes the characteristics of a former (corrupt) style of religious performance to reveal its inferiority and its

need to be placed "[u]nder the correccyon of them that letteryd be."
If part of the Protestant program for stamping out Catholicism included a process by which "the images" of the older faith "neede[d]
to be presented in order to be literally or ritualistically destroyed"
(White, 1993, 15), then the drama of the older faith may have been
approached with a similar attitude of exposing a corrupt use of religious performances in order to distinguish a proper understanding of
(and attitude toward) such performances. At the very least, Poeta is
highly attentive to (and at pains to acknowledge) the fact that the play
and its production are offered up willingly to a revision process connected primarily to scriptural authority. Like Paul himself, play, performance, and audience can also be subjected to a conversion process
stressing revelation and religious reform, and focused on illustrating
the appropriate use of and response to religious theater.

One of the play's most problematic elements, a processional that
apparently embraces its audience as Paul's contemporaries by conflating past and present, further demonstrates the possibility of alternative performance styles and audience roles. When considered as a
remnant of a past performance history that displays the corrupt practices of the medieval Church, the audience involvement required by
the processional becomes a textual relic of the kind of participatory
style that the reformists sought to critique and dispel. The extant text
of the *Saint Paul,* in fact, comes as close as it can to offering alternatives to the audience-engaging processional without entirely eliminating it. Certainly, the "si placet" direction added to the right margin of the main text (f. 39v) may once again disclose the ability of the
play to adapt to different "playing conditions" (Baker, 1989, 25); yet
the direction also suggests that the sponsor of the play may simply
reject involving the audience directly in the action, while nevertheless leaving the processional intact as an archaic oddity of Catholic
practice and performance ritual.

Moreover, Poeta's paradoxical endorsement yet critique of the
procession also reflects these conflicting, though strangely conflat-
ed, attitudes toward the procession and the role of the audience in
relation to it:

Besechyng thys audyens to folow and succede
Wyth all your delygens this general processyon;
To understand this matter, wo lyst to rede
The Holy Bybyll for the better spede,
There shall he have the perfyth intellygens . . .

(156–60)

"This matter" to which Poeta refers remains enigmatic. While Poeta seems to use the Bible to endorse "this general procession" (which stands grammatically in direct apposition to "this matter"), he also seems to replace procession and performance with a reading of the biblical account. On the one hand, he seems to endorse the "perfyth intellygens" to be gained from participation in the processional; on the other hand, he seems to critique procession and performance while replacing it with the "perfyth intellygens" to be found only in Scripture. Poeta's entreaties regarding the processional seem, at once, as in John Marshall's description of a 1986 performance of the *Saint Paul,* capable of making an audience "literally followers of Saul," encouraged by "the Poet's instructions and Saul's journey in the most natural commingling of spiritual theme and physical action," and yet alternatively adaptable to a presentation "with perhaps less audience involvement at a single sight" (1994, 305–6).[20] To contemporary critics, this flexible portion of the play should also hint at an internal complexity of performance layers: the original processional, part of an alternative style of performance, remains either as an intact memorial to that use, ready to be employed again, or, as the "si placet" indicates, to be critiqued and purged away, either literally halted or merely referenced as a earlier misuse of the play.

Thus, rather than eliminating all allusions to what would have been considered a misguided role for the audience, a possible reformist use of the *Saint Paul* might have elected to convey what dis-

20. This production even used the marginal "daunce" directions as a means for moving the audience from station to station. For complete reviews of this production, see Meredith (1982) and Happé (1982).

tinguished the old faith from the new faith. Such a choice reveals a truly reformist conviction: it is not enough merely to replace old with new; the wrongs of the earlier religion must also be exposed and used as a justification for religious change and revision. Tyndale, for example, seemed involved in and dedicated to just such a process of revelation and critique. Describing what he sees as the dangers of popish rituals, he accuses the clergy of "car[ing] for no understanding; it is enough if thou canst roll up a pair of matins, or an even-song, and mumble a few ceremonies." He further asserts that clergy and rituals alike "bring us from the true faith, that is in God's word, unto a superstitious and false belief in our own imagination," thereby causing the people to "ascribe heaven unto their imaginations and mad inventions; and receive it not of the liberality of God . . ." (1848b, *Obedience*, 243, 226, 185). The rituals and ceremonies of the old faith, marked by audience engagement and active physical as well as mental participation, encourage human capacities of unruly thought and speech and therefore mislead people who lack the true way to "the perfyth intellygens" that must be found through a different program of communication and reception based more fully and directly upon the truth of Holy Scripture. If Poeta's acquiescence to the authority of Scripture endorses Protestant tastes, his treatment of the performance and audience provides a fortuitous "correction": a public purging of the earlier faith's mistreatment of religious performance linked to worship practices considered superstitious ritual and lascivious spectacle too dependent upon human emotion and response.

In *The Conversion of Saint Paul,* then, both hero and "Poet" devise, explain, and assert a style of communication and reception that can be distinguished from an alternative use of the same play— a use related to the ceremonies and rituals of the faith that Bale, Tyndale, and other reformers were keen to condemn as misleading indulgences and misuses of human capacities. Described as dangerous and blinding influences based upon spectacle and worldly pleasure, Catholic worship practices conflict with the sacred truth and eminent authority of Scripture. The reformists' emphasis upon the truth and perfection of God's Word therefore seems to have necessitated an ideological shift in worship practices, in the form by which the everyday Christian interacted with the divine. The drama of the earlier faith, consequently, may have emerged as a particularly effective tool for communicating this shift which required a different understanding of the role and responsibility of audiences in relation to sacred performance and the reception of sacred truths and meanings.

Reformed Audiences, Reformed Saints

The theological impulses that apparently shaped Protestant revisionist attitudes toward the drama of the earlier faith, moreover, may have similarly influenced reformulations of sainthood. Just as the reformists' adaptations of the earlier faith's drama worked to differentiate an appropriate style and use of religious performance from an inappropriate visual, physical, and emotional engagement of audience and players, so too did they work to create an idea of sainthood that would replace the personal intercession characteristic of Catholic belief. According to Tyndale, in *The Obedience of a Christian Man*, those who worship in the Catholic faith "turn themselves from God's word, and put their trust and confidence in the saint and his merits; and make an advocate, or rather a god of the saint; and of their blind imagination make a testament, or bond, between the saint and them . . . and this-wise imagine in their hearts saying: The saint for wearing such a garment, and for such deeds, is become so glorious in heaven. If I do likewise, so shall I be also" (1848b, 184). Tyndale's description of Catholic saint worship as a close bond between human worshipper and heavenly saint resembles the earlier faith producing a religious drama that similarly required the active involvement of (and identification with) sacred events and holy people. Tyndale's complaints about saint worship again critique the promotion by the earlier faith of a misguided use of human imagination. Indeed, the "bond" that Tyndale describes invokes the same kind of temporal and spatial continuum promoted in the early English drama by the active visual, verbal, and physical participation of the audience in performance. Requiring active involvement on the part of the worshipper and the re-creation of past actions by present actions, the bond constructs a fluid continuum between saint and worshipper, past and present, sacred and mundane. Tyndale also describes this belief and practice when he upbraids those "ceremonies, which some imagine their ownselves . . . saying . . . Such holy persons did thus and thus, and they were holy men; therefore if I do so likewise, I shall please God" (1848c, *Pathway*, 16). The spiritual stance and response role expected of a Catholic audience member and/or saint worshipper, however, conflicts with (and must be distinguished from) the humble reception of scriptural truth, described by Protestant thinkers.

In fact, the Protestant (re)definition of sainthood—of what constituted true holiness for the reformed faith—celebrates the perfectly reformed audience member, quietly receiving, accepting, and embodying the truth of God's Word. Thus, the reformists recast their saints as flawless examples—*exempla*—made perfect by their spiritual reliance upon God's Word and their ability to manifest this reliance. Anne Askew, for example, a woman burned for her apparent adherence to Scripture, becomes in Bale's description a saint, because "Askewe and her fellowship had none other relics about them . . . but a bundle of the sacred Scriptures enclosed in their hearts" (1849, 190). The actual *ingestion* of Scripture, an actual "bundle" in the heart, demonstrates the reformist's definition of a proper reception role for any true Christian. Similarly, in Lewis Wager's Protestant version of the life of *Marie Magdalene*, faith is God's gift "sealed" in the individual's heart:

> This faith is founded on God's promission,
> And most clerely to the mynde of man revealed,
> So that of God's will he hath an intuition,
> Which by the holy ghost to his heart is sealed.
>
> (1992, 46, ll. 1485–88)

Likewise, Paul and Poeta privilege the absolute authority of Scripture while guiding their audience to a role more controlled by God's Word, and therefore less physically and sensually participatory, than the role validated by the play's diabolical characters. Paul himself, once converted, exemplifies Bale's own hopes for a revised notion of sainthood: "that saints [might] be used as a means of teaching, of clarifying the nature of the Word." As Peter Happé comments, Bale "was ready to substitute some new Protestant saints whose power would rest upon the veracity with which they transmitted the Word" (1986, 214–15). Anne Askew and her adherents are thus the perfect audience—the whole, complete receptacles of the Sacred Scripture that has determined and guided their spiritual lives. Not surprisingly, then, near the end of Bale's *King Johan,* Nobylyte declares:

> Englande hath a quene, thanks to the Lorde above,
> Whyche may be a lyghte to other princes all
> For the godly wayes whome she doth dayly move
> To her liege people through Gods wurde specyall.
> She is that Angell, as Saynt Johan doth hym call,
> That withe the Lordes seale dothe marke out hys true servauntes.
> Pryntynge in their hartes hys holy wourdes and convenauntes.
>
> (1985, 2671–77)

Emphasizing textual authority and the direct reception of "holy wourdes," Bale transforms Elizabeth into a Protestant saint, her perfection embodied in her reception and communication of "the Lordes seale."

The writings of Wager, Bale, and others disclose a Reformation ideology that authorized an interpretive and stylistic adaptation, useful for Protestant polemic, of *The Conversion of Saint Paul*— a relic of the past faith that serves to reveal and critique the evils of Catholicism, as well as to correct and replace them with beliefs and practices aligned with the reformed faith. Mirroring this process of revelation, criticism, and replacement, the Protestant reformulation of sainthood, along with a redefinition of the medium of spiritual life, recast the relationship between word and image, mind and body, divine and human. In their elimination of intercession, in their privileging of Scripture and direct access to it, the reformists attempted to repudiate what they considered misleading, superstitious rituals and attitudes by demonstrating their faults from within the very texts and traditions that had originally disseminated them. Critiquing what they saw as worship practices erroneously founded on human imagination, spectacle, and mere entertainment (on recreation as much as re-creation), reformists stressed the absolute authority of Scripture, believing that scriptural access would fill the people with the truth of God's Word.

Yet, almost paradoxically, reformists worked from within the very tradition that they sought to dispel, drawing peoples' attentions with the very spectacles, imagery, and engaging forms and practices that they sought to condemn. More subtle than the blatant destruction of the earlier dramatic tradition often connected to iconoclastic reforms, these reformulations of theater, performance, and reception were more insidious, claiming as they did to know the proper way to reveal, communicate, and receive the word of God.

Part II

Sanctifying Response

The Church and the "Real Presence"

Chapter Three

Accessing the Divine in the Croxton
Play of the Sacrament

"Whanne we pleyin his miraclis as men don nowe on dayes"[1]

THE CHESTER CYCLE and the Digby *Conversion of Saint Paul* reveal attempts to remake the religious drama of the earlier faith in order to suit emerging Protestant beliefs regarding audience roles and responsibilities, and the connection of these to appropriate forms of worship and devotion. Seeking to characterize a Catholic use of the plays as, in fact, an idolatrous and diabolical misuse, reforming forces, rather than completely condemning the religious drama, chose to portray the dramatic form itself as an imminently redeemable form of religious practice. The plays of the vilified faith become themselves a clever force for modeling and encouraging religious reform—if they are used properly by audiences eager to seek the truth of Scripture. Recycled as a means for distinguishing appropriate from inappropriate response, and proper from im-

---

1. The quotation is from Davidson (1997), 101, l. 48. All future references are from this edition and will be cited parenthetically by line number.

proper religious faith, the plays themselves call upon their audiences to overcome, through a shift in response roles, the corrupting and misleading influence of the earlier religion with the truth and clarity of the new one. Thus, although the Catholic religious drama was often simply eliminated or halted, it was also revised and reformulated (as was sainthood) to aid Protestant forces in demonstrating the superiority of the new religion to the old one, and the dawning and realization of the true faith. The Middle English religious drama was reshaped as Protestant polemic, communicating and supporting changing theological sensibilities particularly concerned with the role of the individual in seeking divine truths.

Protestant attempts to distinguish the use of the religious drama from that of the earlier faith should not, however, blind us to the possibility that such a dynamic and lay-oriented form of worship may have also proved problematic for Catholic clerical leaders. In fact, as I work to demonstrate in this chapter, audience roles and concerns over proper responses to and uses of the drama were not uniquely Reformation or Renaissance preoccupations. Rather, as this chapter reveals, medieval clerical authorities were likewise attentive to the potential power of audience response to shape, define, and even challenge devotional experience. This attention to reception aesthetics in the late medieval period thus provides a precedent for Reformation and Renaissance forces eager to tap into the drama as a strong force for shaping religious meanings and experiences. Focusing in this chapter on the *Tretise of Miraclis Pleyinge* and the Croxton *Play of the Sacrament,* I argue that these two texts, once examined together, indicate a considerable tension between Catholic lay and clerical claims to the drama as a potential embodiment of transubstantiation belief and power. The *Tretise,* the most important piece of theoretical commentary on the drama in Middle English, and the *Play of the Sacrament,* focused on a transubstantiation miracle and a resulting conversion, complement each other and display a fundamental link between the religious drama and the transformative power of the Eucharist. More specifically, they attest to potential struggles over clerical and lay claims to (and uses of) the drama intricately connected to Eucharistic piety during the late Middle Ages and played out through powerful audience responses to the Sacrament. Such struggles demonstrate a fundamental understanding of the religious drama as a transformative devotional exercise tied closely (and perhaps competitively) to the miracle of the transubstantiation. Thus, "miraclis pleyinge" engaged a kind of "transubstantiation aesthetic" that provided its participants the power of *corpus Christi*. The writers of the *Tretise* offer a worried response to this understanding and use of the drama as a potential substitute for transubstantiation ritual and clerical authority. Rather than an unmitigated condemnation of the drama inspired entirely by Lollard belief, then, the *Tretise* may reveal instead a complex attention to a style of production and audience response associated with the religious drama that threatened the Church's universal claim to mediate the sacred and the mundane. Emphatic about identifying "miraclis pleyinge" as a misuse of Christ's body, the writers explore an issue similarly central to the Croxton *Play of the Sacrament:* How should the miracle of that body be used, and by whom?

This chapter then reveals another example of the fundamentally re-creative aspect of the late medieval religious drama—an aspect previously discussed initially in conjunction with the Chester cycle: the belief in the power of the drama to bring together past and present and thus for audiences to relive the salvific power of sacred history and the miracle of Christ's birth. Yet, working recursively, this chapter also attends to the larger and pervasive meanings of that essentially audience-driven capacity of the sacred drama within its original late medieval context. Rooted firmly in Incarnation belief and devotion to the Eucharist, the potentially miraculous power of the drama, while rarely denied, was often a point of considerable contention for various groups—lay and clerical alike—who sought ownership of that power and access to its origin in the most central of Christian mysteries.

Christ's Passion and the Misbehaving Players of Miracles

Contained in the British Library's Tenison Manuscript, a collection of documents copied in the early fifteenth century,[2] the *Tretise of Miraclis Pleyinge* divides into two parts, each composed by a different author.[3] While both sections have potentially Lollard or Wycliffite leanings, each also contains ideas aligned with orthodox beliefs.[4] Even if, as Clifford Davidson has argued, Part I is "not demonstrably heterodox" and Part II is "much more characteristic of Wycliffite writings" (1997, 4), the two authors share several concerns regarding the activity of "miraclis pleyinge." Both assert that "miraclis pleyinge," because it stages sacred topics and miracles, assumes an improper intimacy between humans and the divine.[5] Encouraging a comparably improper mingling of flesh and spirit—a conflation achieved only by Christ—"miraclis pleyinge," according to the

2. Davidson (1997), in his introduction to his edition of the *Tretise,* places the original writing of the *Tretise* between 1380 and 1425. The extant text, British Library Ms. Add. 24, 202, fols. 14r–21r, was copied in the early fifteenth century. For a bibliography of scholarship on the dating of the manuscript, see Davidson's Introduction, 34, n. 1.

3. See Davidson's Introduction (1997), 4–34, and Johnston Jr.'s discussion of the dialects of Parts I and II in Davidson's edition, 53–84. Clopper (1990) sees a fundamental disparity between the two authors' attitudes regarding what makes "play" appropriate (896–98).

4. Davidson discusses this issue at length in his Introduction, as does Davis (1990). Davis also argues that both parts of the *Tretise* were composed by a single author. Hudson (1988) questions the Wycliffite characterization of the *Tretise* (38). Nisse (1997) reasserts a Lollard origin for the text. See also Davis (1982). Clopper (1990) does not address the Lollard issue and, instead, follows a line of interpretation that anchors the objections to "miraclis pleyinge" found in the *Tretise* in "papal and ecclesiastical opposition to indecorous behavior and the sins that accrue from attendance on such affairs" (898).

5. While Clopper (1990) has raised important doubts about whether the religious drama was the *Tretise* writers' object of concern, most critics consider "miraclis pleyinge" a reference to the religious drama and, in general, I agree with that majority opinion. The definition of "miraclis pleyinge," however, is not my chief focus in this chapter, but rather the beliefs and behavior that, according to the writers, encourage and accompany the activity. I contend that the writers were concerned with a religious attitude and practice for which the religious drama provided a specific example. The term "miraclis pleyinge," therefore, might include other activities

writers of the *Tretise,* provokes its audiences and participants to treat Christian doctrines lightly, to disregard the authority of Christianity's leaders, and to ignore important distinctions between humanity and divinity. Whether condemning "miraclis pleyinge" for its potential to usurp the sacramental priority of the Church and its leaders (a possible concern of an orthodox writer) or for its misuse of a sacramental power (in which a Lollard writer might not believe), both writers see "miraclis pleyinge" as a challenge to the larger Christian community, disrupting fundamental Christian structure and authority (and enabled, in large part, by late medieval audiences' misuse of and inappropriate responses to the religious drama).

In the *Tretise,* Christ's Passion, despite its fortunate result for humanity, emerges as the ultimate, condemning consequence of humans assuming an irreverent access to the divine. Such an irreverent access (resulting, in this case, in the torture of divine flesh at human hands) both writers of the text describe as a chief characteristic of "miraclis pleyinge." Similarly, in the late-fifteenth-century Croxton *Play of the Sacrament,*[6] cursory treatment of Christian doctrines, disregard for Church leaders, and assumed access to the divine (embodied in the sacred object of the host) result in a bloody version of Christ's Passion, marked by human mishandling of sacred objects and topics. The *Tretise* thus offers the Passion and the soldiers' brutal treatment of Christ as a damning end to (and ultimate condemnation of) the evils of "miraclis pleyinge." Yet the Croxton play also transforms what seems an inadvertent reenactment of the Passion into an opportunity for redemption, carefully shepherded and controlled by Church representatives who invoke the very doctrines

---

and behavior that indulged the same desires as did the religious drama. Davidson (1997) also discusses the interpretive difficulty of defining *miraclis* in his Introduction (1–4). More recently, Clopper (2001) has continued methodically to examine the issue of terminology and its central importance for early drama studies.

6. Norman Davis (1970) believes that the Croxton play was likely composed soon after 1461, the date presented in the manuscript for the events the play details. Davis dates the copy originally contained in Trinity College, Dublin, f. 4.20, Catalogue no. 652, ff. 338r–56r, now stored separately, to the early sixteenth century (lxxxiv–lxxxv and lxx–lxxv).

and embody the very structure that the writers of the *Tretise* see as threatened or undermined by "miraclis pleyinge." While the Croxton play does not condone the behavior of its misbehaving "players," it also does not portray their actions as ultimately threatening to the larger Christian community. Instead, that Christian community—its beliefs, doctrines, and authority embodied by an audience and sponsorship of believers—enables the story of the Croxton play to be told without fear of damnation. The Croxton *Play of the Sacrament* stages and illuminates a number of the chief points of the *Tretise* writers regarding the sacramental use of the religious drama and its fundamental connection to *corpus Christi*, transubstantiation ritual, and right of access to both. Yet what the writers of the *Tretise* see as the dangerous precedent of "miraclis pleyinge"—inappropriate human engagement of sacred objects and topics—the Croxton play embraces as potential site for indulging spiritual desires and exploring religious belief, while reassuringly asserting the fundamental stability and authority of Christianity.[7]

"Pley not with Me but Pley with Thy Pere": *"Miraclis Pleyinge" as Mistreatment of Christ*

To illustrate the dangerous nature of "miraclis pleyinge," both writers of the *Tretise* invoke various analogies, but the most visceral portrayal of the threat of "miraclis pleyinge" arises when the writer of Part I compares those who engage in "miraclis pleyinge" to the Jewish soldiers who tortured Christ in the Passion: "sithen thes miraclis pleyeris taken in bourde the ernestful werkis of God, no doute that ne they scornen God as diden the Jewis that bobbiden Crist, for they lowen at his passioun as these lowyn and japen of the miraclis of God" (133–37).[8] Like the soldiers who treated divine spirit as

7. Cf. Beckwith's treatment of the Croxton play (1986). While Beckwith sees Croxton as an exploration of doubt, I see it as an exploration of belief. More recently, Beckwith (2001) has also examined the sacramental role of the religious drama. See also Beckwith (1994 and 1996).

8. For the connection between the Passion and "Hot Cockles," a children's game, see Davidson (1984), 107–9.

mere human flesh and thus beat and tormented Christ, participants in "miraclis pleyinge" also mistreat the divine and injure the center of Christianity. The Passion is also singled out for special comment in Part II, whose writer asserts that "men schulden not bourden with the figure of the passion of Crist" (683–84, 689) because such "pleyinge of the passion of Crist is but verre scorning of Crist" (692–93). For both writers, the threat of "miraclis pleyinge" emerges from the apparent attempt of its players to do Christ's work. Staging religious themes requires human representation and engagement of sacred topics, acts that for the writers of the *Tretise* are an unlawful mingling of flesh and spirit. Such acts scorn Christ because, in essence, they potentially usurp Christ's singularity as divine flesh and miracle maker. In Part I, for example, the writer asserts that Christ and his saints performed miracles "heere in erthe," whereas humans who "usen in bourde and pley the miraclis and werkis that Crist so ernystfully wroughte to oure helthe . . . errith in the byleve, reversith Crist, and scornyth God" (24–27). Similarly, the writer of Part II describes the effect of "miraclis pleyinge" as a reversal of the Old and the New Testaments. Identifying "miraclis pleyinge" as "pley of the fleysh" (472), he explains that "the Olde Testament, that is testament of the fleysh, may not ben holdun with the Newe Testament, that is testament of the spirit; and yif it be hooly kept with the testament of the spirit, it doith awey verre fredom and bynimmeth the heretage of hevene" (474–79). The reversal, it seems, stems from the attempt to bridge a gap through human flesh that only Christ can close through divine spirit. Throughout the *Tretise,* the mingling of flesh and spirit, of human and divine bodies, is described as a particularly dangerous, if not blasphemous, characteristic of "miraclis pleyinge" that emboldens much of the critique of sacred enactment within the document.

For both writers of the *Tretise,* then, to engage in "miraclis pleyinge" is to assume wrongly an intimacy with things divine and heavenly, and to close what should be an inviolate distance between flesh and spirit. Thus, for the writer of the first part of the *Tretise,* one who plays at miracles is like a servant who plays with his lord—one whose actions are objectionable because of the difference in rank: "[W]hanne we pleyin his miraclis as men don nowe on dayes, God takith more venjaunce on us than a lord that sodaynly sleeth his servaunt for he pleyide to homely with him. And right as that lord thanne in dede seith to his servaunt, 'Pley not with me but pley with thy pere, so whanne we takun in pley and in bourde the miraclis of God,' he, fro us takinge his grace, seith more ernestfully to us than the forseid lord, 'Pley not with me but pley with thy pere'" (48–56). A parallel analogy asserts the importance of a schoolmaster's authority in relation to his pupils (76–86). Both examples communicate the loss of discipline and authority the writer sees accompanying "miraclis pleyinge." Dread of God is lost (41), as is the discipline required of faith and belief in God's authority (76–86). Similarly, the author of Part II sees the disruption of the lord-servant relationship as analogous to "miraclis pleyinge" (501–5) and provides the story of Ishmael and Isaac as another example of inappropriate acquaintance with and breach of spiritual hierarchy, as "the pleyinge of Ishmael with Isaac is figure of the pleyinge of the fleysh with the spirit" (496–97). These analogies communicate the writers' feelings about "miraclis pleyinge" as a disruptive activity that encourages a disregard for a Christian authority and structure based upon a fundamental distinction between divine and heavenly bodies—a distinction, according to Christian doctrine, overcome only by Christ himself.

When the writers of the *Tretise* condemn "miraclis pleyinge" by comparing it to Christ's Passion, they also point to its origins in the Incarnation, in the meeting of divine and physical bodies that those who play at miracles attempt.[9] The text thus suggests both a regard for incarnational power, for its ability to maintain Christianity's authority and structure, and a fear of its attraction for the lay pop-

9. While Anthony Gash (1986) has explored the representation of Corpus Christi within the larger community of town and village in the later medieval period, I argue that the space of Christ's body and its conflicting meanings affect the mediatory space of the religious drama's performance. This performance space not only attempts access to the divine and sacred, but also determines the nature of that access. See also Peter Travis's discussion of the role of the social body of Christ in the cycle plays (1985).

ulation—those whom Christian leaders sought to control. As Miri Rubin, Gail MacMurray Gibson, Sarah Beckwith, and others have demonstrated, the later Middle Ages, influenced by an emphasis upon Christ's worldly and physical presence, reevaluated the spiritual potential of worldly and human experiences.[10] As the authors of the *Tretise* reveal, moreover, those who play at miracles seem to privilege these types of devotional values, seeking emotional and physical immediacy in their religious experiences. A section of Part I that describes a defense of "miraclis pleyinge" demonstrates the high value placed on human emotion and interaction for participants: "[B]y siche miraclis pleyinge men and wymmen, seinge the passioun of Crist and of his seintis, ben movyd to compassioun and devocion, wepinge bitere teris" (162–64). Likewise, the devotional utility of "pleyinge" is compared to the visual immediacy of paintings of sacred subjects: "[S]ithen it is leveful to han the miraclis of God peintid, why is not as wel leveful to han the miraclis of God pleyed, sithen men mowen bettere reden the wille of god and his mervelous werkis in the pleyinge of hem than in the peintinge? And betere they ben holden in mennes minde and oftere rehersid by the pleyinge of hem than by the peintinge, for this is a deed bok, the tother a quick" (179–85). The writer here refers to the then-current belief that "seeing" meant coming into direct visual contact with the object;[11] he therefore describes the "pleyinge" of "miraclis" as a more lively (and thus more effective) form of devotion than even that achieved through paintings that are "deed bok[s]." While he will proceed to criticize the activity, this author of the *Tretise* is aware of the high value placed on "miraclis pleyinge" as a devotional practice because of its emphasis upon visual, emotional, and physical immediacy, and the active involvement required of its participants. Connected, I believe, to what Gibson (1989) has called an "incarnational aesthetic" (1), and what Rubin (1986) has described as "a sacramental world-view" (52), neither the powerful desires of "mira-

10. See Gibson (1989, esp. 1–18); Rubin (1991); Beckwith (1993); Zita (1988); Robinson (1965); and Aulén (1960).
11. Davidson (1997), 133–34, note to lines 179–85.

clis pleyinge" nor its popularity are denied by the writers. Rather, the authors deny the players' right to act on those desires using the meeting of divine and human as precedent.

Performance as Miraculous Corruption: The Clergy and the Lay Audience

The *Tretise of Miraclis Pleyinge* bears witness to the irony of a late medieval belief system where an emphasis upon Christ's humanity ensured Christianity's popularity among the laity but also encouraged them to see the divine and the sacred as more directly accessible, and thus to engage in activities that merged "flesh" and "spirit." In the *Tretise*, "miraclis pleyinge" is portrayed as one of the more alarming and revealing of those activities because, in part, it seemingly proceeds without the control and supervision that the clerical establishment sought to maintain over its followers' belief patterns and worship practices. As the references to irreverent servants playing with lords attest, the writers of the *Tretise* perceived "miraclis pleyinge" as a disruptive activity whose participants willingly disregarded the authority and structure of traditional Christian doctrine. According to the writer of Part I, "miraclis pleyinge" is a disorderly activity that "reversith discipline" (116), and encourages lechery, debate, "bodily mirthe," and gluttony (118–22), while "it suffrith not a man to beholden enterly the yerde of God over his heved, but makith to thenken on alle siche thingis that Crist by the dedis of his passion badde us to forgeten. Wherfore siche miraclis pleyinge, both in penaunce doying in veryy dicipline and in pacience reversyn Cristis hestis and his dedis" (123–28). This disruption of authority and doctrine that apparently accompanies "miraclis pleyinge," coupled with what the writers of the *Tretise* represent as its participants' misuse of the incarnational example of Christ, illustrates the paradoxical position of the late medieval Church in relation to an increased devotional attention to the Eucharist ironically encouraged by the Church. For in attempting to solidify the special position of the priesthood as the sole handlers of Christ's body—as Beckwith

(1986) describes, "the keepers of its miraculous powers" and "the necessary medium of transformation" ("Ritual," 66)—the Church placed special emphasis upon the Sacrament, thereby allowing the laity to embrace its more homely qualities.[12] Connected with the worldly and physical nature of Christ that made the divine and spiritual seemingly more accessible, the host becomes tangible proof of incarnational belief and power: a tactile object that demonstrates the potential of humanity.[13]

Accompanied by a growing attention to the physical as well as the spiritual nature of Christ's life, incarnated body and host came to represent and enact a fluid space between human life and spiritual redemption, mediating between the mundane details of this life and the eternal salvation yet to come. The laity sought a contemporaneity between sacred topics and human life—between divine forces and physical realities for which the Incarnation, Passion, and Eucharist provided powerful precedents. Their actions drew upon the power of the transubstantiation yet often proceeded unmediated by clear clerical presence or authority. Extending from the use of the host in healing rituals, folk remedies, and blessings of crops and animals, to its encompassing, centralized presence in the Feast of Corpus Christi,[14] a use of sacramental power unmediated in its mingling of divine and human bodies (and of sacred and mundane properties) captured the attentions of the *Tretise* writers.

While these associations with the body focus on the physical and emotional involvement required of participants in the playing of miracles, they also persistently display the complex relationship attested to in the *Tretise* between "miraclis pleyinge" and Christ's

12. Rubin (1986) provides a detailed overview of Eucharist devotion and controversy originating in the eleventh century.

13. Devotion to the Eucharist was also, of course, linked to the affective piety movement in the later Middle Ages and the emphasis of the movement upon personal identification with Christ through his human sufferings and qualities. Clarissa W. Atkinson (1986) provides a religious and historical background of the affective piety tradition and movement (129–56). See also Beckwith (1986b, "A Very Material Mysticism"); and Salter (1974).

14. See James (1983).

body. According to the writer of Part I, "miraclis pleyinge" reduces divine bodies to human status, so that the "pleyinge" of religious topics actually "reverse[s]" Christ's actions and the use of his body for sinners in the Passion: "[S]iche miraclis pleyinge reversith Crist. Firste in taking to play that that he toke into most ernest. The secound in taking to miraclis of our fleyss, of oure lustis, and of oure five wittis that that God tooc to the bringing in of his bitter deth and to teching of penaunse doinge, and to fleying of feding of oure wittis and to mortifying of hem" (57–62). Using human senses and faculties to re-create and reexperience sacred scenes, topics, and meanings—"taking to miraclis of oure fleyss, of oure lustis, and of oure five wittis"—encourages a spatial misuse of the physical body, of Christ's form in the Incarnation, and of his actions in the Passion. "Pleyinge," therefore, is a human corruption of Christ's use of the human form. According to the difficult logic of the *Tretise,* human bodies ought not to play at the actions of the God-become-man because such play is merely disruptive mimicry that reduces—or reverses—spirit to flesh. Not only do human and divine bodies meet unsuitably, but the space of enactment comes dangerously close to reversing Christ himself. In the attempt to meld sacred and mundane, the space of performance is portrayed as a corruption of the original miracle of the Incarnation—a corruption due at least in part to the attempted engagement of a mediatory power intended for the priesthood alone.

Though they do not plan to enact the transubstantiation on their own, the laity, hopeful of redemption, nonetheless participate in devotional practices dedicated to fulfilling the sacrament's transformative capability in other venues, including perhaps the staging of miracles and sacred topics. Such stagings or enactments were charged with "re-creative" promise: the hope that representation might result in miracle. Much of the Middle English religious drama illustrates this "re-creative" capacity through the desire to meld present audience and playing space with events from sacred history, to invoke spiritual topics in order to access their spiritual meaning and miraculous potential. What troubles the writers of the *Tretise* is the indeterminate, independent nature of such activities, which blend mundane realities with religion and worship. The "danger" of "miraclis pleyinge," as David Mills (1983) has written, "lay in its still ambivalent status, its dangerous resemblance to functional forms of religious worship and instruction, and in its widespread appeal to a community, with all the dangers that the community would redirect it to serve its own self-interest" (91).[15] I have argued, furthermore, that both writers of the *Tretise* are concerned with "miraclis pleyinge" as an activity that ignores spiritual hierarchies and proceeds recklessly with little regard, if any, for a controlling religious authority. The orthodox writer of Part I seems particularly preoccupied with this unstructured and unchaperoned aspect, and his attention to priests who actually engage in plays suggests his special interest in the threat of "miraclis pleyinge" to clerical authority. Referring to the ability of an Old Testament woman such as Sara to keep herself away from plays and players in order to maintain her chastity and suitability for the sacrament of marriage, the writer asserts that a priest of the New Testament should strive even more to keep himself from plays and players to maintain his special position as minister of "ne only . . . the sacrament of matrimonye but all other sacramentis and names sithen him owith to ministre to alle the puple the precious body of Crist" (262–78).[16] Certainly, as Lawrence Clopper (1990) has asserted, this argument communicates the writer's belief that the priest who participates in plays invites "his parishioners [to] have regard neither for him nor for the sacraments" (899). Moreover, and more specifically, the writer's focus on the Eucharist demonstrates his particular concern for the threat "miraclis pleyinge" poses to clerical control over the host and the circulation of its sacramental powers. Not only, therefore, do priest and sacrament lose public regard, but such participation in playing relinquishes the priesthood's singular connection to the host, as "keepers of its miraculous powers" and the "necessary medium of [its] trans-

---

15. Mills's essay contains the only other comparative study of these two texts of which I am aware.

16. See Clopper (1990, 898–99) for a useful discussion of this passage.

formation" (Beckwith, 1986, "Ritual," 66): "[T]his holy womman Sara at the day of dom schal dampne the pristis of the Newe Testament that givis heem to pleyes, reversen hir holy maners aprovyd by God and al holiy chirche; therfore sore aughten pristis to be aschamyd that reversen this gode holy womman and the precious body of Christ that they tretyn in ther hondis, the whiche body never gaf him to play but to alle siche thing as is most contrarious to play as is penaunce and suffring of persecution" (281–88). The priest who plays endangers his distinct claim to the Eucharist and its power. Indeed, such priests "reverse" both their "holy maners" and "the precious body of Crist" because they relinquish their authority over the transformative potential of Christ's body. By indulging in plays and not distinguishing themselves from other players, such priests suggest that the Eucharist and its sacramental power are accessible. "Miraclis pleyinge," understandably, becomes a salient consideration for those bent on maintaining the priesthood's sole claim to the Eucharist.

Responding to the apparent availability of sacramental power enabled by an increased emphasis on Christ's body and primarily engineered by the clerical establishment, "miraclis pleyinge," as described in the *Tretise,* becomes a particularly potent threat to what Rubin (1986) has called "the exclusive right of the clergy to mediate the grace of redemption, the shared Creator and Savior, to dispense of supernatural power through rituals performed by [the] clergy alone" (46).[17] Yet while the writers of the *Tretise* attempt to condemn "miraclis pleyinge" as mere physical play, or as an activity that must always devolve into mere entertainment,[18] their critique does not conceal what seems to have been at least the initial desire of its participants to create a spatial miracle—to tap into the transformative power originally designated for the "clergy alone." The participants in "miraclis pleyinge" want to bring flesh into contact with spirit. They seek the kind of physical and emotional im-

17. See also Zita (1988), 60.
18. The author of Part 2 extends this point to include a comparison of "miraclis pleyinge" with the Israelites' worship of the Golden Calf (ll. 586–663).

mediacy (162–65) that will help them to "bettere reden the wille of god and his mervelous werkis" (181–82). Although the writers of the *Tretise* characterize its participants as irreverent, even impudent, revelers with slight regard for authority figures, they do not deny completely the participants' reverent intentions for "miraclis pleyinge": that representation might result in actual miracle. Even the strongest condemnation of "miraclis pleyinge" offered by the *Tretise,* its comparison to Christ's Passion, while gruesomely frightening, maintains powerful connections between the spatial miracle of Christ's body and the hope that "miraclis pleyinge" can draw upon that miracle.

Reasserting Belief through Bloody Miracle: The Croxton Play of the Sacrament

In the *Tretise* the torture and mockery endured by Christ at the Passion come to represent the dangers of assuming with the sacred too close an intimacy that is invoked improperly when one plays at miracles. Yet, when the Croxton *Play of the Sacrament* stages a re-creation of the Passion, that closeness becomes a topic for exploration, complicating the assertion that miracles ought not to be re-enacted. The Croxton play presents its own contemporary versions of the Jewish mishandlers of Christ who, having purchased the host from a greedy (though Christian) merchant, put the host to "a preve."[19] As the Banns describe, these Jews "grevid our Lord gretly on grownd,"

> And put hym to a new passyoun;
> With daggers gouen hym many a greuyos wound;
> Nayled hym to a pyller, with pynsons plukked hym doune.
>
> (37–40)

19. Davis (1970), 64, ll. 208 and 442. All future references are from this edition and will be cited parenthetically by line number.

More than a bloody and sensational display, this treatment of the host, as enacted in the play, results in a miraculous re-creation of Crucifixion, Passion, and Resurrection that calls upon the audience as participants in and enablers of the miracle. Actors and audience play with and upon the space of Christ's body as the initially small and vulnerable wafer comes safely and surely to encompass both the redemptive potential of the Jews' own gruesome curiosity and the space and experience of the play's audience. While in the *Tretise* access to Christ's body in the Passion represents a blasphemous reversal of belief resulting from "miraclis pleyinge" and its desire for contact with the sacred, the re-creation of the Passion in the Croxton play represents a celebratory reassertion of belief, empowered by a tactile intimacy with the sacred object that is the host.[20]

As a play about handlings and mishandlings of the host, the Croxton *Play of the Sacrament* considers numerous issues regarding concerns over the circulation of and access to sacramental power revealed in the *Tretise*. Indeed, we may view the Croxton play as a treatise in its own right, one that explores sacramental access and the playing of miracles from a late medieval perspective. Prevailing upon a climate of spiritual confidence and curiosity amplified by East Anglia's economic prosperity, the Croxton play approaches its subject with considerably less dread and fear than the *Tretise*.[21] Where the *Tretise* writers portray "miraclis pleyinge" as a misuse of Christ's body, accompanied by a loss of clerical control over the Eucharist, the Croxton staging plays at miracles to explore how such misuse can disclose not only the sacramental potential of the Eucharist but also the stability of Christian belief.[22]

20. Thus, like Nichols (1988), I depart from those who have interpreted the play as a response to Lollardy and/or anti-Eucharist belief. Critics who see the Croxton play as a response to Lollardy or to sacramental doubt include Cutts (1944); Gibson (1989), 34–42; and Beckwith (1986a, "Ritual"). Donnalee Dox (1997) has also re-opened this issue.

21. Gibson (1989) examines the specific spiritual attitudes of fifteenth-century East Anglians.

22. The Croxton play is self-commenting and self-reflexive. As Seth Lerer (1996) remarks, the play is "a kind of metadrama, a play about the possibilities of theater and its symbols" (47).

A Dangerous Merger of Flesh and Spirit:
Aristorius and His Playing Priest

When Aristorius, a wealthy merchant, opens the Croxton play with an invocation to "Christ, that is our creator" (81), he seems a good Christian, attentive to his subordinate position as layman and merchant. However, he quickly begins a boasting sequence, listing for the audience the cities and countries where he does business. Deeply involved in his secular pursuits and accomplishments, he resembles the familiar boasters and tyrants of the cycle plays; but, unlike most of these, he is also a Christian whose material success has curiously infiltrated his religious attitude and life. Financially successful, he believes that he has God's blessing on all of his activities: "No man in thys world may weld more rychesse; / All I thank God of hys grace, for he that me sent" (117–18). Uniting mercantile activities and religious duty, Aristorius's enticing yet troubling conflation of worldly and spiritual abilities also may have been particularly resonant for an East Anglian audience whose own centers of worship owed so much to the economic prosperity of the region's cloth trade. While the region's elaborately styled parish "wool churches," funded by wealthy cloth merchants, can be seen as a response to guilt over material prosperity, they also illustrate the entanglement of worldly and spiritual pride exhibited by Aristorius—and in which his audience members are likely complicit. With their complex (even ostentatious) architecture, the "wool churches" were late medieval monuments to the hope that material success might engender spiritual success and that both could be displayed together.[23]

Given his confidence in both his worldly and religious dealings, Aristorius's wealth and prosperity, his "weld" of "rychesse," extends its influence to controlling his priest, Sir Isodor, who, Aristorius as-

---

23. See Gibson (1989), 23–28, for an important discussion of the "wool churches." Similarly, the detailed wills of East Anglians, also discussed by Gibson (67–106), with their elaborate provisions and bequests made possible by earthly acquisition, suggest a belief in the potential influence of worldly wealth upon one's final fate, a hope that earthly success might translate to heavenly achievement.

serts, "wayteth vpon me to knowe myn entent" (120). After drug-
ging the ineffectual priest with food and wine, Aristorius obtains
the host from the local church and, after bargaining over its price
with five curious Jews, sells it to them. Such action illuminates intriguing parallels to the concerns expressed in the *Tretise* regarding
clerical loss of sacramental power. Sir Isodor, whose slumbering and
lack of authority over his parishioner permit the merchant to obtain
the host, resembles those priests described in the *Tretise* who "givis
hemm to pleyes" and who "reversen . . . the precious body of Crist
that they tretyn in ther hondis" (281–88). Sir Isodor's behavior exemplifies those inattentive and "pleyinge" priests described in the *Tretise* whose actions compromise clerical authority and a loss of clerical control over the use and space of Christ's body. As described in
the *Tretise,* and as enacted in the Croxton play, the laity—represented by Aristorius, whose vocation implicates the play's East Anglian
audience—approach the sacred with little, if any, reverence. If in the
Tretise "miraclis pleyinge" abuses the potential of Christ's body, here
Aristorius instigates an economically charged playing sanctioned by
an attitude that has already dangerously merged worldly with spiritual pursuits. Aristorius, in effect, takes the host into his own hands
in a prideful conflation of economic and spiritual profit that the *Tretise* associates with the conflation of flesh and spirit characterizing
"miraclis pleyinge."[24] His treatment of the host seems quite similar to those profit makers who "to han wherof to spenden on thes
miraclis and to holden felawschipe of glotenye and lecherie in siche
dayes of miraclis pleyinge . . . bisien hem beforn to more gredily
bygilen ther neghbors in byinge and in selling" (604–8). So entan-
gled is his faith with his business, so confident is he in his materi-

----

24. My characterization of Aristorius here and my analysis of the following passage has been aided by Davidson's gloss in his edition of the *Tretise* (1997, 152–53, n.
to ll. 607–8). He comments that "sponsors of civic drama were hardly able to separate spiritual profit from economic profit gained from the festivities which brought
a large crowd of outsiders to the city on such occasions as Corpus Christi," and asserts that the *Tretise* writers condemn such conflation as they do the mixing of flesh
and spirit.

al and spiritual success, that Aristorius seems to think himself perfectly justified in tricking his priest, obtaining the host, and selling it
to his Jewish customers. In order to treat the host as a material object to be sold for economic profit, Aristorius must conflate the sacred with the mundane, the spiritual with the physical. Treating the
host, the symbol and embodiment of the miracle of the Incarnation, as a material commodity is an example of placing sacred and
mundane on the same level—the joining of spiritual and physical
spaces, divine and human qualities that comprises the activity of
"miraclis pleyinge." However, unlike those who play at miracles to
gain an access to sacramental power (seemingly available through
Christ and the Eucharist) that will enable them to attempt on their
own a redemptive meeting of flesh and spirit, Aristorius is so sure of
his right of access that he exchanges sacramental power for earthly
profit, confident that such profit reflects well on his spiritual as well
as his worldly position.

Christian Dread and Christian Wonder: The Staging of Audience Belief

Secure in his religious as well as his business success, Aristorius
relinquishes the sacrament and its attendant power to his customers, the curious Jews who wish to put the host to a "preve." Surely
implicated in the Jews' torturous treatment of the host (indeed his
conflation of business and religion has authorized it), Aristorius is
never directly involved in their physical abuse of the host. Although
the merchant displays attitudes regarding flesh and spirit that the
Tretise writers associate with "miraclis pleyinge," unlike its participants as they are described in the *Tretise* he stays at a safe distance
from the "playing"—from the torture that allows for miracle in the
play. Despite his heinous actions, Aristorius remains a part of the
Christian community, clearly distinguished from the Jewish outsiders whose treatment of the host, while staged by Christian actors
and viewed by a Christian audience, can be explained as the actions
of nonbelievers, as those who in medieval Christian tradition con-

sistently sought to desecrate the host and mock Christ.[25] In holding its Jewish characters chiefly responsible for re-creating the Passion, the Croxton play ostensibly keeps all of its Christian participants at a safe distance from what the writers of the *Tretise* assert is the precedent that condemns "miraclis pleyinge" and its participants' desire for contact with the divine. The re-created Passion of the Croxton play—in essence the staging of a staging—thus allows its audience and actors to examine, without direct recrimination, what amounts to the danger as well as the potential of "miraclis pleyinge."

For all practical purposes, the audience of the Croxton play are mere observers of a staged scene of torture that, in turn, re-creates a miracle. Even if they identify with Aristorius and question the impact of their material success upon their religious practices, their status as Christians and as viewers remains intact. Nevertheless, they are subjected to an extended scene that may very well have indulged their own spiritual desires and fears—from a safe distance. Influenced, as were many late medieval Christians, by an increased devotional attention to the physical nature of Christ, the audience of the Croxton play no doubt viewed the Jews' intimate machinations with both dread and wonder. More specifically, the play's presentation of the host as a mercantile object whose nature and quality are priced, tested, and measured by human touch may have been particularly charged for East Anglians whose livelihoods were based upon a tactile good, cloth, whose quality was also a measure of human hands.[26] Though protected from culpabil-

25. See Cohen (1983), Rubin (1992), and Davis (1970, lxxiii–lxxiv).

26. The motivations of the Jews approximate those of the Doubting Thomas who, as Gibson (1989) explains, was transformed in the later Middle Ages into a positive image of spiritual devotion among the laity. Embodying the "sensory concreteness" of fifteenth-century piety in England (16), Thomas's touching of Christ's body and wounds can be seen as a precedent for the physical and tactile—if extreme—actions of the Jews. Furthermore, the empirical desires of the Jews to test the host rather than merely destroy it (as do their continental counterparts) suggests that they have more in common with late medieval Christians than might immediately be expected. For a discussion of the Croxton Jews and other Jewish desecrators of the host, see Norman Davis (1970, lxxiii–lxxv). See also Beckwith (1986, "Ritual," 68 and 83–84, n. 14).

ity as Christian observers, the audience (and its actors) are thus partial participants, inheriting a role that the performance itself cannot
always deny. The Jews' diligent work, for example, is accompanied
by a graphically specific narration which seemingly assumes little if
any gulf between actor and audience space (385–525, 653–716). In
addition, at one point, in order to stop the host's miraculous bleeding—the result of its physical piercing—Jonathas, the Jews' leader,
attempts to throw the wafer into a kettle of boiling oil, only to have
it adhere to his hand (489ff.). When, according to the stage directions, "*he renneth wood, with the Ost in hys hand*" (s.d. after l. 503), no
doubt he is meant to approach the audience directly, holding out
for them the physical representation of the very miracle-enabling
space that all participants currently (if temporarily) inhabit. The
Jews may be represented as those who play at miracles, but the audience is also implicated in a process that extends the sacramental potential of the Eucharist to the space of the performance. The host
and Jonathas's crazed running about encircle all in the dangerous
yet perhaps miraculous power of unlicensed play within and upon
the space of Christ's body.

In the scene following Jonathas's injury, the audience, in fact, is
addressed directly by a physician's servant who, along with his master,[27] will remain attentive to the audience throughout the scene.
Full of descriptions of the doctor's sexual pursuits and his inadequa-
cies as a healer, the comic scene, perhaps meant to offer a reprieve
from the graphic episode that has preceded it, also presents a familiar parable to the audience, one that they are called upon to recognize and authorize by refusing the doctor's request for patients
(601–22). When Jonathas also refuses his services, he signals to the
audience the possibility of his redemption; this refusal parallels the
audience's response to the quack doctor and foreshadows the potential of true healing as well as the eventual appearance of Christ,
the spiritual healer who replaces all fleshly physicians. Since the par-

---

27. The Doctor figure has no precedents in other versions of the play. See Davis (1970, lxxv).

able is never directly communicated, audience recognition is important for the progression of the scene and the play; their belief is invoked to ensure a redemptive movement forward that, again, contrasts with the *Tretise* writers' assertions that flesh will reverse spirit.[28] Indeed, before Christ appears, Jonathas and his companions engage in additional flesh-oriented pursuits: throwing the host with attached hand into a cauldron that then boils over with blood, and then attempting to bake the host in an oven in order to stop the bleeding. When, instead, the host transforms into a bleeding and speaking image of Christ that bursts from the oven, the audience and their Christian belief system seem, in part, to have compelled and predicted the transformation—their belief transfigures the disbelief of the Jews and enables miracle. As a speaking image that offers forgiveness and redemption, physical and spiritual healing, the Christ image is a miraculous incarnation of the audience's recognition, driven by their belief, of the parable of the physician.

Like the bishop called in to return the Christ image to bread, to establish order, and to complete the Jews' conversion and redemption, the audience, by maintaining Christian belief, also contributes to the completion of the miracle process through an understanding of the Incarnation miracle that the Jews, despite their direct access to the host, do not have. While Episcopus thus mourns over the "new passyon" (803), he also sets about seeking its miraculous completion by calling for a display of belief that demonstrates an understanding of Christ's sufferings:

> Now, all ye peple that here are, euery man,
> On yowr feet for to goo bare,
> In the devoutest wyse that ye can.

> (810–12)

Entreated to help restore order, to join in a Corpus Christi procession to the local church, audience members assert a confidence they have had all along in a belief system that, in contrast to the opin-

---

28. See lines 57–62, 109–28, and 461–544.

ions expressed in the *Tretise,* sees the human and fleshly elements of Christ's Passion not as a dangerous opportunity for reversal but as a step toward divine and spiritual redemption.[29] The gruesome acts exhibited in the play, while shocking examples of disbelief, can also be viewed as opportunities to explore belief and to renew it, to celebrate the depth and potency of the inherent sacramental power of the miracles of Incarnation, Passion, and Eucharist.[30] The Croxton play's staging of host desecration, of what amounts to an extreme example of unlicensed physical play with sacred object and divine body, may thus actually provide an opportunity for displaying and asserting that belief.[31]

In their separate examinations of "miracle playing," both the *Tretise of Miraclis Pleyinge* and the Croxton *Play of the Sacrament* are each concerned with clerical control of the Eucharist and with the Jews who mocked and tortured Christ at the Passion. In the *Tretise* these two issues disclose the dangers of "miraclis pleyinge": the attempt of its participants to transfer, without authorization, the power of the Eucharist to sacred enactment is an abuse of Christ, a mocking of what he alone achieved in the Incarnation. In staging its own version of the Passion, set in motion by a priest's loss of the Sacrament, the Croxton play elucidates the concerns expressed in the *Tretise* but also complicates their connection to the staging

29. While it is possible that the procession is merely a staging that does not involve the audience, I believe that the audience become participants whose belief helps the narrative progression of the play to move from disbelief to belief. See also Beckwith (1986, "Ritual," 77–80).

30. As Beckwith (1986a, "Ritual") claims, the "very act of profanation, the very act of torture, has merely produced the means of salvation in this Christian economy of redemption" (68).

31. If, in fact, the *Tretise* writers' examples of Ishmael and Isaac, Old Testament and New Testament, represent, as Nicholas Davis (1990) describes, "the two human covenants with God, 'fleshly' (Jewish) and 'spiritual' (Christian)," and their mixed "play," the "persecution of 'those born after the spirit' by 'those born after the flesh'" (128), the Croxton play seems to overcome this opposition with its communal procession, with a progression from Old Testament faith to New Testament belief (as both Jew and Christian participate) that proceeds from flesh to spirit but also incorporates both.

of miracles. Employed by the *Tretise* writers as doctrinal evidence against "miraclis pleyinge," both clerical control of the Eucharist and the Passion become in the Croxton play opportunites for performance and spiritual exploration precisely because they *are* points of doctrine. Included, in fact, in the Constitutions of the Fourth Lateran Council,[32] the document which in 1215 first defined transubstantiation as a point of faith for the Christian world, are decrees concerning the safekeeping of the Eucharist (number 20) and the punishment of contemporary Jews who mock the redemptive power of Christ (number 68). In emphasizing the importance of keeping chrism and Eucharist under lock and key so that they cannot be reached by any hand that might do them harm, Constitution 20 contains sentiments strikingly similar to those expressed by Episcopus as he restores order (and addresses the repentant Sir Isodor and Aristorius) near the end of the Croxton play:

> And all yow creaturys and curatys that here be,
> Off thys dede yow may take example
> How that yowr pyxys lockyd ye shuld see,
> And be ware of the key of Goddys temple.
>
> (924–27)

In addition, the Constitutions contain two other decrees taken up by the Croxton play. Sir Isodor's gluttony and drunkenness—which allow Aristorius to obtain the host—clearly violate the decree against clerical gluttony and drunkenness (number 15), and the scene that dispenses with an earthly healer in favor of the heavenly physician echoes the language of Constitution 22, which commands "physicians of the body, when they are called to the sick, to warn and persuade them first of all to call in physicians of the soul." Animating issues that had, in essence, already been anticipated and legislated, the Croxton play provides for its East Anglian audience yet another safe venue for exploring contemporary religious concerns.

---

32. All references are to the online version of the Constitutions available at http://www.ewtn.com/library/COUNCILS/LATERAN4.HTM.

Emboldened by an economic prosperity that may have strengthened a fundamental confidence in Christianity's authority and structure, the Croxton play may have been a planned staging of disbelief that allowed East Anglian Christians to indulge spiritual desires and concerns connected to that same economic prosperity and an increasingly material culture.[33] The Christian beliefs held by the play's audience and actors can thus be seen to enable the miracles, based upon liturgical language and the doctrine of transubstantiation, that result from the Jews' tampering with the host. As the play progresses from desecration to miracle to eventual redemption, it becomes increasingly dependent upon an audience of believers whose belief status originally kept them from direct implication in the Jews' actions. In the *Tretise,* "miraclis pleyinge" ends with and is condemned by the Passion, with what the *Tretise* writers assert is an abuse of Christ and the Christian faith on the part of its participants. In the Croxton play, however, the miracles that follow such abuse are fulfilled by a sacramental and redemptive power that enlists the emotional and physical participation of its believers in a process that perhaps redeems "miraclis pleyinge" as well as Jew.

33. In a presentation at the International Congress on Medieval Studies, Kalamazoo, Michigan (May 2000), Mark D. Holtz explored a similar idea in relation to the larger phenomenon of bleeding hosts. In the later Middle Ages, he argued, bleeding hosts "do not need to bleed for believers."

Chapter Four

Devotional Response and Responsibility in the York Cycle

"Al . . . that walkis by waye or strete"[1]

LATE MEDIEVAL AUDIENCES attached to the religious drama a transformative power founded upon their own devotion to the Eucharist and belief in transubstantiation. The late medieval Church had willingly encouraged this devotion, with the goal of strengthening the hold of the priestly classes upon this transformative power made so explicitly important to late medieval Catholic belief; however, they apparently did not anticipate the laity's creative appropriation of this power. Such an appropriation could, paradoxically, and did challenge the Church's ostensibly exclusive control of *corpus Christi*. Bearing witness to clerical concerns regarding lay beliefs and practices associated with the host and the Eucharistic sacrament, the *Tretise of Miraclis Pleyinge* and the Croxton *Play of the Sacrament* reveal lay appropriation of, and belief in accessibility to, the transformative

1. Beadle (1982), 321, ll. 253. All future references are from this edition and will be cited parenthetically by pageant and line number.

power of transubstantiation. The religious drama relied upon its participants—its sacred players—to actively engage a response role that, like the transubstantiation itself, transforms and transcends body and spirit, humanity and divinity, mundane present and sacred past. The drama, consequently, becomes the vehicle for a fundamentally laic claim to the Eucharist and the Incarnation. The Croxton play, specifically, can be seen as an attempt on the part of the clergy to reclaim an exclusive right and power that (as it is portrayed in the play itself) has been dangerously and incorrectly transferred outside the realm of Church control. By emphasizing the necessity of control and containment, the culminating scene of the play portrays an attempt to return the re-creative potential of Christ's body to the locked pyx and altar, and away from the hands, bodies, and daily lives of the drama's participants, whose appropriation of that potential is likened to the Jews' horrific treatment of the host.

Yet, as I also argued in the previous chapter, while there is no doubt that that use of the drama as a perhaps lay version of the clerically controlled ritual of transubstantiation is systematically condemned in the *Tretise,* the Croxton play can be seen both as an avid enactment of that clerical criticism and as a redemptive and joyous response to it. While it portrays the potential dangers of laic claims to the powers of transubstantiation and the miracle of Christ's body, the play also affirms the re-creative potential of the religious drama as a devotional exercise fundamentally grounded in sacralizing the elements of everyday life and experience. Both the *Tretise* and the Croxton play, then, attest to the existence of a use of the drama that clearly linked it to belief in transubstantiation—a use that could prove both compelling and problematic for negotiating relationships between the Church and its lay population. Moreover, like the *Tretise of Miraclis Pleyinge* and the Croxton *Play of the Sacrament,* the York cycle provides a powerful example of the re-creative aesthetic that engaged audiences of the late medieval religious drama and which—as demonstrated by the efforts of Expositor in the Chester cycle and of Paul and Poeta in the Digby *The Conversion of Saint Paul*—at least some reformist and Protestant authorities were eager to define, revise, and vilify. At the same time, like the *Play of the Sacrament,* the particularly emphatic attention to audience roles and response in the York cycle must be examined in light of its own staging as late medieval sacred drama. More specifically, the York cycle illustrates an active engagement of sacred playing that likewise attests to the popularity of this employment of the religious drama as a sanctifying force, seemingly powerful enough to usurp even the day officially dedicated to the city's Corpus Christi procession.[2]

Civic Duty, Spiritual Duty: The Late Medieval Work of the York Cycle

The manuscript of the York pageants, known as the "Register," compiled in the third quarter of the fifteenth century from guild copies of individual pageants, is (as Richard Beadle has asserted) a text of the cycle from that time period: the later fifteenth century. Evidence suggests that during the sixteenth century the Marian pageants were likely suspended and then eventually eliminated. The Register, however, does not demonstrate any direct forms of censorship, and thus, as Beadle describes, the text does not offer "a fully accurate record of either the content or the organization of the cycle" past the late fifteenth century (1994, 92). I will not argue that the York cycle provides some untouched "essence" of the Middle English religious drama, or that its texts have preserved the drama in some "pure" form. Indeed, such an approach is, as I suggested in my Introduction, an impediment to study of this drama. Rather, the "dated" circumstances of the Register (which is the extant text of the pageants), coupled with the basic freedom of the pageants from the influence of Protestant (and earlier, Catholic) authorities, encourage us to approach the surviving texts mindful of the local uses that the citizens and city of York made of its incarnational dra-

2. Between 1465 and 1476, the procession was moved from the liturgical date of the first Thursday after Trinity Sunday to the day after Trinity Sunday. See Johnston (1973–1974) and Beadle (1994), 90.

ma. These various uses become more explicit through examination of the wealth of documentary materials connected to the cycle and its performance.[3]

The familiar presence of the York pageants in everyday lives, activities, ordinances, and processes of civic order, moreover, reveals an awareness of the potential ability of the sacred performance to sanctify common occupations and activities. Close connections between the pageants and the craft guilds of York are well evidenced by the carefully prepared lists contained in the city's A/Y Memorandum Book and by the head notes appearing at the beginnings of individual plays in the city Register.[4] For practical as well as spiritual benefits—and for an essential conflation of both—the performance situation of the play brought sacred people, events, and objects into proximity with homes, businesses, and even the casual passerby, who would have been drawn into the sacred work invoked and enabled by worshipful reenactment. This performance situation, together with the complex relationship between the pageants and the craft guilds, and thus the daily occupations and livelihoods of all citizens of York, reveals much regarding the function and meaning of the play, described cryptically but suggestively as "maintained and

3. See Beadle and King (1994), xv: "The 'Ordo Paginarum,' though much altered and revised, reveals that the cycle had by 1415 assumed the shape and scope it was to have for the rest of its career. Comparison with the text in the Register reveals that a number of plays were revised during the fifteenth century, and that some were reasssigned to other guilds. . . . However, the general aspect and scope of the cycle remained the same, as it was to do until its decline and eventual abandonment in the latter half of the sixteenth century." More recently, Happé (2004), in an essay addressing potential Protestant changes to the cycle plays, has contrasted the largely Catholic sympathies of York's city council with the "less traditional . . . outlook" at Chester where evidence of direct Protestant influence was more pronounced (20).

4. Contained in the A/Y Memorandum Book is the *Ordo Paginarum,* a list of the guilds and the pageants they performed with an accompanying short description of each pageant. A second and similar list that contains shorter, one-line descriptions of the pageants follows the *Ordo Paginarum* in the A/Y Memorandum Book. The head notes appearing at the beginning of each play indicate the name of the responsible guild or guilds. See Beadle (1982), 23–25, 16, 416–64. See also Beadle and Meredith (1983).

brought forth in their order by the crafts of the . . . city for the benefit of the citizens of the same city and of all strangers coming there
of the aforesaid feast, especially for the honor and reverence of our
Lord Jesus Christ and for the profit of the said citizens" (Johnston
and Rogerson, 1979, 713).[5] The pageants, beyond their annual performance, seem to have maintained a familiar presence in daily life
in York, demonstrating a potent (if commonly accepted) connection
between civic and spiritual duty. In addition, more than sanctifying
spaces within the city, pageant performances and their sacred players created opportunities for both spiritual and economic profit (and
their likely conflation) as the city and its citizens expected their Corpus Christi play to provide sacramental meaning and benefit both
within and beyond any set performance.

Audience Address and the Re-creative Experience

As I noted in my Introduction, the audience-address figures of
the York cycle are particularly ubiquitous, mediating between the
audience and the dramatic re-creation of spiritual events and experiences, yet moving fluidly between contemporary York and salvation
history. Emboldened by the spatial and physical immediacy within
the small, narrow streets of the city, York's audience attentive figures take advantage of this particular performance situation to demonstrate what Beadle calls the cycle's "duality of perspective" (1994,
87), its metadramatic quality (86, 89), and the consistent emphasis of
that perspective upon the presence and involvement of the contemporary city and audience. The audience of the York cycle is therefore

5. The original text, in Latin, appears in Johnston and Rogerson, 28. For more
on the particularly "civic" quality of the York plays, see Stevens (1987), 17–87. See
also Clopper (1989), 111–12: "Cycles of religious drama . . . seem to have appeared
in northern England in those cities that established strong governments centered in
the trade guilds. In those cities and towns where civic government had to compete
against powerful ecclesiastical establishments or where religious rather than trade
guilds dominated, cyclic drama does not seem to appear . . . . The conclusion that
can be tentatively drawn is that cycles of drama are to be identified with the secular
or lay guild government, perhaps as an expression of civic control, civic pride, and
civic concern for the religious education of the townspeople."

moved toward what Sarah Beckwith describes as "a process of ritual participation" (1995, 66). Characters such as Herod (who comments upon those spectators fighting for a good view [31. 1–5]), Judas (who offers his explanation to the audience for his selling of Christ "for therty pens" [26.152]), and Christ himself (who from the cross addresses all participants, linking, of course, audience with players [35.253–64; 36.118–30, 184–95]) help us to identify this "process"— a kind of salvific work which, in turn, transforms the space of city and audience into their own venues of spiritual mediation and sacramental transformation.[6] As they did for medieval audiences, the address and guide figures of the York cycle bring us into the re-creative movement and sacred work of its plays, prompting the audience to participate along with the cycle and its players in order to produce not only the literal version of the Fall and the Redemption, but also its spiritual meaning and benefit. Influenced by the incarnated Christ's transformative work in the world, so powerfully illustrated in the transubstantiation (including the laboring expanse of Christ's own body), the space of the city of York and the participant bodies that occupy that space move fluidly between sacred past and mundane present in a process of creation and re-creation.

The immediate participation of the audience in helping to conflate the time and space of York with that of sacred history is, in fact, all but demanded by several audience-address figures whose expectations for direct audience involvement are reminiscent of similar figures found in the Chester pageant of *Balaam and Balaak*.[7] Working to get the attention of the audience, as well as to engage the audience in the re-creational aesthetic and response role necessary for the spiritual success of the plays, these figures attest to a fundamental devotional use of the pageants: a transcendence of time and space linked to the mingling of sacred and mundane, divine and hu-

6. On the audience interactive nature of the York cycle, see also Collier (1978). Beckwith (2001) has also recently expanded her work on the York cycle with a special emphasis on its sacramental quality. Moreover, Happé (2004), in distinguishing "Catholic preoccupations" from "Protestant ideas," identifies in the York cycle "a closeness between what is enacted and the life of the city" (25).

7. See Chapter One above.

man found in the Incarnation and the Eucharist and reminiscent of
Jeffrey's description of "recurrence" history (1973, 72). When, for
example, Pharaoh opens *Moses and Pharaoh*, he "addresses not only
the Yorkshire spectators, but also the people of Egypt" (Diller, 1992,
122). Moreover, in his call for quiet, attention, and order, Pharaoh
fuses his response to the practical situation of the performance atmosphere to his own historical power, subjecting past and present
audiences to boastful descriptions of his worldly dominion:

> O pees, I bidde that no man passe,
> But kepe the cours that I comaunde,
> And takes gud heede to hym that hasse
> Youre liff all haly in his hande.
> Kyng Pharo my fadir was,
> And led the lordshippe of this lande,
> I am his hayre as ele will asse,
> Evere in his steede to styrre and stande.
> All Egippe is myne awne
> To lede aftir my lawe,
> I will my myght be knawen
> And honnoured as it awe.
>
> (11.1–12)

Similarly, at the beginning of *Christ before Herod,* Herod's call for quiet and order brings his historical power, fierceness, and pride into
the contemporary York street—"this broydenesse inbrased"—while
his command "plextis for no plasis byt plate you to this playne" ap-
plies directly to those audience members fighting for a good view
of the pageant wagon (31.1, 5). More than mere passing references
to performance conditions and audience, this conscious bringing of
the past to bear upon the present comments upon the production
of these pageants as a concerted form of worship, founded upon
the sacred responsibility to achieve and maintain an aesthetic of re-
creation. Subjected to Pilate's physical threats as he brandishes a
weapon (an audience attentive behavior again found in the Chester
Balaak and Balaam) in *Christ before Pilate I,* the audience may be ad-

dressed on a comic level, but their active participation in aiding the pageant's conflation of past and present is also demanded and its necessity reasserted (30.1–4). In *Christ before Pilate II*, in fact, Pilate's speeches demonstrate his assumption that the audience members are his subjects and active witnesses to the events leading up to the Crucifixion: "Loke to youre lord here and lere at my lawe— / As a duke I may dampne you and drawe" (32.4–5). In opening *The Death of Christ,* moreover, Pilate takes the audience's participation a step further. Not only does he call for quiet and attention—

> Sees seniours, and see what I saie.
> Takis tente to my talkyng enteere.
> Devoyde all this dynne here this day
> > (36.1–3)

—but he also implicates the audience, as well as Caiphas and Annas, in the events of the Crucifixion:

> His blodde to spille
> Toke ye you tille,
> Thus was youre wille
> Full spitously to spede he were splite.
> > (36–39)

In company with other braggarts and tyrants from sacred history who populate the York pageants, these figures, then, use the reality of performance conditions to establish a foundation for direct involvement by the audience in a process of transformative work, linked ultimately to Christ's own labors.

The Laborer as Sacred Worker

A primary example of re-creative performance as devotional exercise, the York cycle reveals a use of the religious drama that calls upon its participants to engage in a sacred and laic transubstantiating work that includes players, spectators, and the time and space of the city itself. Consequently, its audience attentive figures disclose an employment of the drama and expectations for its audience that would likely agitate (for different reasons) not only the Protestant revisers of the Chester cycle and the Digby *Saint Paul,* but also those Catholic clergy responsible for the opinions regarding drama and the Eucharist communicated in the *Tretise of Miraclis Pleyinge* and the Croxton *Play of the Sacrament.* Moreover, the use of the drama as a devotional means available to the laity for bridging human and divine, mundane and sacred, daily life and salvation story becomes in some pageants a means for critiquing one type of worldly labor while praising another. In their attempt to claim and align their type of labor with the transformative, redemptive work of Christ (and, by extension, of Corpus Christi play), the manufacturing classes of York illustrate how deeply the drama as re-creative devotional exercise and sacred labor permeated late medieval society in England.

As Beckwith has argued, a number of the York pageants contain a potential "artisanal ideology which place[s] importance on manufacture, or on making, rather than on the control of exchange mechanisms through the manipulation of networks of supply and distribution" (1994, 265). The partial result of a desire of the laboring classes to sanctify their own work, and a secondary effect of this artisanal ideology (so bound up in the transformative and re-creational work of the drama itself), was a subtle maligning of the activities of the mercantile elite who were the primary members of city government and who closely supervised and manipulated the physical logistics of the cycle's production.[8] Portrayed as static, controlling, and motivated selfishly by earthly profit—rather than by the sacred acts required by true participation in the ritual of religious theater— the work of the mercantile elite emerges, at least in some pageants, as a restrictive force, a form of antiresponse, undermining the city's economic and spiritual livelihood joined so fluidly through the transcendent mechanism of York's Corpus Christi cycle.

As the work of Sylvia Thrupp (1948), Jacques Le Goff (1980),

---

8. See Stevens (1987), 19ff.; the Introduction to Beadle (1982); and Beadle and King (1984), xii and ff.

and Heather Swanson (1989) has suggested, there were ongoing controversies and conflicts throughout the Middle Ages regarding the legitimacy and morality of the merchants' work, as opposed to that of the laborers' work. While in the later medieval period, as Le Goff points out, with "urban expansion" mercantile activities came to be more "justified" by their contribution "to the common good" and proper place within "the *familia Christi,* which bound all [kinds of] *good* workers together" (61), the work of merchants certainly remained suspect in quarters that saw them as disadvantaged by comparison (Le Goff, 1980; my emphasis). The concept that "man's work was supposed to be in the image of God's"—a concept that circulated throughout much of the early and high Middle Ages— did not necessarily lose its hold upon the laboring classes, especially when it might be to their spiritual and economic benefit to seize as their credo the belief that since Creation was "God's work," a vocation "which did not create was bad or inferior. It was imperative," argues Le Goff, "to create, as the peasant, for example, created the harvest, or, at least, to transform raw material, like the artisan, into an object. If there was no creation, then there should be transformation *(mutare),* modification *(emendare),* or improvement *(meliore).* The merchant who created nothing, was thus condemned" (61).[9] Perhaps in no other pageant of the York cycle are physical exertions and the toil of work, as well as its transformative and salvific potential, made so explicit to the audience than in the cycle's retelling of the Crucifixion (35). The soldiers, occupied in fitting and nailing Christ to the cross, approach their macabre work with a close, careful, and methodical devotion that, accompanied by their ongoing detailed description of their labors, consistently reminds the audience of their own duty as participatory agents working to connect past and present, sacred and mundane, divine presence and human body. Staged, fittingly, by the Pinners, who "made small metal objects, mostly with sharp points, such as pins" (Beadle, 1982, 452), *The Crucifixion* presents the activities of workers—pinners, soldiers,

9. See also Le Goff (1980), 302, n. 21.

actors, audience members—attentive to the specifics of their work and the tools and labor it requires to bring about redemption.

Moreover, even before the soldiers begin their task, Christ seems to bless their work both within and beyond the Crucifixion and the pageant itself in a speech that exemplifies the essence of the re-creational goal of the religious drama. As he refers to the pain that he will experience because of Adam's "plyght," Christ also seemingly alludes, indirectly and perhaps punningly, to the activity of "pinning." In a beseeching prayer, he declares:

> Almyghty God, my fadir free,
> Late this materes be made in mynde;
> Thou badde that I schulde buxsome be
> For Adam plyght for to be pyned.
>
> (35.49–52)

The pinners, because of the connection between their livelihood and the action required to attach Christ to the cross, display their work in this pageant as responsible both for its present performance and, at least in part, for the original event. Focusing their work on the space of Christ's body, the soldiers *cum* pinners demonstrate its transformative and (as the audience knows) redemptive potential. Furthermore, by focusing energetically on the specific details and tools of their work, the soldier-workmen transpose the transformative and redemptive potential of Christ's body onto the space of performance and audience, onto the work of everyday craftsmen and audience members who, in turn, are acknowledged as sacred laborers. The "arma Christi," those symbols of the weapons of Christ's death and suffering (as well as triumph) often portrayed and invoked in late medieval literature and art, become in the York *Crucifixion* tools for work, and for accomplishment and creation.[10] Familiar objects such as nails, hammers, wood, and rope become sacred tools and render the soldiers' exertions re-creative as well as salvific work. As Beadle has noted, "[T]he ignorant, physical, painful work of man in the

10. See Davidson (1984), 101.

cause of sin and death is transfigured into the sublime, spiritual work of redemption in the cause of life everlasting" (1994, 103). Rather than condemning the work of the pinners and other laborers in the city who use such tools and toil every day with similar exertion, the soldiers' careful, if cruel, attentions to their work with Christ's body actually sanctify such manual labor, making it part of (and necessary for) the Resurrection of Christ and the redemption of humankind.

The spiritual significance of the work of York's laboring classes, linked with the transformative work of Christ's torturers and laboring soldiers, gains further importance and influence when, in his address from the cross near the end of *The Crucifixion,* Christ calls out to "Al men that walkis by waye or strete" (35.253), thereby making contemporary these events of salvation history—part of the presence of the everyday streets, actions, and spaces of York and its citizens. Like Christ's torturers, and like York's laboring classes who are held up here as the true claimants to the re-creational power of Christ and drama, the pageant spectators are workers in their own right, contributing to the meaning of the Crucifixion both within and beyond its original occurrence. Locating the events of his death within the streets of contemporary York, Christ, referring to the particulars of his "head," "hands," and "feet," and re-creating, in a sense, the work of his torturers, connects the space of his body with city and audience. He thus encourages his spectators likewise to become the transforming workers of those redemptive tortures. "Beholdes," Christ says, "myn heede, myn handis, and my feete,"

> And fully feele nowe, or ye fyne
> If any mournyng may be meete,
> Or myscheve mesured unto myne.
>   (35.255–58)[11]

The audience is thus called upon to "measure" the significance of the Crucifixion across a span of time and space that meets in the

---

11. Christ also addresses the audience from the cross in *The Death of Christ* (118–30 and 184–95).

particular moment of the pageant performance, but that also extends into and beyond their own streets, homes, and storefronts.[12] The audience, therefore, as much as the actors, are seen as generating the meaning and salvific power of the pageant, and the successful merger of mundane and spiritual labor toward which the pageant and its participants work will enable spiritual knowledge, and ultimately salvation.[13]

Similarly engaging its audience in a clear example of transformative craftsmanship, the York pageant of *The Building of the Ark* (8)—staged appropriately by the city's shipwrights—serves not only to demonstrate the historical significance of the shipwrights' vocation but also to sanctify the importance of their work beyond the pageant's performance. Allowing for an extended construction scene for the ark that displays the tasks and tools of the York shipwrights, Noah's story and the events of the Flood are divided into two separate pageants. Moreover, God's own self-described construction of the world—"My werke I wroght so wele and trewe" (8.18)—is linked a few lines later to Noah's construction of the ark when God commands him: "I wyll thou wyrke withowten weyn / A warke to salle thiselfe wythall" (8.35–36).[14] Noah as laborer is thus presented as sal-

12. Cf. the illustration from the Villers Miscellany and the accompanying discussion in Lewis (1996), 204–9.

13. As Le Goff has commented, "Christ brought the certainty of eventual salvation with him, but collective and individual history must still accomplish it for all, as well as for each individual. Hence, the Christian must simultaneously renounce the world, which is only his transitory resting place, and [yet also] *opt for the world, accept it and transform it, since it is the workplace of the present history of salvation*" (1980, 31; my emphasis).

14. Cf. Beadle (1994), 87: "[T]he closing words of the script embellish what has been the playwright's intention throughout, to blend the daily labor of the York Shipwrights with the divine scheme of redemption, for they revolve around a felicitous play on the word 'craft,' which signifies both the play-Ark, the vessel which has just taken shape before the audience's eyes, and at the same time the divinely-inspired craft or mystery of shipbuilding within which God has taught Noah. . . ." Stevens (1987) expresses a similar idea: "[T]he demonstration of [a] ware or skill . . . as part of the anachronism of playcraft linked the performer with the play and created a larger meaning for the performance. The linkage helped to incorporate the city's ordinary purpose—its daily ritual of work and human intercourse—into the play action and thus into the grand design of salvation history" (29).

vific worker, partaking of what Le Goff has called an evolving late
medieval "theology of labor" that "attempted to demonstrate that
labor had its positive roots in God because . . . the Creator's work . . .
was genuine labor . . . a creation, but one which entailed the usual
painful consequences as seen in the fact that the creation was a *labor* from which God had to rest on the seventh day. God was the first
worker" (1980, 115). Noah's concentration upon his task, his detailed
description of his work (8.89–119), and his perseverance even at the
end of the pageant ("[a]bowte this werke now bus me wende"; 148)
places the audience in a role of craftsmanship that suggests at a very
intimate level that careful, proper attention to the space and nature
of one's sacred work as audience member ought to extend to one's
worldly occupation—and that both ought to enable the events and
outcomes of Christian history. A precursor to Christ's body in *The
Crucifixion* pageant, the ark becomes a space of work, construction,
transformation, and re-creation. And, like the soldiers in *The Crucifixion*, Noah, through his involvement of the audience in the specific
details, tools, and measurements of his labors, extends the working
space of the ark, the pageant, and sacred history to include the space
of audience, city, and its working classes.

Merchandizing the Sacred: The Stations of York and the Body of Christ

In contrast to the transformative and redemptive potential associated with the work and occupations of the city's laborers communicated in *The Crucifixion* and *The Building of the Ark,* the York *Conspiracy* pageant (26) seemingly condemns worldly occupations and
business practices while asserting a large gap between spiritual and
earthly pursuits. But when examined more closely, especially in connection with York's practice of leasing to certain of its citizens performance and viewing spaces for individual pageants along the cycle's route in the city, *The Conspiracy,* with its emphasis on money,
profits, and spiritual as well as earthly economics, helps reveal both
the danger and the potential of connecting civic and spiritual duties.

More specifically, in offering to its audience a use and treatment of Christ, of his body, and of the sacred performance (the play of Corpus Christi itself) in conflict with that presented in such pageants as *The Crucifixion* and *The Building of the Ark, The Conspiracy* provides a lens for viewing disputes over claims to the sacralizing power of the York performance. These disputes are complicated by the desire of the laboring classes to assert Christ's transformative work as more closely related to their own vocations.

The performance of a pageant within York and related spaces outside its gates—within the context of daily life and work—could infuse the specific spaces of performance (including, importantly, the audience's position and role) with sacred meaning and potential. Laying claim to a good performance and audience space, then, could be economically desirable, and financial reasons undeniably motivated the citizens of York to lease these spaces in order to sell spots to those who wished preferred access to a pageant. Meg Twycross's work with the station lists reveals that certain individuals consistently rented stations, and that this "impressive amount of short- and middle-term continuity . . . suggests that hiring stations was a profitable affair" (1978, 10–33). Yet these records may testify not only to struggles over money-making opportunities, but also to conflicts over who gains and controls access to the pageants' potential for spiritual (as well as economic) opportunity. The performance of a pageant at or near one's door—the twenty-five existing station lists (dating from 1399 to 1569) detailing lessees often indicate in this way the annual performance places—might provide one more access to the sacred, thereby making one's property, home, or business location a sacred space, and bringing the owner one step closer to God and salvation.[15] While Eileen White asserts that "everyone [in York] would be exposed to the fact of the performance" and "the whole city was given over to it, with a holiday from work" (1987, 57), Beckwith elaborates specifically upon the ability of the

15. For example, the 1399 station list states: "Secundo ad ostium Roberti Harpham" and "Tercio ad ostium Iohannis de Gyseburne"; the 1569 list: "ij[de] ageynst mr Henrisons hows" (Johnston and Rogerson, 1979, 11, 356).

wealthy (likely the mercantile elite who either held leading governing positions or had close ties to those who did) to gain better "ex-
posure," and therefore apparently more substantial access, to the
sacramental, and potentially transubstantiating, power of the pageants. "Wealthy householders," she says, "through paying money to
the city, could literally inscribe their own property into the very in-
scription of the route of the Corpus Christi pageants, because their
houses were part of the processional staging of the cycle" (1996,
72).[16] Can one buy access to sacred spaces, to a pageant and its sacred potential, to God and to salvation? Can this purchase actually substitute for the sacred work that the Middle English religious
drama so often called upon its audiences to undertake as devotional
responsibility, itself an avenue to the transcendent and miraculous
meanings of Incarnation and transubstantiation? These questions,
charged with conflicts over sacred space and city space, spiritual and
worldly profit, and linked to disputes between the laboring classes
and the mercantile elite of York, are dynamically examined in the
York *Conspiracy* pageant.

When Pilate opens *The Conspiracy*, the first play in the York Passion sequence, he does so with a familiar assertion of his power and
dominion that is meant to be heard and understood by actors and
audience alike:

> Undir the ryallest roye of rente and renowne
> Now am I regent of rewle this region in reste,
> Obeye unto bidding bud busshoppis me bowne
> And bolde men that in batayll makis brestis to breste.
> To me betaught is the tene this towre-begon towne,
> For traytoures tyte will I taynte the trewthe for to triste.
>
> (26.1–6)

As in (for example) Herod's address in *Christ before Herod* and Christ's
address from the cross in *The Crucifixion*, Pilate provides a space-
specific reference that joins the region that he rules with contem-

16. See also Crouch (1991).

porary York. In each of these cases, the speaker assists the potential efficacy of the city streets and spaces. Moreover, at the very beginning of his address, Pilate asserts interestingly that he rules under a king, meaning Herod, who has the most "rente," or revenue, as well as the most fame. Having merged his and Herod's kingdoms with "the towre-begon towne" of York, Pilate here suggests that he and Herod may claim any profits that this area of the city itself ("this region") makes. Pilate begins the pageant on a ponderous note for its participating audience; he indicates an attention to past and present revenues that seems to include the very space that the play and performance occupy, and which most certainly would have been leased by one of the city's citizens for financial profit. On the one hand, Pilate's presence and the presence of the pageant itself can sanctify the city space, presenting opportunities for spiritual gain; on the other hand, his claim and Herod's claim to the space's economic revenues almost seem to question the legitimacy of using such a type of revenue to gain such spiritual profit. In this sense, then, Pilate's words seem to critique and condemn the motives of those whose (perhaps rather limited) participation (or work) in the play is linked primarily to the money they make as lessees.

While Pilate invokes a limited, indeed nonproductive, nontransformative use of the space of York and its play, Judas's treatment of Christ and his body is similarly focused on mere economic profit. Unlike the soldiers' work with (and upon) Christ in *The Crucifixion,* and unlike Noah's creation of the ark (a precursor to Christ's body), Judas's work statically centers on a business proposition with those who seek to destroy Christ. Perhaps like those who place a limited, monetary value on pageant stations, Judas places a limited value on Christ's body, thus reducing Christ's importance to his own personal profit. In essence, Judas turns Christ's "laboring body" into a mere "commodity," restricting its value and space in an interesting contrast to the soldiers' eventually successful attempts to stretch Christ's body to fit the poorly proportioned cross.[17]

17. See Sponsler (1997), 142.

Judas's potential association with the merchant classes is perhaps particularly revealed, in addition, in the monetarily charged explanation he provides for his selling of Christ. Asserting that he was the "purser" of Christ's money from whom he stole a "tente parte" (26, 136, 137), Judas argues that money was wasted on the expensive ointment used by Mary Magdalene to anoint Christ's feet (129ff.). As he laments the "thirty pens" that he would have kept for himself if the ointment had been sold for its value of "iij hundereth" (141ff.), Judas reveals his attention to pricing, market value, and exchange rates. Moreover, he communicates a value system that defines his selling of Christ as a type of compensatory transaction, one that makes up for his previous financial losses: "But now for me wantis of my will / That bargayne with bale schall he [Christ] by" (139–40). Reducing to a business transaction what will become Christ's ultimate sacrifice to humankind, Judas seemingly cannot see beyond earthly profits, cannot find a bridge between worldly and spiritual work. When he asserts that "for I mysse this money I morne on this molde, / Wherfore for to mischeve this maistir of myne" (147–48), he reveals his wholly earth-bound position, resulting in his inability—and thus, perhaps, the merchant classes' inability—to balance spiritual and worldly activities, including the profits of the current Corpus Christi play. When wagering with Pilate, Caiphas, and Annas, he declares, "I wolde make a marchaundyse" (214) and then announces "[f]or if ye will bargayne or by. / Jesus this tyme will I selle you" (219–20). Judas's focus on his own personal profit— on work that creates nothing, transforms little, and restricts Christ's reformative message to purses and pence—causes him to sell off his salvation that is Christ. Ironically, he is unaware that his own worldly motives and actions are actually provoking the real spiritual "bargayne": God's gift of salvation.

Taking a cue from the re-creative and transformative work of the cycle, the laboring classes of York, in a laic claim to the powers of Incarnation and transubstantiation, suggested in some of their pageants that the regulatory and restrictive handling by the merchant class of workers, goods, city, and Corpus Christi play opposed the real, salvific meaning of Christ's life and resurrection as transformative, transcendent miracles. In York, moreover, the governing authorities, consisting primarily of the mercantile elite, seemed eager to use the city's Corpus Christi cycle as a form of punishment, as a restrictive measure for regulating the craftsmen and artisans of the city whom they oversaw and employed. The records pertaining to the York cycle's productions contain, for example, several references to this use of the cycle as a form of punishment for, in particular, individual guilds that exceeded the space, time, and/or limits of appointed craft or work. A 1388 decree declares that if any fletcher should do any work and/or display any of his work for sale on Sunday, he will be fined and half of the money donated in support of the fletchers' pageant.[18] Similarly, a 1411–1412 entry uses support of pageant as a penalty for those bakers who try to sell their wares outside of a city-specified place of business.[19] And transgressing candlemakers and ironmongers in 1417 and 1420, respectively, were dealt a punishment that requested financial support for their assigned pageants.[20] As Le Goff and other scholars of labor in the Middle Ages have noted, the merchant classes asserted themselves as control-

18. Johnston and Rogerson (1979), 6: "[N]ul ffleccher de yceste Citee ne ouerara desormes ascun dymenche ascunes oueraigne appartenant a lour dite Artifice ne ne mettera ascunes setes boltis nautres lours darres pur auaunt pur monstrer vender ascune dymenche sure peeyne de xl d appaiez lun moite a la chaumbre & laure a lour pagent de corpore christi. . . . [N]o fletcher of this city will work henceforth any Sunday at any work belonging to their said guild, nor put any arrows, bolts, nor other of their dars in front to show for sale on any Sunday on pain of 40d to pay, one half to the chamber and the other to their pageant of Corpus Christi . . ." (692).

19. Johnston and Rogerson (1979), 16: "[N]ullus pistor ciuitatis aut aliquis de suit portet bel portari faciat extra loca sua aliquod genus panis venalis ad domos fenestras vel habitaciones alicuius regratarii infra ciuitatem istam vel suburbia eiusdem sub pena iij s iiij d vsui communitatis & artificio pistorum ad sustantacionem pagine sue & aliorum onerum suorum . . . . [N]o baker of the city or any agent of his should carry or cause to be carried outside his [specified] place any type of bread available for sale, to the houses, windows, or dwellings of any regrater within this city or the suburbs of the same, under penalty of 3s 4d, for the use of the commons and for the craft of the Bakers for the support of their pageant [or] of their other burdens . . ." (702).

20. Johnston and Rogerson (1979), 30–32, 35.

lers of time, space, and length and amount of work. From the thirteenth century on, the merchant classes who were almost without exception "employer[s] of labor," began to rely increasingly on systems of "communal clock[s]" that were "instrument[s] of economic, social, and political domination wielded by the merchants who ran the commune. . . . For the merchant, the technological environment superimposed a new and measurable time, in other words, an oriented and predictable time, on that of the natural environment, which was a time both eternally renewed and perpetually unpredictable" (1980, 35). Using the cycle play as a vehicle for restriction and control, city authorities thus may have provided an arena for the laboring classes to critique mercantile work and intentions as fundamentally antithetical to the sacred labor of Christ and Corpus Christi play. The laboring classes of York could therefore align their own work with that sacred labor and seize upon certain pageants as opportunities for portraying this opposition, while still encouraging and maintaining an allegiance to the drama as a form of sacred work that required an understanding of labor as transformative and re-creative occupation.

Part III

Gendering Response

Christ's Body and God's Word

Chapter Five

Incarnational Belief and Gender in the Digby *Killing of the Children*

"Ferse" Women and "Gentylle" Men[1]

FOR THE SACRED PLAYERS OF THE YORK CYCLE—both the actors and the audience who watched them perform—the space of Christ's body infused the streets of their city with a salvific potential that was engaged through an aesthetic of audience participation and response—one that mediated boundaries between past and present, divine and human, heavenly and earthly. The audience of the Digby *Candlemas Day and the Killing of the Children of Israel* (referred to by most scholars as *The Killing of the Children*) seems to have been encouraged to connect that salvific potential to a fluid approach to gender that could also aid them in uniting the meaning and power of Christ's birth and death with the present-day experiences of the drama's participants. The York cycle thus bears witness to a populist claim to the transformative powers of the Incarnation and the Eucharist—powers that, through an active devotional par-

---

1. Baker et al. (1982), ll. 311 and 259.

ticipation in the sacred drama, might be made accessible to (indeed, might actually be enabled by) the city's laboring classes. *The Killing of the Children* suggests that a similar transformative power might be applied to another social hierarchy, that of gender and gender roles.

As I will discuss in my concluding chapter, *The Killing of the Children* contains evidence that supports a Reformation reworking of its religious meaning and performance use (one that may correspond to a 1562 staging with the Digby *Saint Paul* and the Digby *Mary Magdalene*). Indeed, in that possible Protestant reworking of the play, gendered behavior as an indicator of religious faith, practice, and meaning indicates something quite different: the masculine and feminine behaviors that are a crucial theme in the play are reinterpreted in light of Protestant polemic. Similarly, as I discuss in Chapter Six, the association with Catholic drama and audiences of certain attitudes regarding gender may have proved to be another means for reformist and Protestant forces to vilify the old faith, and thus distinguish and define the righteousness of the new faith.

Yet, the revealing combination of episodes that is the Digby *Candlemas Day and the Killing of the Children of Israel* speaks primarily to the worship and performance goals of late medieval Catholicism (and to the time period revealed by the date of 1512 found within the manuscript itself).[2] Contained in Bodleian Library Ms. Digby 133 (along with its companion plays: *Mary Magdalene, The Conversion of Saint Paul,* and a fragment of *Wisdom*), *The Killing of the Children* in its extant form consists of two episodes whose pairing scholars have often found puzzling: the massacre of the innocents and Mary's purification and presentation of Christ at the Temple. In fact, the linking of these two episodes contrasts Herod's brutish inability to accept the miracle of the Incarnation with the joyous celebration of Christ's dual nature at the temple ceremony. This contrast, in turn, encourages the audience to explore alternative forms of gendered response as a means for aiding and experiencing the

2. See Baker et al. (1982), lii–liii, and Baker and Murphy (1976).

transformative potential of the Incarnation and of the religious drama itself.[3] While Herod's rigid adherence to a brutal form of masculine behavior is linked to a form of response that denies the miracle of the Incarnation, those figures in the play who do accept and respond favorably to the miracle—ultimately acknowledged and celebrated in the purification/presentation episode—display intriguingly fluid characteristics of gender. The audience is likewise encouraged to integrate such fluid characteristics into their roles as interactive believers intent upon re-creating a miracle of temporal and spatial transcendence offered through participation in the religious drama. Seen as an extension of the powers of the Incarnation and the Eucharist to transcend the boundaries of humanity and divinity, the ability to experience a combination of gendered emotions informs the devotional responsibilities of these participants who seek to recreate, as sacred players, the transcendent power made accessible through Christ, the Eucharist, and the play.[4]

3. The Poeta's incorrect ordering of the plays in his opening address suggests that the plays may have been performed in the reverse order in which they are presented in the manuscript. Yet the two performances are clearly paired in the manuscript, with *The Killing of the Children* preceding the Candlemas play, leaving little doubt that they correspond in some significant way. See also Baker (1989), 25–28, and Marshall (1995), 126–27. For other analyses of the relationship between the two episodes of the Digby play, see Mills (1983), 164–65; Woolf (1972), 196; and Harrington (1995), 67–80. In addition, the *"Vacat ab hinc"* (Omit from here [on]) note that appears before the Candlemas play seems to indicate that it may not have been performed with the play it accompanies "on at least one occasion" (Baker et al., 1982, lx). I discuss the potential implications of this omission near the end of Chapter Six.

4. Following Stallybrass and White (1986, 58), the process is not one of inversion but rather of combination, or what Stallybrass and White refer to as "hybridization," an experience that "produces new combinations and strange instabilities in a given semiotic system. It therefore generates the possibility of shifting the very terms of the system itself." See also the work of Carolyn Walker Bynum (1982, 1987, 1989, 1991, 1995). In *Jesus as Mother* (1982, 162), for example, Bynum asserts that "[m]edieval authors do not seem to have drawn as sharp a line as we do between sexual responses and affective responses or between male and female. Throughout the Middle Ages, authors found it far easier than we seem to find it to apply characteristics stereotyped as male or female to the opposite sex." Karma Lochrie (1997, 194) also cites this passage and argues that "[t]he polymorphousness of Christ's body, with its feminine genital wound and its simultaneous masculine prop-

Echoing the devotional experiences of late medieval peoples evidenced in such audience-involved, popular, and highly influential
texts as the *Prickynge of Love* and the *Mirrour of the Blessyd Life of
Jesu Christi,* the combination of episodes in *The Killing of the Children* presents gender as a category of response available for those
eager to participate in the salvific potential of the religious drama
and its links to the Incarnation, the Crucifixion, and transubstantiation.[5] Appending a fluid notion of gender (as a form of devotionally
motivated behaviors available to both men and women) to this sacred work as a means for accessing, comprehending, and celebrating the power of the divine, *The Killing of the Children* indicates that
gender may thus have played a useful role in aiding the kind of participatory response that the religious drama likely asked of its audiences in the late medieval period. The gender crossings of *The Killing of the Children* invoke the boundary-breaking nature of the late
medieval religious drama; indeed, this osmosis was fundamental to
the drama's identity as a devotional exercise that asks its participants
to complicate the role of reception aesthetics in the Middle English
religious drama. This role connected the ability to respond like a
woman as well as like a man to the ability to comprehend and benefit from the ostensibly incomprehensible: the presence of the divine
in a human child born to a human woman.[6]

---

erties, introduces confusion at a very foundational level of religious language and,
therefore, of religious devotion."

5. For the popularity and influence of the *Prickynge,* see Kirchberger (1951), 15,
and Beckwith (1993), 64. For the popularity and influence of the *Mirrour,* see Salter
(1981), 115, and Sargent (1992), lix.

6. A number of scholars have argued for an emphasis upon female presence
and traditionally female concerns (see, e.g., Coletti, 1999; Gibson, 1989; and Ashley,
1990). While the partnering of episodes in the play may testify to the importance
that late medieval communities placed upon social constructions of womanhood,
closely linked with alternative and conflicting images of sexuality and mothering,
profanity and purity, I am more interested in this study in issues of gender fluidity
and performance and their impact on audience response.

Herod's Blind Response

Like his counterparts who populate the early English religious drama, the Herod of *The Killing of the Children* proclaims himself to the audience through a boisterous opening address that implicates his listeners in the process of the play they will be experiencing. Delivering a type of speech that, as we have seen elsewhere, draws upon an audience's willingness to aid in the dramatic attempt to link past with present in a re-creational devotional exercise, Herod turns his "audience" into his "subjects." The audience thus plays the part of those who were disempowered by Herod's past tyranny and claims to earthly power and dominance. Herod emphasizes his "bronde bright" and vows violent physical vengeance upon any "erthely wretches" who challenge him ("ther flesshe shalbe alle torent"); he thus subjects the audience to a tyrannical exhibition of what could be termed "hypermasculinity."[7] Linking worldly dominance to masculine display, Herod proclaims that he is "[m]ost strong and myghty" (62), the "most bedred [dreaded]" (64), and that "no conqueroure nor knyght is comparid" to me (68). Whether male or female, then, audience members would likely feel themselves urged into a position and response role requiring submission and silence, a role more characteristically "feminine" than "masculine." Moreover, this approach to response (and to gendered experience), which includes a worshipful identification with those who are perceived, at least from a worldly perspective, to be among the weakest members of society, becomes an important first step in the process of the play as devotional exercise. A fully interactive audience of *The Killing of the Children,* intent upon invoking the transcendent power of the religious drama, would thus embrace the opportunity to experience the disempowered and potentially emasculated state

---

7. Baker et al. (1982), 98, ll. 64, 73, 76. All references to the play are from this edition and will henceforth be cited parenthetically by line number within the text. While Coletti (1999) has similarly argued that the world of Herod's court demonstrates an "image of society [that] measures success in terms of the acquisition and display of manhood" (4), she takes her analysis in a direction different from mine.

Herod's brutish treatment seeks. Such a state, in terms of an inter-active response role characterized by submission and humility, pre-pares an audience for comprehending at firsthand an aspect of the Incarnation that was especially resonant for late medieval laypeo-ples: the disruption of corrupt earthly hierarchies of power, rank, and gender that the miracle of Christ's birth implied, relying as it did upon a simple mother and child to help enable the salvation of humanity.

Revealing the gendered dimension to Herod's tyranny and to his treatment of the audience, the opening scenes of the play fur-thermore characterize Herod's negative portrait of hypermasculin-ity as a form of engineered blindness and brutality whose fuller im-plications are revealed in his reactionary and murderous response to the miracle of Christ's birth: "Sle alle the children, to kepe my liberte!" (96). Incapable of perceiving that power (and, indeed, sal-vation) might transcend earthly and masculine boundaries, Herod thus resorts to slaughter in his highly articulated response to the birth of his potential rival. He models a reception role distinctly in opposition to that required of an audience hopeful of tapping into the transcendent power of the religious drama through their will-ing participation in its re-creative potential. Unwilling to believe in or to participate in the miracle of Christ's birth, Herod turns instead to earthly power and to murder in order to eliminate his boyish ri-val. Requiring his soldiers to share in his response to Christ's birth so that his plans may be carried out, Herod in fact instructs them in this form of response, aligning its brutality and violence with a definition of manhood that likewise requires a vision dangerously limited by earthly power and glory. These orders further demon-strate the gendered aspects of his response and include more than the killing of children: Herod also requires his soldiers to prove such conventional "masculine" qualities as strength, valor, and prowess through an act that seemingly requires a process of desensitization and a deadening of response. Drawing upon traditionally masculine equipment to prepare his soldiers, Herod commands his knights to "arme" themselves "in stele shynyng bright" (106), but he also encourages them to arm themselves emotionally: "Make alle the children on your swerdes to dey! / I charge you, spare not oon for mercy nor pyte" (115–16). Just as the massacre itself foreshadows Christ's Passion and Crucifixion, Herod's emphasis on worldly weapons similarly invokes the weapons and instruments associated with the latter: in marked contrast to the arming of Herod's knights, the "arma Christi" encode a message of empowerment through subjugation and submission.[8] Thus Christ's version of knighthood—and by extension his manhood—is subtly set against the brutal versions portrayed by Herod and his knights.

Rigid in his adherence to earthly (and therefore brutal) forms of power and masculinity, Herod presents gender as a "politically enforced performativity" (Butler, 1990, 146) that blinds him and his soldiers to the miracle of Christ's Incarnation. In contrast, by playing the role of Herod's lowly subjects, the audience engage a distinctly different response to the Incarnation, one that connects humility (and, perhaps, the ability to take on a conventionally "feminine" perspective) with the capacity to understand and benefit from the miracle of the Incarnation that anticipates, as does the massacre, the model of empowerment through submission found in the Passion and the Crucifixion. Readers of the *Prickynge of Divine Love* are similarly urged to cultivate a state of meekness and subjugation modeled by Christ's own response to the culminating events of his earthly life: Christ went to the cross as a man

unmyghtiest & out-cast . . . and of this considerynge a man taketh councel & reed for to folwe aftir sum-what as for to withdrewe his herte fro all mysrewled disire of worship & pope of the world, from welthe of worldeli

8. In addition to the *Prickynge*, which emphasizes the devotional rewards of meditating on and cultivating as one's own experience the submissive nature of Christ (most actively demonstrated through the Passion and the Crucifixion), see "Symbols of the Passion," a late medieval poem that details the effects of the "arma Christi." *Legends of the Holy Rood* (1871) contains two versions of the poem. Such devotional themes can also, of course, be found in the *Ancrene Wisse*. See also the discussion of the "arma Christi" in Lewis (1997) and Woolf (1962), as well as Mills's assertion that "Watkyn's pretensions arise from the cynical perversion of chivalry by Herod" (1983, 164).

rycchesse. Hee fleeth worshipes & favoures of the world as venyme & uggeth [dreaded] preysynge & vein plesynge as a stynkande post. (Kane, 1983, 42–43)[9]

More specifically, in fact, the contemplative in pursuing such a state is urged to "holde thyself as no man but as a wilde beeste unworthy [of] felowschipe of men & parchaunce if thou meke thyself soo he that loked on the mekenesse of his hand-maiden shal loke on the mekenesse of this soule and accepte thi mekenesse" (18–19). Prompted therefore to identify with those who are at the mercy of Herod's earthbound wrath and limited worldview, the audience can see themselves as participants in the ongoing miracle of Christ's birth, in which a *mere* child born to a *mere* woman can (as the play itself will reinforce) overcome even Herod's immense power.

In ordering his knights to "sle alle the children that come in your sight, / Wiche ben within two yeere of age," Herod believes, however, that an earthly massacre of children will ensure a "conservacion of my tytelle of right" (110–12). He and his knights thus represent a form of antiresponse to the transcendent power of the Incarnation and the Crucifixion. Choosing to oppose himself to the miracle, he refuses to participate in its meaning and potential and remains mired in an unbending display of earthly (and ultimately empty) power. Such an opposition, in fact, is offered for contemplation in the *Prickynge of Love*. While "veyne plesynges & preisynges of the world" are "ful perlous," and "flateries & worshipynge and suche worldly favoures . . . maken a man blynd . . . and poyson hym with venymous pride temprid with hony of feyned holynesse," an active search for a state of meekness is offered as an alternative: "what is thenne more profitable than thus [to] be mekid through felyng of thyn owne wrecchidnesse and thus ben hyghed through sight of cristes goodnesse. Crist is lowhe & criste is high; if thou wole go in hym lowe thou shal come to hym high" (Kane, 1983, 97). Likewise, in the *Mirrour,* the reader is reminded that Christ "shal be grete, noght in temporele

9. I have modernized some spellings and punctuation when quoting from Kane's edition of the text throughout this chapter.

lordshipe & worldly dignity" (Sargent, 1992, 24), and the cultivation of meekness is offered as an antidote to worldly sins and states of mind—with Christ as the highest model of perfect meekness (9, 49, 52, 66).[10] Similarly, the speaker of the *Mirrour*, who invokes the earthly trappings of kingship and high-status manhood (servants, trumpets, "& alle other wirchipes & pompes of the world"), asks why Christ willingly eschews these trappings—those elements that would "kepe [him] from the comune people"—and instead consciously adopts a lowly position: "Whi . . . go ye thus symply alone & on the bare erthe?" Answering his own question—"Sothely the cause is . . . ye have made your self as one of us . . . ye become a servant to make us kynges"—the speaker's portrayal offers Christ as a chief model for the reception role urged upon the audience of the Digby play (65). Aligned with the lowly status of one of Herod's subjects or victims, the members of the audience, like Christ himself and the contemplative associated with the texts of the *Prickynge* and the *Mirrour*, may seek access to a power that transcends earthly rankings of social status and gender.

Watkyn: Manliness as Performance and the Divine Fluidity of Response Roles

When Herod's messenger, then, having witnessed his ruler's exchange with his knights, seeks to raise his own social status through a display of manhood that he believes will match the qualities Herod has voiced and required of his soldiers, it seems initially that the audience is presented with another figure whose glorification of worldly power and status has blinded him to the Incarnation miracle. Yet, as his exchange with Herod reveals, Watkyn the messenger provides another example of the fluid nature of response as he seeks to elevate his status through an attempt to display characteristics and attitudes that indicate, primarily, his manhood.[11] Present for Herod's

10. I have modernized some spellings and punctuation when quoting from Sargent's edition of the text throughout this chapter.

11. My discussion here builds upon the work of Coletti (1995), 245–48.

preparation of his knights, Watkyn perceives that Herod mandates the characteristics that define the true men of his kingdom, so he "aske . . . a bone" of him, requesting that the ruler "make [him] a knight!" (136). Watkyn then follows his request with a description of the behavior requirements that he believes will convince his superior of his qualifications:

> For oon thyng I promyse you: I wille manly fight,
> And for to avenge your quarelle I dare undertake;
> Though I sey it myself, I am a man of myght.
> And dare live and deye in this quarelle for your sake!
> For whan I com amonge them, for fere thei shalle quake!
> And though thei sharme and crye, I care not a myght,
> But with my sharpe sworde ther ribbes I shalle shake,
> Evyn thurgh the guttes, for anger and despight!
>
> (137–44)

Ostensibly hoping to impress Herod with his willingness to kill children, Watkyn also presents an extended description of how Herod himself has responded to Christ's birth. This description fundamentally connects that response to a rigid adherence to a definition of manhood that celebrates brute force, violence, and mercilessness. Providing an apt example of what Marjorie Garber (1992, 16) has called "category crisis," Watkyn, in his attempt to transcend his class status, is also portrayed as potentially transgendered; in wanting to become a knight, Watkyn reveals that a "man" is also something one becomes—a fluid process that implicates the role of gender in response. Not only, Watkyn says, will he be able to kill children in a "manly" fashion, but his response to them, and to the action, will also be appropriately brutal. As Watkyn draws attention to the fact that he will try to perform like a man, he exposes gender itself as a kind of performance—a role one may play in order to achieve one's desires. In Watkyn's case, his desires are decidedly more earthly than heavenly.

Given his assertions of "might" and manliness, and his apparent lack of sensitivity to the pain and suffering of his future victims (assertions willingly expressed in violently graphic language), Wat-kyn thus seems capable of performing Herod's gruesome order and thus proving his manhood and potential for knighthood. He seems just as willlfully blind to the Incarnation miracle and its disruption of earthly hierarchies of social status and gender as are Herod and his knights. Yet, in his next exchange with Herod, Watkyn's contin-ued claims to strength, valor, and bloodlust are strongly mitigated by his admission that he is, in fact, frightened of women. I will go, he insists, "[a]nd arm myself manly . . .

> And if I fynde a yong child, I shalle choppe it on a blokke!
> Though the moder be angry, the child shalbe slayn!
> But yitt I drede no thyng more thanne a woman with a Rokke!
> For if I se ony suche, by my feith, I come ageyn!
>
> (156–60)

In fact, throughout the remainder of Watkyn's conversation with Herod, each assertion of the messenger's abilities as a fighting man is tempered by further indications of his fear of mothers. Although at one point he states that he will not spare one child "[i]f the fad-er and moder wille lete me have my wille!," his concern is focused chiefly on "the wyves" (180). Desiring a different status in life, one that will bring public acknowledgment of his possession of charac-teristics traditionally valued in men, Watkyn nevertheless continues to voice feelings that don't fit with that "masculine" role. "The most I fere," he says, "the wyves wille bete me!" (205). Although he appar-ently desires worldly status, then, Watkyn reveals, perhaps in spite of himself, an insight that links him, along with his lowly position, to the audience. Watkyn's awareness of the potential of women to resist even in the face of weapon-wielding men suggests the ability of the divine, especially as demonstrated in the Incarnation itself, to overcome and even to invert traditional boundaries and hierarchies. The messenger who would be a knight thus offers the audience a further opportunity for contemplating what role gender may play in achieving the type of response role necessary for accessing the tran-scendent and redemptive powers of the divine.

For Herod, however, Watkyn's revelation—that he wishes to be a knight while admitting that he fears women—amounts to a betrayal. He is shocked to discover that his servant, whom he thought to be "[a] bold man, and an hardy" (1.164) can be intimidated by a woman:

> What! Shalle a woman with a rokke drive thee away?
> Fye on thee, traitour! Now I tremble for tene!
> I have trosted the[e] long and many a day—
> A bold man, and an hardy, I went thu haddist ben!
>
> (161–64)

Having previously "trosted" what Watkyn appeared to be, Herod now discovers that he may have been deceived by Watkyn's gender performance. This deception emerges, moreover, as a potential threat to the power structure of Herod's realm—a realm in which being a "man" requires the ability to kill children without fear or remorse. Despite Herod's insistence that Watkyn "quyte . . . like a man" rather than "pley the coward" (196–97), the messenger figure thus remains a curious combination of qualities: he wishes to obey Herod's orders and "act like a man" (or at least the kind of man Herod requires), but he nonetheless harbors a fear of women that comically undermines the manly status to which he aspires and suggests a disruption of traditional societal roles for men and women. Mindful of the extremes to which Herod takes conventional definitions of masculinity—and, as we have seen, he requires the same brutality from his "true" knights—Watkyn's indefinite gender status may be read, then, as more than comic relief. If, as Judith Butler (1990, 146–47) has argued, gender, "[a]s the effect of a subtle and politically enforced performativity . . . is an 'act' . . . that is open to splittings, self-parody, self-criticism, and those hyperbolic exhibitions of 'the natural' that, in their very exaggeration, reveal its fundamentally phantasmic status," then Watkyn, it seems, is an exaggerating figure who discloses gender as "enforced" and "open to splittings." In order to maintain his political power and position, Herod needs Watkyn and his soldiers to "act like men"; but Watkyn's gender slippage indicates that this action may be mere performance, rather than "natural" ability and desire.

In his comic yet telling inability to mimic completely the type of response that Herod insists is required of men and knights, Watkyn thus maintains a connection with the audience that charges their own response with a sacred potential. Encouraged to seek a response role significantly different from that demonstrated by Herod and his soldiers, and therefore more aligned with feminine characteristics, the audience, having encountered Watykn's gender slippage voiced through his portrait and fear of rebellious mothers, are thus prepared for the massacre scene (and the event through which Herod intends to demonstrate his worldly power) in which both the rigidly brutal soldiers and the trepidacious Watkyn will participate. In addition to his inferior status and his familiar mediatory position as a messenger figure in the religious drama, Watkyn suggests that some of the lowliest and weakest members of society—the mothers of the soon-to-be-slain innocents—may actually have access to a power that can threaten Herod's realm. This suggestion echoes the miracle of the Incarnation and amplifies the devotional meaning of the audience's willingness to take on a response role outwardly characterized by submissiveness. In order to participate fully in the meaning and miracle of the massacre scene that will soon take place, the audience are thus prepared to identify with the mothers themselves, who, despite their ostensibly complete vulnerability to soldiers and weapons, will display a resistance that is miraculous as well as darkly comic. This hybridization of gender characteristics, moreover, is echoed in the portrait of Christ and his life as a combination of power and disempowerment ("prosperite & adversite"), worshipped by kings, yet born "in that stable among bestes in poverte, wepyng as a nother child of a simple mannes" (Sargent, 1992, 51–52).[12] By actively taking on a response role connecting acceptance of the Incarnation miracle with feminine characteristics (or at least those that oppose Herod's definition of manliness and rigid in-

12. See n. 4.

comprehension), the audience can more closely experience the ability of the divine to challenge and overturn earthly hierarchies.

Mary and Joseph: Suspending Gender Boundaries

In his inability to play by the rules that his earthly society uses to determine knighthood and manhood, Watkyn, the messenger who would be a knight and a man, thus initiates a discourse that associates the ability of salvation history to overcome Herod's great act of murderous evil—his response to the Incarnation—with definitions of masculinity and femininity less narrow than those espoused by the ruler and his soldiers. The ability to participate in the miracle of salvation history through the re-creative potential of the sacred drama is thus also connected to an audience's willingness to suspend boundaries of gender, as well as those of past and present, divine and human, spiritual and material. Following Watkyn and Herod's discussion of manly and knightly qualities, the scene between Mary and Joseph reinforces the importance of such suspension, offers alternatives to the behavior modeled by Herod and his knights, and further prepares the audience for the climactic massacre scene in which an openess to fluidly gendered response roles will be tested and ultimately rewarded.

While the Angel who warns Joseph about Herod's plans offers the foundational example of a hierarchical suspension (if not a form of emasculation)—the trumping of an earthly king by a "child [who] hath lordship" (245)—the flight into Egypt scene similarly builds upon the gender slippage voiced by Watkyn by portraying Mary as the more assertive member of the holy couple. Preceding the staging of the massacre, and thereby providing the audience another opportunity to explore the potential of shifting gender roles and their availability for achieving a successful devotional response, the scene between Mary and Joseph features Mary's apparent influence over both her husband and their impending journey. The scene also engages the comic and redemptive potential of Watkyn's assertions regarding feminine power. The relationship between Mary and

Joseph has been altered by the miracle of Christ's birth, by the arrival of a child who has lordship—who, as described in the *Mirrour*, had "gret thinges . . . prophecied of him as of god almighty" only to be "beden of the angele to fle fro Heroude into Egipte as [if] he were a pore man withoute might" (Sargent, 1992, 52). Consequently, the relationship suspends gender role hierarchy, demonstrating a harmony and flexibility that accompany, acknowledge, and celebrate the power of that miracle. As in the cycle versions of the episode, it is Joseph who receives the Angel's warning; in the Digby scene, however, Mary seems the more active initiator of the family's journey into Egypt:

> Now, husbond, in alle hast I pray you, go we hens
> For drede of Herowdes, the cruelle knyght.
> Gentylle spouse, now do youre diligens,
> And bryng your asse, I pray you, anon right,
> And from hens let us passe with alle our myght.
>
> (257–61)

In addition, Mary presents the audience with alternative models of manhood: contrasting the "cruel knight" Herod with her "gentle spouse" Joseph, she offers her husband (and his response to herself and the child Christ) as a corrective to the brutal reception to Christ's birth earlier demonstrated by Herod and his knights. Joseph is humble, appreciative, helpful, responsible. Admittedly, his acquiescence to Mary's requests—"Mary, you to do pleasuance without any lett" (265); "to plese you with all humylite" (279)—reflects both Mary's devotional following in the later Middle Ages and the medieval tradition of portraying Joseph as a comically aged cuckold. Yet Joseph's humble nature in the scene also contrasts significantly with the alternative image of masculinity portrayed by Herod and his knights.[13] Initially challenged, if unwittingly, by Watkyn, Herod's

13. For discussion of the Joseph-as-cuckold tradition, see Vasvari (1995); Hahn (1986); Filas (1962); and Doucet (1956, 1957). Hahn's analysis counters the comic elements of Joseph's portrait. On the cult of Saint Joseph, see also Herlihy (1983), 127–28; and Warner (1976), 188–90. Perhaps the most complete survey of the Joseph cult

response to the Incarnation is here preempted by the holy couple's harmonious relationship, assisted, in large part, by Joseph's willingness to take on what may appear at first to be a comically emasculated role. Yet, as with Watkyn, the humor of the scene is infused with a strong devotional message: the ability to transcend one's earthly gender role—at least temporarily—may be not only a redemptive requirement, but also a way to activate the transcendent potential of the sacred drama.

Perhaps influenced by changes to his portrait in the later Middle Ages, the Digby Joseph, in fact, emerges as a particularly resonant figure for sacred playgoers wishing to experience the devotional usefulness of alternative gender roles. Increasingly portrayed in the later Middle Ages as responsible, nurturing, and productive, Joseph comes to be "associated with a cult of the feminine maternal" based upon Mary herself. If, as Rosemary Hale (1996, 113) has argued, this image offered Christian males an opportunity to seize upon, and perhaps co-opt, the devotional power associated with Mary and the domestic realm, a similar role playing and gender shifting may have found its way into the experience of playgoers intent upon exploring the re-creational, transcendent, and miraculous possibilities of the sacred drama. If such possibilities were at least in part aided by audience members' willingness to participate in the dismantling of temporal and spatial boundaries—as well as the dismantling of boundaries between human and divine—then one's devotional duties to the drama might likely include a willingness to suspend boundaries of gender: to allow one's self to respond like a woman, as well as "like a man," in order to experience more fully the far-reaching implications of divinity and Incarnation.[14]

---

is Seitz (1908). Devotion to Saint Joseph was especially supported by Peter d'Ally (d. 1420); his follower, Jean Gerson (d. 1429), who sought a feast day (sanctioned in 1479 for March 19); Bernardine of Siena (d. 1444); and Isidor de Isolani (d. c.1530). For d'Ally's writings, see *Tractatus de duodecim honoribus S. Joseph, Summa Josephina*, 1079–1102; for Gerson, see *Opera Omnia*, 7 vols., ed. Louis Ellies du Pin (Hildesheim, 1987); for Bernardine, *Sermo de s. Ioseph, Summa Josephina*, Art. 1–2; and for Isolani, see *Summa de donis Sancti Ioseph* (Rome: Polygot Press, 1887).

14. For "domestic" images of Joseph in the later Middle Ages, see Gibson (1989)

While Herod and his soldiers display the brutish failings of conventional masculinity taken to a violent and dehumanizing extreme, then, Joseph's masculinity is rewritten as fluid and flexible.[15] At the same time, Mary, as the assertive and commanding partner in the marriage, also presents a combination of gender and parenting roles that challenges traditional images of femininity and motherhood. As an empowered figure, she thus offers the audience further encouragement for their willingness to take on the disempowered role of Herod's subjects. Taking charge of the journey into Egypt ("from hens let us passe with all our myght" [261]), she shares a strong vocality with the mothers of the massacre scene soon to be enacted. Likewise, her condemnation of Herod—"that cursid wight" (263)—also connects her with the mournful yet powerfully vengeful wom-

---

on the *Josefshosen*—the stockings of Saint Joseph—which he is portrayed as removing so that they might be used to swaddle the new-born Jesus (58–59).

15. Ashley (1990) has also noted a contrast between "Joseph's gentleness" and "the bloodthirstiness of Herod" (123), but she does not pursue the contrast. Elliott (1993) discusses Mary's and Joseph's relationship as a potential paradigm for chaste unions between real men and women (180ff., 299ff.). While Elliott's analysis emphasizes the ongoing subjugation of women even in the face of models and circumstances (such as "spiritual marriage") that may have temporarily empowered women (for Elliott, the Joseph cult encouraged a weakening of Mary's characteristics and position), there are numerous occasions in her study where she concedes that there are important exceptions to this general rule. See, for example, her discussions of Dauphine and Elzear (283ff.), of Robert Malatesta (249ff.)—who is "a poignant reminder . . . of how fragile gender constructions are, in general" (250)—and her concluding comments on the durability of "female defiance" and its challenge to patriarchal authority (301). Much of Elliott's approach is founded, understandably, upon the assumption that women's lower-class status in the Middle Ages was often based on (mis)understandings of sexuality that indicate that any liberation and/or empowerment for women required a transcendence of sexual identity portraying women as subordinate to men. I explore here, however, how societal attention to— even emphasis upon—gender practices may have, occasionally, achieved what spiritual marriage could not: an exploration and engagement of gender as fluid, flexible, and therefore redemptive. Compare, also, Gibson's work (1989) on the popular theme of Joseph's Doubt (152–66). Simultaneously engaging the comic capacity of a cuckolded husband—a potential disruption of conventional gender roles—with the miracles of the Annunciation and the Incarnation, Joseph's doubt seems to point ultimately to an empowering of Mary, whose abilities Joseph initially fails to comprehend and can only come to understand through divine aid. Coletti (1993) has also written about the plays of Joseph's Doubt or Troubles in the English cycle plays.

en, foreshadowing the mothers' curse upon Herod that seems to be the direct cause of his death (360–88). Mary, as she attends to her child and family, also demonstrates a maternal assertiveness that anticipates the mothers' response in the following scene. This strong and flexible image of woman and motherhood fortifies the mothers' imminent response with spiritually redemptive significance. Moved to explore devotional responses that draw upon alternative expressions of gender, the audience is thus prepared through Watkyn's gender-shifting challenge to Herod and through the fluid gender roles presented by Mary and Joseph to forge a strong identification with the ostensibly most disempowered of all the characters in the play: the mothers of the slain innocents.

The Mothers of the Innocents: The Meek, Like Christ, Will Rise

Preceded by the positive portrayal of refigured forms of masculinity and femininity exhibited in the exchange between Joseph and Mary, the mothers' resistance to Herod's soldiers, along with their retaliation focused upon Watkyn, becomes more than a humorous interlude. Assertive from the very beginning of the scene, the Digby mothers present an alternative to the gender convention of female submission and passivity. More than a temporary, and therefore comic, suspension of patriarchal authority, their willingness and ability to resist the armed soldiers finds its source in the miraculous ability of a mere child to challenge and usurp the authority of a man and a king, an ability consequently aligned with the transcendent powers of the Incarnation. Despite Herod's earlier dismissal of Watkyn's warning about women with children and distaffs, and despite the soldiers' aggressive threats (punctuated with references to their masculinized equipment),[16] the women respond with their

16. *Miles 1:* Herke ye, wyffys! We be come your housholdes to visite,
   Though ye be never so wroth [angry] nor wood,
   With sharpe swerdes that redely willy byte,
   Alle youre children within to yeere age in oure cruelle mood,
   Thurgheout alle Bethleem to kylle and shed ther yong blood,

own forceful words and resistance, urging the audience to identify
with and even participate in such resistance:

> *Mulier 1:* Fye on you traitours of cruelle tormentrye,
> Wiche with your swerdes of mortalle violens
> *Mulier 2:* Oure yong children, that can no socoure but crie,
> Wylle slee and devoure in ther innocens!
> *Mulier 3:* Ye false traitours! Unto God ye do grett offens,
> To sle and mordere yong children that in ther cradele slumber!
> *Mulier 4:* But we women shalle make ageyns you resistens,
> After oure powere, youre malice to encomber!
>
> (297–304)

Reminiscent of the play's earlier portrait of Watkyn, whose own indeterminate gender status commented on the potential strength of
mothers and foreshadowed the suggestive treatment of the Holy
Couple's flexible gender roles, the women here demonstrate both
"feminine" and "masculine" traits, creating a situation in which "the
constructed status of gender is theorized as radically independent
of sex as gender itself becomes a free-floating artifice, with the consequence that *man* and *masculine* might just as easily signify a female
body as a male one, and *woman* and *feminine* a male body as easily
as a female one" (Butler, 1990, 6). At the same time, the audience
of the play, having taken on the role of Herod's disempowered subjects and thus having opened themselves up to an experience and

---

As we be bound be the commaundement of the kyng!
Who that seith nay, we shalle make a flood
To renne in the stretis, by ther blood shedyng!

Miles 2: Therfor, unto us ye make a delyveraunce
Of youre yong children, and that anone!
Of elles, be Mahounde, we shalle geve you a myschaunce!
Oure sharpe swerdes thurgh your bodies shalle goon!

Watykyn: Therfor beware, for we wille not leve oon
In alle this cuntre that shalle us escape!
I shalle rather slee them everychoon,
And make them to lye and mowe like an ape!

(281–95)

response role more feminine than masculine, might likely identify with the rebellious women, seeking alternatives to earthly hierarchies of gender, class, and other social roles.

In addition, Watkyn continues, throughout this scene, to serve as a mediatory figure who negotiates boundaries between masculinity and femininity, as well as boundaries between play and audience. In his attempt to signify his body as singularly "male" and "masculine" (and therefore as knighthood material), it is he, appropriately, who challenges the women about the seemingly "masculine" role they have chosen to play. He seems to wish to restrict their gender identity to their apparently biologically and socially determined situation. At the same time, however, he seeks this restriction upon the women in order to distinguish and assert the gender identity he so wishes to act out and claim as his own:

> Peas, you folysshe queyns! Wha shuld you defende
> Ageyns us armyd men in this apparaile?
> We be bold men, and the kyng us ded sende
> Hedyr into this cuntre to hold with you bataile!
>
> (305–8)

Why should defenseless women—"folysshe queyns"—attempt to defend themselves against armed men? In posing the question, however, Watkyn points to a binary opposition of male power and female powerlessness: he voices the assumption on which the binary is based, and therefore makes it available for questioning, for challenging, for overturning. He thus indicates not only the physical reality of the soldiers' arms and armor, but the potentially negotiable social conventions that accompany the conditions of manhood and womanhood. Espousing the social construction of those conventions—the performance of masculinity displayed by Herod and his soldiers—Watkyn's warning, rather than frightening the women away, renders the opposite effect both for the mothers, played by males, as well as for the audience, made up of men as well as women. The "male" mothers do not respond through socially constructed conventions for women; instead, they claim roles for themselves that portray them as the aspiring knight's physical and social superiors—more powerful and "masculine" than he and, by extension, his companions:

> Fye upon the[e], coward! Of th[e] I wille not faile
> To dubbe the[e] knyght with my rokke rounde!
> Women be ferse when thei list to assaile
> Such prowde boyes, to caste to the grounde!
>
> (309–12)

Asserting that women can *choose* to be fierce, and reducing both Watkyn and Herod's "real" knights from men to "boys," the mothers' retaliation suggests that gender characteristics are a selected course of action, an instance of choice, what Butler (1990) calls an "act . . . that is open to splittings, self-parody, self-criticism" and "a kind of persistent impersonation that passes as the real" (146–47; vii). In addition, the reduction of men to "boys" echoes the gendered implications of the Incarnation miracle; the ability of a mere boy to overcome a king is here reversed in order to demonstrate, in turn, the potential of mere women to challenge social (and therefore earthbound) conventions that place power in the hands of armed men.

Representing, if unwittingly, the devotional potential of response roles that engage a range of gendered emotions, Watkyn is an enabling force for both mothers and audience. Having identified with the lowly and the powerless, the audience is now free to experience the powerful (if darkly comic) resistance of the mothers, mimicking the miracle of Christ's lowly birth and the power of an infant to overcome an earthly king. The ability to respond like a woman, then, contains the essence of the Incarnation miracle and gives the audience an opportunity to experience that transformative essence. Thus, in the hands of the mothers, even the lowly distaff, a traditional symbol of women's subservience, is transformed into a symbol of incarnational meaning and power. Wielded by mothers whose rebellion can be seen and engaged by an audience as a form of devotional response that seeks to oppose the actions of Herod and his followers, the distaff reveals its connection to both Eve as spinner and her role prefiguring Mary's "spinning" of Christ's humanity in her womb.[17] At the same time, the conflation of submission and rebellion, humility and resistance that the mothers embody and their distaffs symbolize may also be compared to the instruments of Passion and Crucifixion, the *arma Christi*—weapons reconceived as measures of Christ's own humility and willing subjugation yet simultaneously associated with the powers of redemption. Indeed, in the *Mirrour*, Christ's willingness as a child to serve as a delivery boy of the cloth his mother spins in order to earn the Holy Family's livelihood while in Egypt suggests a meaningful connection between his eventual sacrifice and the distaff as a tool of servitude as well as a symbol of redemption (Sargent, 1992, 53–54).

Presenting gender as potential devotional exercise as well as social practice, the Digby version of the massacre, moreover, partakes of the exploratory spirit of a late medieval custom likewise attentive to gender and gender fluidity. The massacre episode stresses the mothers' resistance (highlighted by their use of their distaffs) to Herod's soldiers and invokes the custom of St. Distaff's Day and its companion event, Plough Monday, in which men and women engaged in comic battles between the sexes.[18] Commemorated at the end of the Christmas holidays, St. Distaff's Day (January 7) and Plough Monday (following Twelfth Day) demonstrate how gender as a devotional and social practice may have been addressed by the Digby staging of its unique pairing of biblical episodes. Both days officially marked the return of women to spinning and of men to the plough, and included encounters between the sexes which, while providing opportunities for fun and festivity, encompassed an important public voicing of gender roles (Wright, 1938, 91–102). Intriguingly, the same men who on St. Distaff's Day set the women's flax on fire (only to have the women throw water on them) might appear as women themselves on Plough Monday, crossdressing ei-

17. See Gibson (1989), 155–68.

18. Gibson (1989), 42–44, connects the Digby play and Saint Distaff's Day. See also Davis (1975); Phythian-Adams (1979), 89–90; Ashley (1990), 124; and Coletti (1995), 246.

ther explicitly or through adorning themselves with multiple colorful ribbons and trimmings. (Some participants, apparently, were so serious about imitating women that in anticipation of the festivities, they let their hair grow long so that it might be curled into female hairstyles.) More than temporary, comic gender battles and/or gender reversals, such occasions may have provided an opportunity for public presentation, testing, and exploration of gender as a significant, powerful cultural practice that could consequently be used for devotional benefit.[19]

The *Prickynge of Love* again presents an interesting parallel: while the text advocates an active cultivation of meekness and subjugation—a position in worldly society whose power derives somewhat from a man seeking a status that is decidedly not manly and perhaps even womanly—it also displays potent examples of the Virgin Mary's adoption of assertive characteristics and behaviors that likewise challenge a woman's (as well as a man's) traditional role.[20] Echoing the actions of both the mothers of the innocents and the female participants of St. Distaff's Day, Mary is sought out by the contemplative as a scourge. Indeed, the contemplative pursues victimhood as a means for connecting with Christ as well as his mother: "Ceertes I wot wat I shal do. I shal fale doun at hir feet & wythoute styntyng be cryinge & by teres I shal crave of hire myn askynge & I wol not leve tyl outher she gyve me his woundes or ellis that she

19. Beckwith (1993) examines Christ's body as a means for navigating and transcending boundaries of humanity and divinity and of the profane and the sacred and asserts that "[i]f, as Mary Douglas has said, 'it is only by exaggerating the difference between within and without, above and below, male and female, with and against, that a semblance of order is created,' then the ambiguating inversion of edges and boundaries surely casts doubts on the reigning classifications dependent on such differences" (61).

20. Urging the contemplative to relive with Mary the Crucifixion, the text also makes a point of referring to Mary's nonconventional decision as a woman to witness the event. In essence, she is breaking a custom for her gender: "[W]er-to [went] thou to the hill of Calvarie? it was not thi custom lady be-fore to renne for to see suche wondrynges. whi withelde thee not at home shamefastnesse of mayden hode? whi lettid not pe vile hede of that place? the ugly sight of mennis synnes? . . . It is not custummable ladi that we punishe wymmen with sice maner deth" (23–24).

with strokis dryve me a-wey from heere & sothely the strokes wil I take & holde as wounds and as ryche jeules" (25). As women, Mary and the mothers of the Innocents illustrate a state of conventional societal meekness that an audience member ought to cultivate, while they simultaneously serve as reminders that the cultivation of such a state implies a hybridization of gender roles sought as a means for devotional enlightenment and participation in the transcendent experience of the Incarnation and the Crucifixion. Though Mary in the *Prickynge* is granted a physical power over the contemplative, it is through meekness and submission that Christ triumphs: "He shlou pride & unbuxumnesse through his wondirful mekenesse and through his obedience" (26). Rather than being figures of humor and/or irreverence, then, Watkyn, Joseph, and Plough Monday's male crossdressers may instead serve as active references to a late medieval devotional practice that extended the re-creative potential of the sacred drama to the role of gender. Transcending past and present, divine and human, heavenly and earthly, Mary and Christ also present an opportunity for an osmotic criss-crossing of gender boundaries perceived by late medieval peoples as a method for achieving spiritual enlightenment and redemption.

More than mere reversals of gender, such portraits, customs, and devotional exercises, especially when considered in light of the ventriloquizing of them in *The Killing of the Children,* may have exposed the rigid and divided conventions of masculinity and femininity, provided an opportunity for experimentation, and voiced potential combinations of gender associations that were granted spiritual meaning in the pairing of familiar episodes from salvation history. In a scene in which "humor, pathos, and terrible violence [are] joined together so wrenchingly" (Coldewey, 1993, 253), the mournful yet significantly powerful mothers of the play succeed in subduing the cowardly Watkyn, who then becomes their messenger, delivering the women's curse that will initiate Herod's death. The staging of gender and its implications for ritual devotion and domestic practice become significantly conjoined in a performance that, in challenging conventional notions of male power and female submission, attempts to involve its audience in an experience reminiscent of the transcendence of divine and human made possible by the Incarnation.

The Cursing of Herod's Blindness

Following the exaggerated masculine portrait of Herod and the flexible genders of Mary and Joseph that stand in contrast to that rigid portrait, the interactions of the aggressive mothers and the shrinking Watkyn communicate a potential for gender slippage that evokes the transformative range of the Incarnation. The women are a mixture of maternal sorrow and manly aggression, while Watkyn is both the extreme of masculine violence that has destroyed their children and an outlet for their pain. "[W]oman and feminine" therefore "might just as easily signify" him (and the mothers) as "man and masculine" (Butler, 1990, 6). The messenger figure represents the masculine force upon whom the mothers wish to take their revenge, and yet provides a body with shifting gender associations upon whom they, and the audience of the play, can heap a suffering caused by the inflexible violence of Herod's truly "manly" knights. If not a completely redemptive figure, then, the gender-shifting messenger does give the mothers an outlet for their suffering and a further venue for demonstrating the power of the divine to empower those who, from an earthly perspective, are without prominence or position. Rescued from the mothers' blows and words by the soldiers he has accompanied, Watkyn cannot shake off his encounter with them; in fact, their suffering and presence stays with him as he carries maternal pain and vengeance to Herod's court. Formerly Herod's messenger, Watkyn now becomes the messenger of the mournful women who delivers their curse:

> In feyth, my lord, all the children be dede,
> And alle the men out of the cuntre be goon!
> Ther be but women, and thei crie in every stede:
> "A vengeaunce take Kyng Herode, for he hath our children sloon!"
> And bidde "A myscheff take hym!" both evyn and morn;

For kyllyng of ther children on you thei crie oute,
And thus goth your name alle the cuntre abought!

(358–64)

Watkyn points to the physical absence of men in the country and quickly asserts that women now pose the real threat to Herod's reign; more than mere victims, they—like the audience who has been encouraged to identify with them—become empowered by their connection to the story of salvation. The mothers' suffering and sacrifice, augmented by the strength implicit in the curse that overcomes Herod, reflect (and prefigure) the combined sacrificial and redemptive power of Christ, as well as the suffering and strength of his mourning mother at the loss of her son.

If Herod believes that dispensing with all *male* children will solve his problems, he underestimates the importance of women's emotions and women's words transformed and empowered by divine plan and spiritual meaning—a transformation and empowerment that (aided by Watkyn) could extend to the devotional experience of an attentive audience. Like Garber's third sex, to which she relates the third actor of Greek classical drama, Watkyn "puts in question identities previously conceived as stable, unchangeable, grounded and 'known'" (1992, 12).[21] Herod's belief that his overtly masculine knights could easily overcome both mothers and a God-become-man is thrown into crisis, initially through Watkyn's eliding gender, and finally, through his delivery of powerful female words as he becomes a messenger, if not embodiment, of women.

Fulfilling the mothers' curse, Herod's weakened state, his pitiful pleas, and his eventual death with which the scene ends contrast sharply with his brutish pomping with which the play began. The triumph of ostensibly meek womanhood over worldly tyranny

21. Garber (1992) cites examples from the Greek classical drama of the third actor, and refers, among others, to a messenger figure who "deconstructs the binary of self and other that was itself a comfortable, because commutable and thus controllable, fiction of complementarity. But—or and—it is not itself *a* third *one;* it is rather something that challenges the possibility of harmonious and stable binary symmetry" (12–13).

thus validates an initially submissive response role for the audience. Giving new meaning to the beatitude that "the meek shall inherit the earth," a transcendence of gender taps into the power of the Incarnation itself and the conflation of submission and empowerment in the Passion and Crucifixion. Such a conflation reifies the re-creational, transformative role of audience member and participant. As Beckwith asserts, "On the one hand, Calvary and its late medieval reproductions and imitations *are* the very origin of sacrality; they are also, however, the place where divinity is systematically debased, humiliated and degraded, where the sacred by lending itself to the humanity that degrades it, traduces its own nature in profanation. Through the condensed imagery of crucifixion, the dynamic interpenetration of sacred and profane can be explored; the passion *is* the metaphoric site of conversion and transference" (1993, 56). Herod, as David Mills has noted, "has an illusion of self-sufficiency which is destroyed when he seeks to control an action directed by God" (1983, 15); this sentiment is likewise conveyed in the *Prickynge:* "he that is prooud thynketh he hath no need of cristes benefices and that is a feendis synne" (60). Related closely to the rigid masculinity he requires of his soldiers, that self-sufficiency opposes and is ultimately overcome by a more fluid representation of gender that aids and accompanies the divine plan directed by God and engaged by *The Killing of the Children* and its sacred players.

Overcome by the words of the sorrowful and by powerfully vengeful mothers, Herod's enforced masculinity—along with his claims to throne, power, and domination—thus fails at the end of the Digby version of the massacre. In fact, the voice of mothers—a voice usually relegated to the quiet, private world of home and family—resounds most assertively in the final scene. As Herod delivers a lengthy concluding speech, his words are full of dejection, loss, and weakness. When the character most resistant to gender fluidity and the miracle of the Incarnation fades toward destruction, the traditionally private world of mothering invades the public world of court, politics, and power. Reinforcing the conflation of nurturing and assertiveness that characterized Mary in the previous scene, the mothers' curse exemplifies the strength and power of mixing gender roles while suggesting that Herod's failure may result, in part, from his own refusal to recognize the dangerous inflexibility of his exaggerated version of masculinity stubbornly linked to his worldly pride and power.[22] Though Herod remains fiercely attached to one side of the dichotomy, Mary, Joseph, the mothers, and even Watkyn (if unwittingly) indicate the possibility and potential of bridging that assumed gap between "female" and "male" worlds. Importantly, in the *Prickynge,* the fluidly gendered act of entering into Christ's wounds is promoted as a remedy for such an earthbound state of pride and unyielding devotion to worldly success, if only so those blinded by this state can avail themselves of the healing experience: "A the gret blyndenesse of adam sones that con not entre into the love of crist bi holis of his woundes. . . . thei travaillen in veyn for worldli thing and wolen not finden the gatis of cristes bodi opened that leded to hevene" (10).[23] Put another way, those who are thus blinded have blocked themselves off from the healing power of the body of Christ, whose open wounds exemplify a significant conflation of masculine and feminine experiences.[24] Herod's pride and his

22. Cf. Garber: "Is to be free and verbal . . . necessarily to be dressed like a man?" (1992, 31). In overcoming the violence and tyranny of Herod's realm through the vehicle of women's speech, the mothers of the Innocents, backed by the powerful words of Mary in the previous scene, engage in a behavior that resembles what Karen Winstead (1997) has identified in virgin martyr legends as one example of "call[ing] into question traditional formulations about gender" (108). In addition, Winstead points to positive portrayals of female saints who were strong, assertive, and vocal. She describes the virgin martyrs as "women who transcended their gender to become manly" and who thus "evoke the mystery of a God become man. Their bodies, torn and made whole, replicate the miracle of the Eucharist" (12). For further connections between Mary and the mothers, see Harrington (1995), 73.

23. See Kane (1982), 156–56, for entering into Christ's wounds and joining with him as a remedy to pride and other worldly sins. The whole chapter is dedicated, in fact, to critiquing "proude men thatte presumen of hem-self" (153).

24. This startling conflation of feminine and masculine experience is also taken up in the mixing of Mary's milk with Christ's blood sought by the contemplative: "And bi-holde owre swete childe Jhesu in his modres armes, sowkande of hire blessid brest & I shal fonde to sowke with him, with al the faith that i have & thus shal I tempore to-gidere the swete mylke of marie the virgine with the blood of jhesu and make to myself a drynke that is ful of hele" (9). Scholars who have explored

strict adherence to worldly conventions, resulting in a decidedly in-. flexible gender role, thus distinguish him from those characters in the play who are presented as fluidly gendered and therefore open to the transformative and transcendent power of the Incarnation and the Crucifixion. This power is made even more credible to audiences in the staging of Mary's purification and presentation of Christ at the Temple with which *The Killing of the Children* concludes.[25]

---

feminine representations of Christ include Bynum (see n. 4 above); Lochrie (1997); Beckwith (1993), who also discusses the *Prickynge* and *Mirrour*; Petroff (1986); and Lewis (1997).

25. Essentially outdone by women whose motherly sorrow overpowers his rule, realm, and supremacy, Herod may also be contrasted with the saint to whom the play is dedicated. Revealing an intriguing combination of gendered associations that provide another precedent for the play's exploration of gender, late medieval portraits of Saint Anne emphasized her successful blending of the traditionally divided worlds of private, domestic (and therefore, female-oriented) life with a public, powerful (and therefore, male-oriented) lineage. (On the late medival cult of Saint Anne, see Brandenbarg, 1995 and 1987, and Ashley and Sheingorn, 1990.) The Saint Anne dedication thus indicates a gender flexibility, illustrated by Anne's successful fusion of the traditionally divided worlds of female home life and male public world that stands in contrast to Herod's narrow masculinity. Coletti (1999) has argued that Anne's connections to both private domestic life and a publicly powerful and noble lineage (as a descendent of David and Solomon and the mother of the Virgin Mary) demonstrate "the binary structure of the Digby play's two parts . . . the massacre's enactment of male status-seeking and consciousness of lineage in the public sphere and the purification's focus on household, family, and women in the domestic realm" (8). Yet the contrast between Herod and Anne has, I believe, as much to do with complicating and transcending that binary as it does with contrasting "male" and "female" worlds. Anne's blending of private domesticity and public lineage provides an important example of gender flexibility, a model for the nurturing and assertiveness of Mary, for the public strength of the mournful mothers and their curse, and for the unconventional conflation of gender traits that characterize Joseph—all of which are presented in the Massacre pageant. As Hale (1996) argues, "The aggregate of virtues and symbols with which [Joseph] comes to be represented draws from the cults of Mary and her mother Anne" (107). Including "household, family[,]and men as well as "women in the domestic realm," that flexibility is portrayed positively in the Holy Couple's interactions and in the mothers' resistance and public mourning, even before we get to the play's enactment of the Purification. Although the binary of male and female gender roles certainly operates in the play, then, I do not believe that this is ultimately the principal opposition around which the play is structured. Instead, the play seeks to contrast gender inflexibility with a willingness to embrace nonconventional roles for men and women and an openness to a combining of characteristics, concerns, and attributes normally

Candlemas: Gender Fluidity as Re-creational Exercise

The Killing of the Children fuses the events from sacred history commemorated in Candlemas ritual (purification and presentation) with the episode of the massacre of the innocents, thereby creating a spiritually powerful venue for exploring the function, meaning, and performance of gender (masculinity as well as femininity) presented to its audience as serious devotional exercise. In particular, the staging and combination of episodes suggest that the meaning of Candlemas expanded beyond its apparently overt associations with women and maternal issues to emerge as an activity that earnestly allowed for a flexibility in understanding and representing gender, involving as it did both sexes in rituals that commemorated a female body's private purification and a male body's public presentation. Candlemas can therefore be considered to celebrate the audience's willingness to take on a feminine response role initially marked by submission but ultimately resulting in a divinely influenced triumph over worldly tyranny. Marked by the ritual lighting of candles, symbolizing the purity of Mary's womb, Candlemas, celebrated annually throughout late medieval England on February 2, commemorated the purification and the presentation events and, importantly, included devotional processions in which all members of the community, carrying those same candles, participated. Cer-

---

divided by their associations with either the masculine or the feminine. The dedication to Saint Anne, therefore, often considered enigmatic, seems explicable due to her association with male and female emphases. Rather than merely pointing to a dichotomy of gender roles in the late Middle Ages, the dedication suggests an exploration of that socialized dichotomy, as well as an attempt to associate an overcoming of that dichotomy with the earthly family and lineage into which Christ was born. Mary and Joseph demonstrate a gender flexibility that enables the safety of the infant Christ and thus the redemption of humanity. Such flexibility suggests an alternative world both that seeks to overcome the binary of male/female and that associates adherence to that world with the attitudes and actions of Herod and his murderous soldiers. In addition to conflating what Coletti (1999) has called "various feminine gender roles" (11), then, Anne's successful combination of domesticity and lineage provides an important link with the gender flexibility portrayed positively in the Digby version of Mary and Joseph's flight into Egypt and, later, in its version of the combined episodes of the presentation and the purification.

tainly, as some critics have argued, Candlemas can be viewed as an empowering event for late medieval women, referring as it did to the Virgin's own celebrated visit to the Temple after childbirth; but more importantly, the ritual exercise and its attention to gender may also illustrate attempts to explore gendered response as a useful devotional tool.[26] If Candlemas enabled a "public privileging" (Gibson, 1995, 144) of women and traditional female concerns, does this not, consequently, suggest a destabilizing of traditional gender roles and characteristics that embraces the men who participated (as did women) in the Candlemas ceremony?

Referring to the Candlemas procession, Nicholas Love describes its participants as "of alle states of mankynde sume, that is to sey of men and women, olde and yonge, maidenes and widowes" (Ragusa and Green, 1961, 48). As such an emphatically inclusive event, the ceremony may have commemoratively linked gender fluidity, in which traditional gender characteristics float freely beyond traditional assignations and expectations, and thus in which "gender itself becomes a free-floating artifice" (Butler, 1990, 6), with a particular spiritual imperative.[27] Like Watkyn, who voices both his desire for manly strength and his fear of manly women, those who process in remembrance and reenactment of Candlemas—a joint celebration of the bodies of Christ and Mary—encounter, if only temporarily, the possibility of shifting gender identities and their connection with the story of salvation. In a commemorative event that entwines a public (and male) ceremony of presentation with a private (and female) ceremony of cleansing, men's bodies join with women's bodies in seeking purification, while women's bodies join with men's bodies in acknowledging the power and significance of both Mary's triumph and Christ's eventual sacrifice. The Feast of Purification "that is cleped Candelmesse" is described in the *Mirrour* as a ritual intended for an active cultivation of meekness. This state of being, this reception role, this "havyng therwith in mynde the

26. Recent work on Candlemas includes Gibson (1995), who draws upon the approach of Cressy (1993), Rushton (1983), and Coster (1990).
27. On the inclusiveness of Candlemas ritual, see Mertes (1987), 132–33.

mekenes the poverte & the buxumnesse" (48) of Mary and Christ child, is similarly laced with the formidable presence of divinity and miracle, and with a re-creative ability that imbues even a ceremony of female cleansing with the power to reconfigure (indeed, rearrange) hierarchies of gender and rule. Candlemas, then, provides a powerful example of and foundation for a late medieval use of the religious drama—one in which participants, worshipers, and audiences actively participated in order to re-create sacred events and to experience the power of the Incarnation to transcend divine and human, as well as, potentially, male and female.

In an important contrast to the ending of the version of the massacre that occurs in the play, in which Herod's worldly realm weakly fades into submission as the instigator and enforcer of that realm dies, the presentation episode begins with a male character openly declaring his submissiveness and obedience. As Herod's form of response was associated with an inflexible definition of masculine behavior, the presentation episode validates a different response for its audience. In contrast to the brutish roles into which Herod talks himself and his soldiers—and which Watkyn fails to imitate successfully, and from which the audience is encouraged to distance themselves—Simeon at the Temple in Jerusalem willingly defers to God's guidance, asking for help in obeying his laws so "[t]hat we unto th[e] do no displesaunce" (389–91). His language echoes Joseph's desire to "plese" Mary (279) and "to do [her] plesaunce without ony lett" (265). Emphatic about God's power, Simeon is also, however, quick to point out the divinity's own willingness to submit himself to an ostensibly less powerful position and role: "From the sterrid hevyn, Lord, thu list come down / Into the closett of a pure virgyn, / Oure kynde to take for mannys salvacion!" (397–99). A similar sentiment is expressed in the *Prickynge:* "thou [Christ] deynyd for us wrecchis to taken oure kynde and be boren in a maydene wombe & of the self mayden to be norisshed and feed" (187). Through the Annunciation "hevene and erthe were coupled to-gidere the highest thing and the lowest crature and creature god & man in a madenys wombe through whiche knyttnge we are ordeyned heyres and bretheren in the kyngdome of hevene" (189–90). God himself, it seems, is the principal model for a response role whose initial meekness succeeds in assisting the powerful triumph of a spiritual redemption that supersedes worldly boundaries, including those that govern gender roles. Simeon describes how the most powerful being in the universe voluntarily subjects himself to the weaknesses of the human form, and he refers to a blending of characteristics that has strong resonances for the gender fluidity explored throughout the play and presented as a beneficial devotional response role.[28]

Simeon, like Joseph, is therefore presented in *The Killing of the Children* as an alternative to the form of masculinity displayed by Herod and his soldiers; moreover, his attention to the gender implications of the Incarnation establishes Christ as the preeminent example of masculine potential and leadership, willing to submit himself to a woman's body. Mixing traditionally feminine-oriented images with traditionally masculine-oriented images, this more balanced view of authority might also be reflected in the fluid images of masculinity portrayed in the Digby portraits of Watkyn, Joseph, Simeon, and Simeon's description of the Christ child. Simeon thus conflates "masculine" images of Christ's strength and power with "feminine" images of his peace and mercy—all meeting in a mother's womb—in order to describe the redemptive power of the Incarnation:

Pes and mercy han [have] set in the[e] here swete,
To slake the sharpnes, O Lord, of rigoure;
Very God and man gun togedire mete
In the tabirnacle of thy modyrs bowere.

(493–6)

---

28. See the similar description of Christ's humility, in his willingness to be birthed by an earthly woman in *The Golden Legend* (1973), 20. See also Julian of Norwich, who identified three maternal functions in Christ, and, like Simeon, focused on the Incarnation, emphasizing his presence in both a female as well as a human body. In addition, through references that resonate with Joseph's attention to the feeding needs of the Christ-child, Julian emphasized the maternal aspect of Jesus's offering of his body through the sacraments (Baker, 1994, 119–33).

Both womb and tabernacle, that "bowere" is also a combined image of feminine shelter and masculine strength, and of feminine strength and masculine shelter. Similarly, as we have seen, in the *Prickynge,* the devotional power and immediacy of such gender fluidity permeates the author's desire to enter Christ's wounds in order to experience both Incarnation and Passion because Christ's body (both feminine and masculine) is a life-giving force that suckles and redeems. Offered in association with the creative and nutritive potential of femininity, Simeon's descriptions demonstrate a combination of qualities that counter the violence and death of Herod's limited (and ultimately unbalanced) view of leadership, discipline, and masculinity. Thus the Christ child brings "triacle and bawme of the best / [w]ith souereigne sugere geyn alle bitter galle" (451–52).

Mary and Joseph reinforce these positive references to Christ's mixed, fluid, and ultimately redemptive nature, as they continue their transgendered interactions. While Joseph, as in the flight into Egypt scene, is quietly obedient and supportive, Mary, as in the earlier scene also, is firmly assertive. She makes sure, for instance, that the "lawe" is followed:

> Joseph, my spouse, tyme it is we goo
> Unto the temple to make an offrynge
> Of oure swete son—the law commaundith so—
> . . . .
> With me to go, I pray you, make purviaunce.
>
> (413–15, 420)

If Joseph and Simeon offer portraits of masculinity that counter the rigid and brutal "manliness" of Herod and his soldiers, Mary, too, plays a significant role in portraying the redemptive potential of gender as "a free-floating artifice" in which "*man* and *masculine* might just as easily signify a female body as a male one, and *woman* and *feminine* a male body as easily as a female one" (Butler, 1990, 6). In the play, Mary maintains her central and imposing role in the combined rituals. If, as Gibson has asserted, Mary's insistence that she undergo the ritual of purification (even after her spouse declares that there is no need) demonstrates a "paradoxical empowerment of meek flesh" as the holy mother "subvert[s] the authority of the Jewish law by submitting to it" (Gibson, 1995, 147), then Mary may be particularly empowered in *The Killing of the Children,* in which her wish to go the Temple is not questioned by her spouse and in which he willingly acknowledges her primary role. "Go forth aforn, hertly I you pray," he tells her, "[a]nd I shalle folue, voide of presumpcion" (426–27). Even at the end of the play, Mary still seems the leader of the family unit, telling Joseph, "Let us go hens, hertly I you pray," to which Joseph replies: "Go forthe afforn my oune wyf, I sey / And I shalle come aftire, stil upon this ground. / Ye shal me fynde plesaunt at every assaye" (528–31).

Mary is equally assertive with Simeon. She boldly offers him the initial greeting of the scene (429ff.), asserts to him at procession's end that "[n]owe" she will "take my childe that is so bright" (509), and announces when the ceremony is over: "Now is myn offryng to an ende conveyed" (517). Like the divine son she helps to bring into the world, Mary herself is a combination of nurturance and leadership, meekness and triumph—and a useful model of devotional response and engagement for the audience. Indeed, for the contemplative of the *Prickynge,* she is a "hunter of soulis," a "conquerour of mennys hertis" who "haste so maskeled [ensnared] us and snarled us with thi good turnes and so homly born up-on us tokenes of love that we may not fle from thee." Followed immediately by an invocation that includes both men and women—"Now thanne bretheren and sistren renne we all togidere in pees and charity" (9)—the contemplative of the *Prickynge* seems provoked to the same kind of mixed-gender celebration set forth for the audience of *The Killing of the Children* in its re-creation of the purification and presentation ritual.

Clearly, the unique combination of episodes in *The Killing of the Children* addresses women's issues; it also, however, addresses them as issues of gender such that male, as well as female, roles are displayed, explored, shifted, and recombined.[29] Though, for example,

29. See n. 6 above.

Anna Prophetissa and (as described in the stage directions) "vir-gynes, as many as a man wylle" (s.d. after l. 464) with candles in their hands initiate the procession—as in annual Candlemas proces-sions—it is Simeon who announces that "Betwyn myn armys this babe shalbe born" (482). An indicator of his intent to convey the Christ child in the procession, "carry" here may well imply Sime-on's wish to facilitate the presentation of the child and Savior to the world. Simeon thus takes on both paternal and maternal roles, much like the men of the community who carry candles to repre-sent both the eternal light of Christ and the purity of Mary's womb. He participates with Mary in bearing, birthing, and bringing Christ to the world. The procession, emphasizing the inclusion of both women and men (Mary and Joseph, Anna and Simeon), also allows for and celebrates the potential of shifting gender identities as an ac-ceptable and desirable form of devotional response.

Candlemas, Sacred Playing, and the Transcendence of Gendered Bodies

In the *Golden Legend,* in a good lady's vision, a procession of vir-gins led by the Virgin Mary participates in a mass in commemora-tion of her purification and offering at the Temple (*Golden Legend,* 1973, 25ff.). Reflecting this Candlemas detail, *The Killing of the Chil-dren* includes, as I have noted, its own company of "virgins" who ac-company Anna Prophetissa in the procession at the Temple. Many critics have assumed that the virgins would have been played by "vil-lage girls."[30] Gibson has furthermore observed that the apparent use of female performers is an important exception to the tradition of all-male performance in the medieval drama, one that might provide additional evidence of the centrality of women to the play (1989, 99ff.). Yet the actual source for the company of virgins suggests a more flexible and devotionally expansive attitude toward the sexu-

---

30. See Baker et al. (1982), lxii–lxiii. See also Gibson (1989), 99; Marshall (1994), 308–9; and Marshall (1995), 129–38.

al identities of those who, as described in the *Golden Legend*, commemorate the purification and presentation. In the story from the *Golden Legend*, the virgins are joined by a group of young men; in the presence of the Virgin Mary, both females and males bear candles, conducting a heavenly version of the ritual.[31] Replaying specific details from the story of the origins of Candlemas contained in the *Golden Legend*, *The Killing of the Children* discloses a particular attentiveness to the event as both spiritual and social ritual—as sacred history both remembered and enacted. Ostensibly, the central subject of Candlemas may be the purification of the female function of childbirth; yet both Mary's intact purity, as well as the participation of men in the commemorative practice of Candlemas, indicate that the meaning of purification extended beyond socially constructed ideas of gender to include both men and women in a ceremony enacted as much in remembrance of the redemptive powers of Christ and Mary as the humbling process of female cleansing. The treatment of the purification and of Candlemas in the *Golden Legend* similarly connects the humility of Christ and that of Mary in following the temple ritual (*Golden Legend*, 1973, 20). As the Simeon of *The Killing of the Children* explains (in another direct allusion to the Candlemas story of the *Golden Legend*), each burning candle embodies the remarkably fluid nature of Christ: "[i]n yone tapire ther be thyng thre . . . wax betoknyth thyn humanyte / and week betoknyth thy soule most swete; / Yone lyght I lykene to the Godhed of the[e]" (486–91). In addition, as detailed in the missal and breviary texts, the Candlemas feast celebrates the power of the divine, miraculously joined with and revealed to the world in a vulnerable infant—a combination that mingles traditional notions of masculine strength and feminine weakness.[32] Such a remarkable mixture of di-

31. Marshall (1995) has argued convincingly that the virgins, rather than played by local girls, were likely local boys from a monastery school. Yet Marshall also concedes that the use of both male and female actors "would echo the vision in the Golden Legend" (130).

32. *Breviarium ad Usum Insignis Ecclesiae Sarum*, Vol. 3, ed. F. Proctor and C. Wordsworth (1862–66), cols. 131–48; *Missale ad Usum Insignis et Praeclarae*

vinity and humanity employed feminine and masculine attributes, ritualizing and authorizing the participation of men as well as women, while celebrating the salvific potential of gender as a fluid spiritual force and response role.

For a people accustomed to seeing men routinely perform women's roles in the sacred drama, what, then, may have been the effect and significance of a liturgical procession, embedded in a staging of events from sacred history, that included both male and female participants—a phenomenon that may have also characterized re-enactments of the purification and presentation by late medieval Candlemas guilds?[33] Do the males merely impersonate females? Do the females impersonate male performers impersonating females? If, in a Candlemas procession or in a Saint Distaff's Day or Plough Monday event, a man might engage and thus perform "womanly" characteristics, and a woman "manly" ones, publicizing gender as a social practice and a potentially spiritual force, the effect of both men and women joining in the culminating scene of the play comments directly upon the celebration of fluidly gendered beings who assist and participate in humanity's redemption through the performance. Sacred playing thus obligates its participants to aid in a transcendence of gendered bodies, as well as of time and space. For Butler, "[i]n imitating gender," the impersonation of women by men, "implicitly reveals the imitative structure of gender itself." It is in

---

Ecclesiae Sarum, ed. F. H. Dickinson (Burntisland, 1861–1883), cols. 696–706. See also *The Golden Legend* (1973), 24.

33. Again, however, we must be careful about making assumptions regarding the sex of participants. Although a late medieval Beverly guild's reenactment of the purification, in celebration of Candlemas, suggests that a female member of the Saint Mary's Guild played the role of the Virgin Mary, the reference to the performer's sex remains unclear. The "quidam de gilda" ("one of the guild")—referring to the person who played the role—seems to indicate a male performer. At the same time, any allusion to the sex of the character might refer to the character alone and not to the performer. Ultimately, however, it is clear that both men and women participated in the Beverly reenactment. The Beverly reenactment is described in the certificate of the Guild of Saint Mary (written between 1388 and 1389), printed in Young (1933), Vol. 2, 252–53. For discussion of the procession, see Duffy (1992), 20–21; Mills (1983), 159–60; Gibson (1995), 141; and Nelson (1974), 88–89.

particular, she says, "the performance of drag" that encourages "a fluidity of identities" that, in turn, "suggests an openness to resignification and recontextualization; parodic proliferation deprives hegemonic culture . . . of the claim to naturalized or essentialist gender identities" (1990, 137, 138). In commenting upon contemporary performances of medieval religious plays in which men have played female parts, John Marshall has suggested that the practice of "men playing women" to a "medieval audience was presumably an accepted custom, validated by tradition," while "today" such a practice "raises questions of sexuality and gender that transform a convention into a theme" (1994, 309–10). I would suggest that the issue of gender in the combined episodes of the Digby *Candlemas Day and the Killing of the Children* lies somewhere between Butler's hope for "a fluidity of identities" and Marshall's cautionary attention to "custom." The customary nature of what we today call "drag" may have allowed in medieval drama for more "openness to resignification" and devotional potential than the shock of (and bias against) a man "acting like a woman," and of a woman "acting like a man," will permit today. Although the male performance of female roles was an acceptable part of medieval theatrical practice, therefore, this does not mean that it proceeded without what Claire Sponsler describes as "the testing and contesting of conventional social roles and cultural categories" (1997, 26). Since, among all the early English plays that present Mary's purification and/or the presentation of Christ, it is *The Killing of the Children* that most closely follows the liturgy for Candlemas and that provides us with the most complete version of a Candlemas procession, its representation of that ritual offers important insights about the social and devotional ritual from which it draws as well as the beliefs that shaped audience responses to and uses of the sacred drama in the late Middle Ages.[34] That

34. The Coventry pageant also exhibits considerable gender conflict and vacillation between Mary and Joseph. Mary, for example, appears to take on a more traditionally masculine role at the end of the pageant when it is she, rather than Joseph, who receives the missing Jesus from the Temple Doctors. See Craig (1957). My work on the Weavers' pageant is the focus of a separate research project.

participants in Candlemas ceremonies invested contemporary belief rituals with sacred meaning is demonstrated by late medieval representations of the presentation and purification in which scriptural figures also carry candles. Clearly, this mingling of belief practice with sacred history informs the Digby version of the events at the Temple—especially as an active re-creation of sacred history, combined with contemporary ritual, and invested in the transcendent power of the drama itself.[35]

Candlemas itself, then, may be what Gibson has called "nothing more nor less . . . than a woman's theater of considerable social and political importance" (1995, 147). Yet the attentive staging of the presentation and purification in *The Killing of the Children* in conjunction with a play dedicated to the events surrounding the massacre of the innocents highlights a cultural attention to gender that includes both men and women in that theater of "social and political performance" (Gibson, 1995, 147). In seeing a "female emphasis" in the Digby text, however, we may consequently run the risk of associating gender exclusively with sex, of isolating femininity to women and masculinity to men, and of mischaracterizing a performance text that, given the "custom" in the medieval drama of an all-male cast, did not and does not necessarily share that association. More specifically, we may overlook the possibility that *The Killing of the Children* offered its participants (both performers and audience) a venue for exploring, testing, and contesting gender conventions, drawing upon Candlemas itself as a potential site of gender transgression and fluidity—all in hopes of re-creating, accessing, and experiencing the transcendent powers of Incarnation and transubstantiation. Arguing that gender and sexual "norms" are only destabilized from within the "repeated

35. See Duffy (1992), 18. Duffy points specifically to the Weston Diptych in the Order of Saint John Museum, Saint John's Gate, London, in which the scriptural purification takes place at a contemporary late medieval parish church and the biblical figures "carry candles, like good fifteenth-century parishioners." Duffy also examines a reprint of a window at East Harling that includes a similar representation of the purification (see Plate 2 in Duffy's text). According to Duffy, these images help to demonstrate "the extent to which popular liturgical observances had come to shape perceptions of the scriptural event which they commemorated" (18).

acts" (141) that sustain what the dominant culture constructs as gender, Butler asks: "What performance where will compel a reconsideration of the *place* and stability of the masculine and the feminine? And what kind of gender performance will enact and reveal the performativity of gender itself in a way that destablizes the naturalized categories of identity and desire[?]" (1990, 139).[36] In partnering the combined purification and presentation with the massacre, the Digby *Candlemas Day and the Killing of the Children of Israel* also connects the apparently gender-regulated exercise of Candlemas with the disruptive gender play of Saint Distaff's Day; it invokes the liturgy for the Feast of the Purification, investing its reenactment of sacred history with a legitimacy validated by Church doctrine and practice. Yet it also incorporates the custom of Saint Distaff's Day, instilling that reenactment with a disruptive potential that provides the kind of compelling performance Butler seeks—a potential site for contesting gender that emerges from within predominant ideologies and cultural constructs.[37]

Outwardly a regulated commemoration of female "otherness," an exercise that distinguishes the female body from the male body in requiring purification after childbirth, Candlemas initially may be considered an institutionalized reprimand—an "interpellation"—of womanhood: a public ritual that constructs and constrains the female gender, even if conducted in a spirit of celebratory remembrance. In coupling Candlemas with Saint Distaff's Day, however, that reprimand is reversed and displaced from, in Butler's terms, its "originating aims" (1993, 121–23). Gender as an indicator of sinfulness or of holiness, of damnation or of salvation, still has a place in the Candlemas ceremony. But late medieval participants in that ritual may have engaged gender shifting as a devotional and social prac-

36. See also 138–41 and 1–34.
37. In his concluding remarks on the play, Mills (1983) comments that "by playing the 'Killing' and 'Candlemas' as a single continuous performance, Digby forces into juxtaposition the modes of comic irony and ceremonial formality [and] compels the audience to recognize and respond to their contrasting efforts and implications" (164–65).

tice, redirecting the meaning of Candlemas away from what Butler calls a "violating sense of 'subjection'" focused on women toward "possibilities of resignification" that might work "against the aims of violation" (121–23). Described in the *Speculum Sacerdotale* as the day "callyd of many men Candylmas. . . . But that is of non auctorite, but of custom of folke" (Weatherby, 1935, 25), the communal ceremony, whose candles were believed to hold special healing and protective powers long after the ritual was over, seems a particularly potent example of resignifying potential at work within the official practice of the feast as condoned and controlled by the Church.

In the context of the reenactment of events from sacred history in *The Killing of the Children,* moreover, it is not only women who are the subject of gender-based reprimand. Watkyn, for example, in the presence of institutionalized definitions of masculinity and its "proper" performance, is a subject of interpellation. Yet he, too, as we have seen, is an instigator of gender fluidity. In his attempt to fulfill his society's expectations for manhood—what Butler calls "a *stylized repetition of acts*" (1990, 140)—Watkyn disrupts those expectations. And in his repeated and ultimately unsuccessful attempts to perform the "masculinity" required by his master, the messenger figure manages (if unwittingly) to redirect Herod's reprimands against the ruler and his realm. Though he wishes to be a knight and a "man," Watkyn also voices his fear of manly women whose mournful words prove strong enough to undo Herod. Working from within his desire to act like a man—to fit his society's definition of true manhood—Watkyn also reveals the instability of gender and disrupts Herod's realm of enforced masculinity. Aided by the gender struggle, reversal, and transgression that is the cultural work of Saint Distaff's Day, the cowardly Watkyn and the fearsome mothers of the Innocents embody a fluidity of gender characteristics that permeates the Digby portrayal of the heroes and heroines of the salvation story. Watkyn prefigures, unknowingly, the gender expansiveness that characterizes Mary, Joseph, and the other willing participants in the Digby version of salvation history, and that may have characterized the commemorative exercise of Candlemas, joining men and women in a public mingling and ultimate transcending of gendered distinctions. In a process similar to Watkyn's disruption of violating gender practices from within his rigidly masculinized world, participants in the exercise of Candlemas, while authorized by the dominant devotional culture of the Church, may have worked subversively from within the practice of an institutionalized activity and belief system. These participants redirected the assignation of the event away from a strictly female focus to a gender expansiveness that late medieval peoples may have associated with Christ, Mary, Joseph, and other key figures in the story of salvation, and which they therefore strove to emulate in their participation in, and sacred responsibility to, religious performance.

Chapter Six

Reforming Religious Performance

"Feminine" Response and "Catholic" Behavior

"H[e]r soule ever after this day to scourge" [1]

IN THE COMBINED EPISODES of the Digby *Candlemas Day and the Killing of the Children of Israel*, behaviors and emotions associated with domesticity, maternity, and womanhood become ways for actors and audience to participate in the triumph of Christ's birth—a triumph that includes the downfall of the earthbound violence and despotism of Herod and his soldiers. By participating physically and emotionally in the celebration of both the infant Christ's presentation and Mary's purification at the Temple, the audience acknowledges the distinctly female side of the Nativity as the power of the divine mingles with domestic and everyday life. While the Digby play prompts its audience to help bring about (as in the York cycle) a convergence of sacred past and mundane present, it extends the potentially transcendent power of play and players to gendered

1. The quotation is from Wager (1992), l. 1424. All future references are from this edition and will be cited parenthetically by line number.

behavior and experience.   Indeed, as the nurturing, maternal roots of Christ's leadership are contrasted with the violent, destructive, and hypermasculine posterings of Herod and his soldiers, the ability to respond to Christ with womanly emotions seems an important factor in the redemptive process.   Pressed upon an audience already acquainted with interacting physically and emotionally with sacred performance, a fluidly gendered response role—one engaging a spiritual desire to transcend the boundaries between male and female and between divine and human—may have seemed a logical and perhaps crucially important devotional step.   To "act like a man" and only like a man, as suggested in the play, limits one's spiritual abilities and the transcendent potential implicit in the religious drama's connection to late medieval eucharistic belief.

Even if the womanly emotions urged upon a participatory audience for the Digby play constitute a borrowing of female devotional practice, the potential of fluidly gendered response is acknowledged in the play, and, indeed, invested with important transcendent powers linked fundamentally to the Incarnation and transubstantiation doctrine. Yet, in Lewis Wager's explicitly Protestant play, *The Life and Repentaunce of Marie Magdalene,* womanly behavior and feminine response become instead points of contention, critique, and religious condemnation.[2] More specifically, in portraying Mary's preconversion state as an epitome of negative female qualities—qualities encouraged by Vice figures with definitive connections to the Catholic clergy—Wager works to effeminize Catholic ritual and practice, making Mary into an emphatically female model of indulged and indulgent Catholic playgoers. Practicing, in her preconversion state, a response role that leads her down a path of corruption and spiritual damnation, Mary must be purged of her feminine—and Catholic—tendencies. She must, in essence—and in significant contrast to the devotional role encouraged by the Digby Candlemas play—be-

2. For the Protestant characteristics of the play, see Happé (1986), 226–34; White (1992), xxvi–xxviii; and White (1993), 81–87. As many critics have noted, Wager's play, while it can be characterized as a "Protestant saint play" or a "Protestant adaptation of a saint play," also borrows from the medieval morality play tradition.

come less like a woman and more like a man in order to become a true Protestant. With her life reinterpreted to suit Reformation and Protestant polemic, Mary becomes a useful means for gendering response, and, by extension, for justifying the manly and righteous triumph of Protestantism over the feminine decadence of the ousted religion (a decadence perhaps given particular credence by the reign of Mary Tudor).

The Magdalene as Model of Feminine Vice and Inappropriate Response

In defense of the drama, the Prologue of Wager's play adamantly asserts the useful didactic purpose of the performance that will follow: founded upon the "Authoritie of Scripture," the play will bring people to "true beleue" through an "example of penance" who will instruct the audience and will move them in the correct religious direction (52–58). Mary, of course, is this example of penance, and while the Prologue may be responding outwardly to Puritan opposition to the drama in the 1560s, the emphasis on the instructional potential of playing also, importantly, informs the audience of *their* role in the drama. They are identified as students who, like Mary, will be taken through a process that will help them to become better Christians. A similar process (as I argued in Chapter Two) seems to have been the goal of a likely Protestant recycling of the Digby *Conversion of Saint Paul,* a play that, for religious reformers, also provided a useful focus on another conversion story. Yet the goal of religious reform that in the *Saint Paul* results from a subtle retooling of a previously "popish" play (indeed, the reforming of the play itself implies the lesson its audience ought to learn about appropriate and inappropriate response roles) in Wager's version of Mary's life is original to the play and its purposes. Moreover, while a Protestant version of the *Saint Paul* might move audiences to associate Vice figures, visual spectacle, and bodily enticements with the inappropriate physical and emotional responses of a popish audience, in Wager's overtly Protestant play such disparaging of Catholic behavior is taken one step further as the preconverted Mary's attraction to spectacle, physicality, and adornment characterize an explicitly feminine response role with which audience members are threatened and exhorted. If Paul is both a guide to and a model of appropriate response, a reforming presence intended to demonstrate the superiority of Protestant reception roles, Wager's Mary may be seen as the direct subject of that reform process—an example of an audience member whose inappropriate, "feminine" response to sacred truths has led her down a path of sin that must be contained, and ultimately vanquished, by the truth and light of Protestantism.

Printed in 1566, yet written prior to 1562, the *Marie Magdalene* provides a useful example of Protestant, if not Puritan, belief in the ability of religious drama (including the religious drama of the condemned faith) to serve as a force of conversion, change, and reform.[3] It provides an important parallel to the likely Protestant recycling of the Digby *Saint Paul* and helps explain why it and its companion saint play the Digby *Mary Magdalene* survived the Reformation and were likely staged safely in Chelmsford in 1562. Yet the Digby *Mary Magdalene*, with its emphasis on Mary's saintly powers, abilities, and interventions that follow her conversion, remains in many ways a Catholic play, one that, not unlike the Digby Candlemas play, might encourage its audiences to explore emotionally interactive response roles not necessarily in keeping with the model of Protestant worship for which the converted Paul provided a useful exemplar.[4] In Wager's hands, in fact, it is Mary's preconverted state that

3. White (1993, 180) dates the composition of the *Marie Magdalene* between 1547 and 1553, while Potter (1980, 196) places its earliest possible composition date in 1550.

4. In the pre-Reformation era, as Happé (1986, 226–27) has noted, "the essence of the [Magdalene] cult was erotic, penitential, and devotional," necessitating a Protestant rejection of this "erotic image, the idolatrous emotionalism, but of course much of this material was also scriptural and so it had to be fitted in with a different context." Similarly, Malvern (1975, 136) asserts that "[t]he paradox inherent in the mystical love shared by the Christ and the Magdalen in second-century writings and in the Digby *Mary Magdalene* Lewis Wager has to eradicate. Through his metamorphosis of his heroine into an example of faith [he] attempts to break the mythologized Magdalen's bond with a goddess of life on earth with the Bride of the

proves most useful to Protestant polemic. If Paul served the reformist cause as the prophetic representative of virtuous (and male) Protestant clarity, mindfulness, and restraint, and as disseminator of the
Word, Mary becomes an especially useful means for characterizing
the indulgent (and female) attraction of the laity to popish forms of
worship and behavior. These forms are perhaps most dangerously
demonstrated in the earlier faith's versions and stagings of the religious drama, but they are also demonstrated and encouraged by
its clerical leaders. Fundamentally, the reforming of Old Testament
culture by the New Testament, a process that served as a precedent
for the reforming of Christian practice embraced by practitioners of
the new faith and which figures prominently in Protestant retool-
ings of the Digby *Saint Paul,* is amplified in the *Marie Magdalene* by a
gendered characterization of the opposing faith that champions the
necessity of replacing feminine vice with masculine virtue.[5]

The Diabolical Femininity of Catholic Performance: Audience Response and Protestant Polemic

Writing during the last days of the reign of Mary Tudor, John
Knox perhaps felt that he had a useful and living precedent for associating female fickleness, pride, and weakness of mind with the
queen's Catholic rule. Enumerating in his *First Blast of the Trumpet
against the Monstrous Reign of Women* the various reasons why wom-

---

Song of Songs." As I argue in this book, however, such "rejection" and/or "eradication" does not mean total erasure. Rather, the process of rejection and erasure is itself portrayed in order to denigrate the older faith and replace it with the new one.
The very associations that Malvern describes aid Wager in his negative portrait of
Catholicism as effeminate and effeminizing. See also Malvern's assertion that the
Digby playwright "does not use the Magdalen as a vessel for the view of woman as
'matter' and consequently 'evil'" (115).

5. This Protestant recycling of typology, often employed by John Bale, is perhaps best described by White (1993, 83): "biblical and historical narrative foreshad-
ow the present (and universal) conflict between the forces of Christ and Anti-Christ.
As with Bale, Christ's struggle with the pharisees is treated as the struggle of the
Protestant preacher against Roman Catholic persecution and the doctrine of justification by works."

en are unfit to reign, Knox asserts that, under a female ruler, all of England's people have essentially been emasculated. They have lost "the spirit of boldness, of wisdome, and of rightuous judgement":

> They see their owne destruction, and yet they haue no grace to auoide it. Yea they are becomen so blinde, that knowing the pit, they headlong cast them selues into the same. . . . . Finallie they are so destitute of vnderstanding and iudgement, that althogh they knowe that there is a libertie and fredome, the whiche their predecessors haue inioyed; yet are they compelled to bowe their neckes vnder the yoke of satan, and of his proude ministres, pestilent papistes and proude spaniardes. And yet can they not consider that whre a woman reigneth and papistes beare authoritie, that there must nedes Satan be president of the counsel. (Knox, 1878, 31)

Yet, John Jewel, writing well into the reign of Elizabeth I in 1567 (and likely in the wake of the Vestarian Controversy), still felt it perfectly acceptable to characterize, and therefore critique, the essentially feminine nature of Catholicism. Commenting, for example, on their elaborate vestments, Jewel claims that the Catholic clergy "'go trimly and finely in their colours as if a spouse should come from her chamber. If thou shouldest suddenly see one of them jetting afar off, wouldest thou not rather think it were a spouse, than the keeper of the spouse?'" (1846, 4.972). Perhaps, given Knox's primary focus on the dangers of the idolatrous religion, rather than the dangers of female leadership in his *Defense* of his *First Blast* (written, of necessity, once Elizabeth came to the throne), he was more interested in finding yet another convenient way to critique Catholicism. While it is certainly an example of antifeminist polemic, Knox's *First Blast* also reverberates with anti-Catholic sentiments and suggests a gendered portrait of Catholic seduction and Protestant reform that may have encouraged the publication and possible recontextualization of the *Marie Magdalene* in 1566. Interested in the effects of female leadership and Catholic authority, Knox conflates the two, describing a feminine state of mind that he associates with diabolical forces and which Jewel, in his extensive defense of the Church of England, later uses to distinguish the virtuous masculinity of Protestantism from the vice-ridden femininity of Catholicism. Moreover, in their concern for defining behaviors, attitudes, and forms of response, Knox and Jewel in their gendering of religious practice draw upon the ability of the religious drama to influence and illustrate an audience's state of mind: how an audience responds to a religious performance determines proper and improper religious behavior, and constructs a discourse for describing such behavior.

Such a discourse is employed in the *Marie Magdalene* when the Vices' seduction of Mary is called "our tragedie" (451). Using a theatrical term to describe the Vices' activities suggests, moreover, that the audience watching the play ought to see Mary as an audience member whose preconverted state is shaped by the drama to which the Vices subject her. Yet, importantly, their ability to shape Mary's state, her behavior, and her attitude, is—as the Vices reveal—based in part upon Mary's willingness to participate actively in her own seduction. This willingness, in its feminine proclivities, demonstrates the spiritual impurity against which the Protestants launched their battle. After engaging Mary in a flirtatious game that occurs soon after he meets her, Infidelitie declares:

> I thanke you mistresse Mary by my maydenhood,
> Lord what a pleasant kysse was this of you?
> Take her with you, I warrant you wil neuer be good
> She is guen to it, I make God auow.
>
> And I trow I shall helpe to set her forward.
> Shortly my ofspryng and I shall her so dresse,
> That neither law nor prophets she shall regard,
> No though the sonne of God to her them expresse.
>
> (313–20)

Exhibiting the kind of nature that will respond favorably to the Vices' plot and play, Mary is portrayed as an audience member more interested in entertainment and pleasure than in spiritual edification. Modeling a particularly active example of the reception role against which the "reformed" audience of a Protestant staging of the Digby *Saint Paul* is warned, Mary becomes a player in the Vices' "tragedie," responding physically, emotionally, and sensually to enticements which, as in a Protestant version of *Saint Paul,* are connected to Catholic ritual and practice. As she grows increasingly attentive to her physical appearance, in fact, Mary swears "By the faith of my body" (515; see also 823), and this escalating focus on her appearance becomes a means for the Vices to work upon her. Yet in the *Marie Magdalene,* that warning to the audience is amplified by the addition of gender. Previously characterized as alluring, deceptive, and spectacle-ridden, Catholic worship is more fully demonized in Wager's play as these anti-Protestant characteristics are associated with the essentially feminine nature of the earlier faith. Mary herself comes to represent the Catholic playgoer and worshipper as a frightening embodiment of womanly tendencies (and impending high-class whoredom).

Thus, when Jewel chooses to critique the Catholic clergy for parading in "'their whore-like fineness, their players' weed'" (1846, 4.971), he emphasizes an association of clerical attire with the deceptive practices of women and players, an association that may have been rooted in the ability of the religious drama to represent and engage alternative response roles that Protestant reformers found useful for distinguishing appropriate from inappropriate religious behavior. As in the Digby *Candlemas Day and the Killing of the Innocents,* late medieval eucharistic piety, accentuated by Christ's humanity, encouraged a use of the drama (and other devotional rituals) that included expansive definitions of gender. Such a use, likewise linked firmly to transubstantiation doctrine, may account for the strongly gendered language charging negative portrayals of Catholic forms of worship, including participation in and responses to the religious drama. Importantly, then, the seductive play to which the Vice figures subject Mary emphasizes garments and coverings (the word "gear" is repeated often in the section of Wager's play dedicated to her fallen state) and associates these with the feminine art of deception. While (as I discussed in Chapter Two) the attention to garments and the possible use of leftover vestments in a Protestant staging of the Digby *Saint Paul* may have distinguished the spectacle of Catholicism from the purity of Protestantism, in

The Life and Repentance of Marie Magdalene the spectacle and adornment that probably characterized Paul's garments before his conversion become distinctly feminized. Convinced to attend increasingly to her physical appearance by Vice figures, who (we are reminded) are connected to both the Catholic clergy and the New Testament Pharisees, and who are conscious of their own appearance and clothing, Mary becomes persistently preoccupied with her garments, her physicality, and her ability to encourage others to engage in bodily pleasures. Yet Mary is both the result and the representation of the seductive activities of the Vice figures whom, despite Mary's fashion-conscious tendencies, are already, through their emphasis on display, deceit, and sexuality, markedly feminine and (as Wager's play communicates) markedly Catholic. When Infidelitie, for example, relates the mere donning of a "garment," "vesture," or "gown" to the many figures he can play—"Of the which some of them to you I purpose to reherse / With bishops, priests, scribes, seniors and pharisies"—he connects the Vices, and their apprentice Mary, to the attire, actions, and dangerously seductive practices of the Catholic clergy (ll.470–71).

These practices Jewel compares to a new bride displaying her finery.[6] Clearly commenting on the elaborate vestments of the clergy, Jewel's negative portrayal, as in the *Marie Magdalene,* moves beyond an indictment of spectacle to an overt emasculation. Like Mary, who declares "I would with all my heart be known, / So that I might be plesant to euery mans eye" (307–8), the clergy Jewel describes dote on their appearance, mimicking the behavior of an attention-seeking young bride. In addition, for both Wager and Jewel, clerical attire is not the only element of Catholicism that reeks of the womanly arts and their association with female bodies and sexuality. When Infidelitie opens the play with a parody of the Catholic Mass and Catholic worship that associates such worship with the theater, he describes his powers of duplicity through a series

6. For a discussion of Protestant recycling of Catholic vestments with polemical intent in plays, see Chapter 2 above; White (1993), 76; and Craik (1962), 56–57.

of colorful analogies that include the alluring yet deceptive coverings enabled by feminine cosmetics: "Enuie I colour with the face of prudence" (128); "Sloth or idlenesse I paint out with quiete" (131); "Lechery vsed for many mens diete, / I set on with the face of loue both farre and nere" (133–34). Both participant in and practitioner of an effeminate state, Infidelitie thus implicates the Catholic clergy in such womanly and misleading pursuits.

For Jewel, moreover, this effeminate state is indicated by more than just apparel. Emphatic about establishing the fundamentally feminine, and therefore corrupt, nature of the Catholic Church, Jewel, in addition to commenting upon the clergy's elaborate vestments, portrays the Church as an active proponent of and partaker in prostitution—an activity that provides yet another basis for Protestant interest in Mary Magdalene.[7] Spending considerable time on the issue of prostitutes in Rome and upon the papacy taking rents or taxes from brothels within the cities, Jewel invokes the common epithet of Rome as "the whore of Babylon" (1846, 4.628), but also refers pointedly to what he characterizes as the frequent practice of priests keeping concubines as a substitute for the marriage restriction. While such references to prostitutes, houses of ill-repute, and sexual misdeeds are offered as general criticism of the sinful character of the Church, Jewel's insistence upon associating the public display of women's sexuality with the Church also attaches such sexuality and other lewdly feminine traits to that institution and its clergy.[8] In Jewel's view, the clergy's fundamental way of life may be seen as based upon brothel culture (1846, 4.630–48). Taking on female qualities as they take on females, the priesthood delights in

7. Happé (1986, 230) comments that "[i]nfidelity links Mary with Malicious Judgement . . . and thus identifies her prostitution with the challenge to Christ's divinity and his ministry."

8. Discussing the actions taken against Catholic belief and practice during the reign of Edward VI, Duffy (1992, 460) refers to "a flood of polemical Protestant literature" that provides a precedent for these associations with prostitution and illicit sexual behavior and references. Much of this literature, Duffy states, rejoiced "in the destruction of image and chantry, but above all attack[ed] the Mass, the Pope's whore who infects all her lovers."

physical pleasures rather than spiritual pursuits. As a result, they are as much seducers as the prostitutes with whom they keep company—a likewise fitting characterization for the Vices of Wager's play, whose rituals and plots and "tragedie" (the theatrical term used to describe their seduction of Mary) are perhaps as much connected to stereotypes of female behavior as are Mary's.

Furthermore, this unflattering connection of the Church and its clergy to sensual womanhood is strengthened by Jewel's attention to Pope Joan in the section of the *Defense* that immediately follows the section on prostitution and the Church. Using Joan as an explicit example of the ungodly state of the Roman clergy, Jewel builds upon his characterization of the Church as a femininized institution, "polluted by a woman" (1846, 4.650), despite that institution's attempts to cover up the "shame lest it should appear in record, and afterword be reported for ever, that a woman, and such a woman, had been bishop of Rome, or that the bishop of Rome had been with child" (4.650). Jewel's insistence on a cover-up elaborates his feminine characterization as the Church, its clergy, and its followers become womanly deceivers, attempting to hide the shame of a faith whose leader's "palace of Lateran in Rome is now become a stew of whores" (4.651) and Rome itself a "mother of lies" (4.655). Even Thomas Harding, the recusant to whom the *Defense* is a reply, is not immune (no doubt given his Catholicism) to a feminine characterization: Jewel refers to his opponent's "vanity" and potential "blushing" (4.652) in response to the Joan issue. Thus, Pope Joan—like Knox's Mary Tudor and Wager's preconverted Magdalene—becomes a central and distinctly feminine symbol for the illicit behavior of papist Christianity.

Condemning "Catholic" Behavior: Reforming Response, Purging the "Feminine"

Yet, as in the *Marie Magdalene*, Jewel is interested in more than a feminine characterization of Catholicism. He wishes to establish a female state of mind that can explain both the dangers and the attractions of the faith he actively condemns and seeks to expurgate, and he does so through language that draws upon the different responses to and uses of the sacred that an audience could engage and display at a religious play. Jewel is concerned with behaviors and attitudes that he can define and contrast. Thus, in describing the practices of the early Church as models for "the same order [that] is this day restored and practised in our churches" (1846, 2.898), he refers to an "order and usage" which, when contrasted with "the usage and behavior" of the Church of Rome, asserts an ideological basis for the attention to audience behavior upon which potential Protestant stagings of the earlier faith's drama (such as the Chester cycle and *The Conversion of Saint Paul*) may have focused. Jewel, furthermore, distinguishes proper from improper behaviors and worship practices through gendered descriptions. Applauding the open reading of Scripture and the reverent silence of the people who "gave ear" in the early Church, Jewel laments both the lack of "heavenly comeliness which St. Paul requireth" and the absence of "the brotherly meeting of all the congregation at the communion of the Lord's supper" (2.898). Associating such behavior traits as openness, restraint, mindfulness, comeliness, and community with masculinity, Jewel asserts that the Church of Rome and its practices (its "usage and behavior") are, by contrast, "'a woman who hath forsaken her wonted modesty, and hath only certain outward shews of that first felicity, and keepeth still the hutches and boxes of precious things, but lacketh the treasure which was in them. To such a woman may the church this day be likened'" (2.899). In Wager's play, Mary, misled by Vice figures posing as virtuous counselors in a deceptive act of theater, perhaps exemplifies such a woman. As Infidelitie describes her, her state of mind, and her "disposition" (1061), she has been

> brought . . . into such a case,
> That she is past the feare of God and shame of man,
> She worketh priuily in euery place,
> Yea and prouoketh other therto now and than. . . .
>
> (1057–60)

Immodesty, deception, and "feminine" trappings characterize and
demonize the leaders of the earlier faith as well as the irreverent,
overly physical style of worship and drama that unfortunately continues to influence English Christians.

The opposite of Jewel's comely, mindful, and reverent male,
Mary is an immodest, body-oriented, and irreverent female whose
overt physicality and concern with visual seduction make her a
particularly damning example for those who might still find merit
in the style of worship and religious drama favored by the earlier
faith. Encouraged to use her body even to the point of misuse—Infidelitie tells her "gyrd your self in the waste . . . . Let your body
be pent, and togither strained, / As hard as may be, though therby
you be pained" (689, 692–94)—Mary must be purged of her ultra-
feminine ways: her "disposition" must be altered. Indeed, Christ's
"[p]urgying" of her devils is not sufficient (1420); Mary requires further cleansing:

> The mercy of Christ thought it not sufficient,
> To forgeue hir synnes, and deuils to pourge,
> But geueth hir grace to be penitent,
> That is, her soule ever after this day to scourge.
>
> (1421–24)

What Faith and Repentaunce emphatically refer to as that which,
in essence, needs ablution is a sinful nature that has distinctly feminine characteristics. Thus, when Mary laments her previously sinful state, she does so through an indictment of tendencies that apply specifically to her feminine proclivities. In times past, she says,
"parts of my body" were "made seruants to all kynd of iniquitie"
(1789–90): "[t]his haire of my head . . . I abused" (1793) and

> These flesly eies which with their wanton lookes,
> Many persons to synne and vice haue procured.
> They haue ben the diuels volumes and bookes,
> Which from the seruice of God haue other allured.
>
> (1797–800)

Describing her feminine wiles as a kind of deceptive doctrine, Mary in her critique of her seductive practices exhibits the language used by Jewel to characterize and condemn Catholicism. Particularly focused on a misuse of the body, Mary likewise echoes the description applied to inappropriate response roles in a Protestant staging of *The Conversion of Saint Paul*—a form of behavior associated with Catholic ritual and forms of worship. Yet in Wager's play Mary provides a living embodiment of that corporeal misuse, an example who, through her decidedly female persona, sends a powerful warning to those who might still entertain an attraction to the ways of the old faith. Indeed, the reality of a male actor playing Mary's role illustrates the threat that feminine behavior can pose to one's manhood.

Emphasizing the ear over the eye, the mind over the body, the reforming figures of the play steer Mary toward behavior more explicitly male and Protestant than that previously promoted. Thus, Lawe and Knowledge of Sin work to turn Mary's attention inward, away from the physical and the visual, toward written texts and, importantly, toward use of her own faculties that reflects the "order and usage" described by Jewel. Indeed, once Lawe enters (1113), the audience of Wager's play is also steered toward a role different from that likely engaged throughout the first half of the play. Resembling the Expositor of the Chester cycle and the Poeta and the converted Paul of the Digby *Conversion of Saint Paul,* Lawe's preacherly tone prompts the audience to keep a respectful distance; his sermon, in contrast to the physical, sexual, and visual nature of Mary's seduction and seductiveness, requires his audience to exercise their listening capacities.[9] Similarly, the process of Mary's repentance stresses the use of her aural over her visual abilities. Whereas the Vices consistently encouraged her to look, see, and attend to appearances, The Lawe tells Mary—and the audience of this new and reforming play of Mary—to "geue good eare" and to "[h]earken diligently

9. As Happé (1986, 231) has noted, "There is very little stress on the visually enacted" at this point in the play.

vnto . . . good discipline" (1286–87), advice echoing Jewel's description of proper religious behavior.[10] Moreover, Wager's Repentaunce delivers a sermon that resembles that of the converted Paul in its concern for distinguishing proper from improper use of the human faculties and bodily senses, including eyes, ears, and speech (1441–60). In a message intended for the audience as well as for Mary, the physical incarnation of that audience, Repentaunce says that "all the imaginations of the mynde, / Which were occupied euill by Sathans arte, / Must hence forth be turned after an other kynd" (1430–32). In Wager's play, that "other kynd" takes on a decidedly masculine character.

Yet, as in *The Conversion of Saint Paul,* the critique of Catholic practice contained in the *Marie Magdalene* is also accompanied by a strong belief in the performative power of religious theater, which, through its own use of aural (as well as visual) details, can encourage its audience to move toward a correct state of faith, mind and body. Clearly, all kinds of playing are not condemned in the play, so the description of the Vices' work as a kind of playing may indicate that part of what is being distinguished, defined, and critiqued (as we have seen elsewhere) is an improper kind of religious theater, accompanied by inappropriate audience behaviors. The Vices play in order to misuse religious language and topics, and in order to disguise themselves as Virtues prodding Mary toward a behavior characterized as a misuse of mind, body, and soul. In response, the Virtues offer their own reformed version of "playing" that seeks to correct this misuse and the "tragedie" of the Vices. Whereas the Vices encourage Mary—and her audience—to practice physical and visual participation, and to attend to spectacle, display, and finery, the Virtues emphasize the the importance of the mind and the ear, of the Word and quiet attentiveness.[11] And in order to make

10. For additional discussions of audience involvement especially in relation to Vice figures in Tudor morality plays, see Jones (1973) and Somerset (1973).

11. White's description of the figures who lead Mary to her conversion and redemption (1993, 87) could also refer to the Expositor/Doctor of the Chester cycle: "clarifying their significance in expository speeches[,] their distinctive physical

the message more effective, they associate a feminine (and therefore corrupt) form of behavior and response with the former, and a
masculine (and therefore commendable) form with the latter. Concerned with defining audience response and reception roles within
devotional practice, Jewel also uses such gendered language to distinguish proper Protestant behavior: "Let us look into the church
of Rome, and behold the usage and behaviour thereof. Where shall
we find that heavenly comliness which St. Paul requireth?" "Where
is the brotherly meeting . . . ?" Thus, to act like a man should be the
goal of every good Protestant. More specifically, a good Protestant,
whether male or female, will demonstrate a state of mind and behavior associated with an audience response role that appropriately privileges masculine silence over feminine noise, manly ears over
womanly eyes: "The holy scriptures were read openly in the presence of the people: the people reverently kept silence, and gave ear,
and understood the will of God, and submitted themselves unto it"
(1846, 2.898). Jewel's writings attest to a tendency among avid reformers and Protestants to portray Catholicism as supremely invested in female culture and behavior. Essentially accusing Catholics (or
those with any lingering Catholic tendencies) of acting like wom-
en (and especially unreformed women), such polemic may likely
have had its roots in the religious drama, providing as it did a useful
means for demarcating and distinguishing religious behavior.

In John Knox's 1559 *Defense* of his *First Blast of the Trumpet against
the Monstrous Reign of Women* addressed to Elizabeth I, then, the
queen's own gendered behavior exemplifies the triumph of Protestantism and the dangers of Catholicism. Entreating the new queen
to be an "exempill" to her people, Knox nevertheless attributes her
conversion from the faith of "Idolatrie" not to her own abilities but
to the "mercy" of God, who "hath covered your formar offence,
hath preserued yow when ye were most unthankfull, and in the end
hath exalted and raised yow vp not onlie from the Dust, but also

---

appearance, properties, and movements, are all utilized to give highly memorable
expression to Wager's evangelical message."

from the portes of death to reull above his people for the comfort of his kirk" (1878, 60–61). Similarly, in Wager's play, after Mary Magdalene has been "purged" of her devils and her soul subjected to the scourging process that will apparently accompany her throughout her days, Mary, describing her "conversion from impiety" (1768), declares:

> To all the worlde an example I may be,
> In whom the mercy of Christ is declared,
> O Lord, what goodnesse dydst thou in me see?
> That thus mercifully thou hast me spared.
>
> (1769–72)

Like Mary Magdalene's self-portrait, then, Knox's portrait of Elizabeth accentuates the power of God and his reforming forces over the capabilities of the queen who, while she is a sovereign ruler, is nevertheless "a weak instrument" who must, given the known weaknesses of the female sex, avoid the trap of flattery (60, 59) into which Mary herself falls in Wager's play.[12] Indeed, in describing the type of "exempill and mirroure" he would like Elizabeth to be, Knox subtly employs a language of gendered behavior that attempts to encourage the queen to act more like a man than a woman: "The mighty Spreit of the Lord Iesus move your hart to vnderstand what is said, geve vnto yow the discretion of spirittes, and so reull yow in all your actionis and interprisis that in yow God may be glorified, His church edified, and ye your self as a livelie member of the sam[e] may be an exempill and mirroure of vertew and of godlie Lief till others" (60). Expressing his hope that Elizabeth will be able to "understand what is said," Knox echoes the efforts of the Virtues in Wager's play to turn Mary's energies inward, toward the mind and away from the body. Like the "discretion" that Knox also seeks and perhaps believes that Elizabeth, as a woman, does not naturally possess, the ability to understand seems a trait that she must also develop to become a good example of the reformed faith. Attempting to defend

---

12. The Vices rely heavily on flattery in order to seduce Mary.

the distinct antifeminine sentiments conveyed in his *First Blast*, Knox desires a reconciliation with Elizabeth based in part on his hope that Elizabeth will, despite her sex, be able to act in a manly fashion because, unlike the "monstrous" feminine and feminizing Catholic reign of Mary Tudor, Elizabeth's rule will shape (and be shaped by) the manly forces of the reformed faith. Perhaps, then, the preconverted Mary was intended in 1566, the year in which Wager's play was finally printed, to symbolize Mary Tudor. Like the converted Mary Magdalene, Elizabeth certainly emerges, contrary to her sister, as a powerful symbol of the abilities of the reformed Church to overcome the limits of femininity and its connections to the popish faith.[13] Justifying the manly and righteous triumph of Protestantism over the feminine decadence of the ousted religion, a woman is deemed fit to take a man's place at the head of a kingdom.[14]

Effeminate and Immature: The Portrayal of Catholicism in Protestant Youth Plays

In the *Marie Magdalene* the treatment of female sexuality and its dangers provides a searing indictment of Catholic worship through

13. Or, that may have been the message of hope (or warning) sent by the 1566 printing of a play potentially written almost twenty years earlier. Given Elizabeth's tendency early in her reign to reinstitute some ceremony and language associated with Catholic tradition, including certain elements of priestly garb, the *Marie Magdalene* may have been viewed as sending an even more apt message regarding religious reform in the mid-1560s than when it was first composed. The theme of priestly vestments, of course, is taken up as well (and more elaborately) in the play *New Custom*. Printed in 1573, but likely composed between 1564 and 1571, *New Custom*, like the *Marie Magdalene*, expresses Protestant fears about the continued impact of Catholic tradition and ceremony, especially in light of the reign of Mary Tudor.

14. As Malvern (1975, 33) has discussed, gender shifting—and in particular the possibility of woman becoming man (or at least more like a man)—has a long history of association with the Magdalene. Pointing to early Christian Gnostic beliefs that defined "spirit" as "male," and which therefore required that a "woman must first become man before she can shed her soul-garments and unite with the transmundane diety," Malvern sees the Magdalene as a prominent (if problematic) representative of this process. "We can see efforts," she says, "to make the heroine a hero in the Gnostic writings starring the Magdalene." These efforts offer interesting parallels to Wager's treatment as well as Knox's attentions to and concerns about his female ruler.

the example of the preconverted Mary who represents the misguided, sensually driven Catholic player, playgoer, and worshipper. Conveying to the audience that Catholicism is a type of indulgence that
effeminizes body and soul, Wager's play provides an opportunity for
portraying the drama of the earlier faith as dangerously feminine,
contrasted with the manly, upright performance aesthetics of his
own Protestant play. In the *Marie Magdalene* while feminine qualities
are assigned to Catholicism, certain types of response and behaviors
are also specifically defined and characterized as feminine. This gendered view of Catholicism thus draws upon an acquaintance with
the sacred drama of the earlier faith in order to gender the nature of
response itself. Indeed, the cleansing process that Mary undergoes
at the hands of the Virtues (and to which the audience of the play is
also subjected) is a lesson in behavior modification—another version
of the message of reformed and reforming response likely communicated in a Protestant version of the Digby *Saint Paul*. Thus, while
the *Marie Magdalene* has been interpreted as a type of didactic play
intended for the edification of aristocratic youth, it also contains instructions for how to leave behind the feminine—and by extension
the immature—tendencies of Catholicism in order to take on the
mature, manly faith of Protestantism.[15] If the potential moral lesson
of the play when it was likely written, near the end of Edward VI's
reign, was directed at the children of well-to-do parents, that moral

15. While Cartwright (1999, 135–66) has argued that the sixteenth-century drama presents more positive images of female characters than, for example, the medieval morality plays, I would contend that these positive portraits are often dependent
upon the female figures ridding themselves of, or at least toning down, characteristics
and behaviors stereotypically assigned to women and replacing them with characteristics and behaviors associated with men. Portrayed as theatrically impressive images of the power of transformation and reformation, women emerge as heroines by
bearing witness to the ability of the new faith to purge the—feminine—excesses of
the old faith. The ability, then, of women to combine "harmoniously . . . male and
female traits" (135) in the sixteenth-century drama can be linked, at least in part, to
a desire to demonstrate the righteous and miraculous results of Protestantism over
Catholicism. For the identification of Wager's *Marie Magdalene* as a teaching play for
aristocratic youth, see White (1992), xxiii–xxiv, and White (1993), 81–84. Happé (1986,
233) considers this possible link to educational drama briefly and then discounts it.

lesson when it was printed more than a decade later, in 1566, may have taken on a more widespread religious meaning. Furthermore, the possibility of the play representing such a lesson and such a goal—the assertion of the righteousness of Protestant behavior, response roles, and worship practices—is suggested by the Prologue's defense of the drama as an appropriate moral activity, a probable reaction to growing Puritan opposition to the theater in the 1560s.

This interpretation of the *Marie Magdalene*—one that views religious plays as a mechanism for representing, distinguishing, and modifying belief practices—can inform approaches to other sixteenth-century educational "youth" plays in which Catholicism takes on the further stigma of immature, foolish youth (in addition to the feminine characterization applied to it in Wager's play). Implicit in such plays, despite their apparent focus on indulged and wayward youth, is a critique of the earlier faith, assisted by a portrayal of its drama and audiences that sought to attach fundamental religious significance to patterns of behavior and response.

If in the *Marie Magdalene* Lewis Wager offered an indictment of Catholicism that linked it to the seductive behaviors of female sexuality, in *The Longer Thou Livest, the More Fool Thou Art,* William Wager (likely Lewis's son) extends this indictment to that other realm of womanhood: mothering and childrearing. Printed in 1569, three years after the publication of the *Marie Magdalene, The Longer Thou Livest* focuses on the doomed figure Moros, whose childishness, immaturity, and feeblemindedness are largely the result of his female-dominated upbringing.[16] Describing his childhood, Moros reveals that his mother emphasized songs, games, toys, and other "pretty things," and that he learned to "ring the saunce bell / And fetch fire when they go to matins."[17] This revelation elicits the following reply from the Protestant Virtue Discipline:

16. Potter (1980, 198) and the other editors of *The Revels History of Drama in English,* Vol. 2, date the composition of William Wager's play to 1559–1568. White (1993, 180) follows this dating.

17. Wager (1967), 8–10, ll. 125 and 164–65. All references to the play are from this edition and will henceforth be cited parenthetically by line number within the text.

Better it were to have no education
Than to be instructed in any part of idolatry;
For there is no part without abomination
But altogether full of sects and heresy.

(166–69)

As in *Nice Wanton* (another play from the middle decades of the sixteenth century that is focused on youth education), which likewise contains a coddling mother who indulges her children in the alleged superstitions of Catholicism, Moros's mother bears the implicit blame for her child's behavior and state of mind. If the play warns against spoiling children, it also communicates an apparently natural connection between indulgent mothers and a Catholic upbringing.[18] This connection maintains the effeminate portrayal of the faith presented in the *Marie Magdalene,* yet it also suggests the dangerous potential of that faith to keep England's next generation of the ruling class in a perpetual state of emasculation, involving immaturity, weakmindedness, and foppishness. While the Virtues in Lewis Wager's play work to cleanse Mary of her natural tendencies toward feminine, and Catholic, behaviors, the Virtues of William's play are focused on training Moros out of behaviors that are strictly unnatural, and inhuman, given his sex. When Discipline tells him to "forget your babish vanity" (139) "and give yourself to humanity" (141), he connects Moros's state to his female-dominated, Catholic childhood and asserts that this state is contrary to nature: Moros's lack of humanity (and manliness) is a lack that both accompanies and is a result of his ignorance of Protestant doctrine and the proper Christian behavior such doctrine requires. Explicit in expressing his belief that the goal of the Virtues is "to alter his mind / And bring [Moros] to humanity" (184–85), Discipline asserts a plan for behavior modification that seeks, as Piety further elucidates, to bring Moros (and others like him) to his natural state:

18. Sanders (1980, 21) characterizes *The Longer Thou Livest* as one of "the moralities of the 1560s concerning themselves . . . with topics such as the implications of the Marian restoration of Catholicism."

All hail, right honorable Discipline.

Well-occupied evermore I do you find,
Instructing one or other with doctrine
According to your natural kind,
Which is both comely manners to teach
And also to minister correction,
If all men unto your precepts would reach,
Soon should be cleansed all infection.

(186–93)

While Mary Magdalene's fall may be seen as a result of her inability to resist the naturally feminine proclivities that make her susceptible to Catholicism, Moros as a male is *infected* with characteristics, behaviors, and weak mental abilities that are caused primarily by a mother's effeminizing, Catholic coddling.

A type of man-child, Moros, with his female-infected and underdeveloped brain and his insubstantial religious background, is thus incapable of responding appropriately to the Protestant-based doctrine in which the Virtues attempt to instruct him. Indeed, the Virtues are systematically interested in Moros's ability to respond and behave properly to such instruction. While Exercitation urges on his fellow Virtues with the advice "Let us give him good information" (241), he tells Moros that "[y]ou may not set your mind upon playing, / But apply yourself to Discipline's counsel" (280–81). Moros does not follow this command. Instead, he responds to the "good information" with which the Virtues supply him with a language and mentality rooted in external pleasures: food, games, nursery songs, birds' nests. Given a Protestant primer, "[t]o pray upon and to learn your Christian beleve / And to amend your manners that be amiss," Moros's first response is to look for the pictures of saints usually found in Hours of the Virgin Mary (467–70)—a subtle yet significant reference to the Protestant critique of the overly visual nature of Catholic worship and belief. Asked by Exercitation to "recite . . . Discipline's counsel and monition" (307–8), Moros offers only mimicry in an extended scene which, while humorous, demonstrates the extent of his infection: an immature child still tied to his mother's apron strings, he is also an incomplete Christian for whom entertainment, games, and physical and visual pleasures substitute for the true faith of the Word and the mind.

Commenting upon what he characterizes as "[t]he greatest heresy that ever was / Hath the pope and his adherents published" (295–96), Discipline asserts that Catholicism itself is based upon a substitution of ceremony for salvation:

> For Christ and his benefits it hath extinguished.
> Example by the wicked Mass satisfactory
> Which to Christ's death they make equivalent.
>
> (298–300)

Similarly, he offers "prayer to saints that be dead" (303) as an example of an improper religious activity, for those who engage in such an empty gesture "forsake Christ which is the head / Who taught to worship in sprite and verity" (305–6). Discipline thus reveals that the reforming process to which he and his fellow Virtues seek to subject Moros likely communicates more than a message to wayward noble youth and their parents. Underlying Moros's empty, foolish responses to religious doctrine is a portrayal of Catholic ceremony and worship practices that characterizes such practices as mere playful, immature, and childish substitutions for the realities of the Christian faith. Moreover, in their continued attempts to modify Moros's response role, the Virtues privilege behavior patterns for determining religious belief that may have been influenced by Protestant efforts to characterize the Catholic religious drama as the supreme example of the empty spectacle of faith that they worked to place at the center of the maligned religion (and one that encourages the state of mind that Moros exhibits).

Like Mary Magdalene, Moros must also be purged of his bad behaviors. Evoking the language used by the Virtues of the *Marie Magdalene* to describe this process (even if he also refers to an actual physical beating), Discipline tells Moros that

The wise man willeth an ass to have a scourge;
You have learned folly many a year,
From the same now I must you purge.
You that have the wit to mock and to scorn,
What wit you have to wisdom I will see.
Upon your sides this scourge shall be worn
Except you will speak rightly after me:
I will love and fear God above all.

(332–39)

Discipline thus asserts to Moros as directly as he can that his immature behaviors and responses—the folly he has learned in the past—must be overcome with alternative forms that are more seemly and dignified. He seeks a "comely" response (Jewel, 1846, 2.898). Moreover, what accompanies these attempts at behavior modification and Protestant instruction is a basic desire to bring Moros to manhood—a state of being that, threatened by the empty faith of Catholicism, has trained Moros to prefer spectacle, games, and physical pleasures over the Word, discipline, and restraint. Yet while Exercitation asserts this to Moros—"For to make you a man we do intend" (406)—perhaps in a last-ditch effort to urge him to reform, Moros remains unreceptive and irreverent. Ultimately, he is capable only of feigning devotion and obedience, and the Virtues quickly realize that, once again, their student merely plays at religion, as apparently do many others like him. Commenting on Moros's attempt to deceive them, Exercitation describes these others:

Certain persons I could rehearse by name
Have pretended a great perfection,
And why? to avoid punishment and shame
Due for their vicious infection.
As some have enter'd into religion,
Wherefore? Because they will not pay their debt
When they are persons of no good devotion,
For upon vanity their hearts are set.

(562–69)

Perhaps a pointed reference to those who merely pretend to be true Protestants (perhaps, specifically, clergy) and do not admit the infection that lingers from prior and/or continued Catholic allegiances, Exercitation's lament suggests, again, that Moros exemplifies more than wayward boys: his behaviors and attitudes vilify Catholicism. Associated with femininity and immaturity, indulgent mothering and feckless youth, the influence of Catholicism likewise encourages the ability to appear religious, to act at faith, to revel in empty externalities. While, as Idleness explains, Moros lacks the ability to see "any virtue," he nonetheless "[i]n plays and games . . . hath no measure" (682–83).

Thus, while Moros does not respond well to the method by which the Virtues wish to bring him to manhood, he is immediately entranced by a similar offer from the Vices. Having disguised themselves as allegedly more appealing qualities—Idleness, for example, becomes "Pleasure," which Moros takes to mean "Play-sure" (806), while Wrath becomes "Manhood"—they tell Moros that "[w]e are come to make thee a man" (780). Unable to respond properly and mindfully to the Protestant doctrine and reforming lessons of the Virtues, Moros is easily seduced by the mere appearance of manhood that the Vices, who are themselves imposters, offer. Aware that Moros is well acquainted with "plays and games," they likewise become actors, drawing him into their drama and requiring his active participation (another parallel to the *Marie Magdalene*). While the Virtues seek orderly, obedient, and mindful responses from Moros, the Vices manipulate a nature already moved to physical and emotional display. The kind of drama they enact with Moros as a fellow player, therefore, differs significantly from that which the Virtues present and with which they hope to make Moros an acceptable audience member and Protestant. Referring to the "many" whom Moros represents, the Prologue of *The Longer Thou Livest* asserts that in their folly, like Moros, they "play that part" (60). While the Virtues seek to purge that part playing from Moros, the Vices emphasize and embody a type of drama that encourages such playing. In contrast to the rather quiet and orderly entrances of the Virtues and their sermonic language and entreaties, Wrath, for example, enters on a wave of physical and emotional immediacy and irreverence, pushing aside the audience: "Make room! stand back in the devil's name! / Stand back, or I will lay thee on the face" (636–37). Likely intended to refer to the physical, emotional, and visual nature of the Catholic religious drama, Wrath's entrance and the Vices' seduction of Moros repeat a Protestant attempt to characterize the earlier faith's use of devotional plays as inherently bereft of true religious intent, and consequently to malign the whole of Catholic belief and worship. Portrayed as empty gestures based purely in body and in spectacle, Catholic stagings illustrate the seductive and diabolical practices of the whole of Catholic belief, while the participants in these plays—actors and audience members alike—demonstrate the differences between improper and proper religious behavior.

In *The Longer Thou Livest,* moreover, the inability of Moros to become a true Christian—his inability to internalize and to behave appropriately in response to the Protestant doctrine that the Virtues present to him—implicates a Catholic upbringing in the potentially arrested development of the nation's male children, as well as its adults. Like the empty gestures of faith that the Virtues know are but "pretend," under the influence of the Vices, Moros merely plays at manhood. Piping "I would look big like a man" (820), Moros foolishly waves a sword (provided to him by the Vices), yet quickly drops that sword when Discipline later approaches and chastises him. Deflated as a mere externality, the swordplay nevertheless continues even as the Vices themselves reveal that Moros embodies but the appearance of manhood, a state further emphasized by Moros's later attention to his attire and look. Described as "gaily disguised" (sd., after 1292), he asks, "Have I not a gentleman's countenance?" (1298), and then becomes foppishly obsessed with obtaining a red feather for his cap which he believes "will make me a gentleman alone" (1544). Despite his eagerness to be a man, then, Moros reveals what might rightly be characterized as an effeminate, immature attention to garb, clothing, "gear" (817)—to external appearances rather than internal knowledge. The product of a female-dominated and therefore Catholic upbringing, Moros does not know what it means to be a true man. Thus when the Vices coyly insist that what will make Moros "appear a man both mighty and wise" (861), and keep him safe from the influence of Discipline and his religion, is the company of women, they build upon an education already characterized by the indulgence of female tendencies and womanly bodies. When Wrath, for example, asserts that Moros's fear of Discipline will be overcome once Moros "is nuzzled in woman's flesh" (992), he links Moros's willingness to consort with prostitutes—one of his lessons in manhood—to his female-dominated childhood through a term that connects motherly nurturing to female sexuality. Likewise employing this term, Incontinence describes how easily Moros is led to vice: "I have nuzzled him in carnality; / A man would marvel to see his readiness / Unto all fleshly sensuality" (1071–73). Similarly, Ignorance—in an assertion that may have been intended to associate "papist" explicitly with the applicable aspect of the female anatomy—declares that "[t]he papists which the truth do know, / Lord, how I have nuzzled them in my science" (1277–78). Strangely and intriguingly, it is this female-dominated upbringing, an upbringing upon which the Vices draw and embellish, that forms the basis for the imposter of manhood and religious righteousness whom Moros becomes.

In the last half of the play, anti-Catholic assertions proliferate as various Virtues lament the dangers and continued influences of the ousted faith, and as Vice figures align themselves with popery and its supposed powers of seduction, disguise, and externally motivated delights. A figure called Antiquity, for instance, comes forward, asserting the Catholic argument for tradition over the Gospel (1309–20), while Ignorance apparently dresses himself as a Catholic priest (1337). Meanwhile, Moros, deluded by the false appearance of manhood and religion in which the Vices coach him—and who are in turn, aided by the female figure of Fortune who asserts that "[a] popish fool will I place in a wiseman's seat" (1065)—continues his decline. Increasingly vain about his desire to look manly, Moros's other external and empty displays of manhood become more volatile and violent; he becomes a parody of manliness who also comes

to rule over his people as a tyrant. Moreover, as Moros falls faster and faster to his doom, the Virtues become more explicit about
pointing to him as an example of a life misled by an adherence to
externalities, physical pleasures, and visual spectacles. In a sermon
that echoes the converted Paul's sermon to the audience in the Digby *Conversion of Saint Paul,* Discipline also refers to Moros's misuse
of his senses, perhaps referring also to audience roles and responses
that indicate and determine one's true religious faith and depth of
manhood. Pointing to Moros, Discipline asserts that he "wilt play
such a foolish part / As shall shame country, father and mother"
(1579–80). Discipline continues:

> In tender age, In Idleness he was nuzzled.
> In adolency, when pubes was springing,
> Touching virtue as a dog that is muzzled,
> Ill-willing to learn and therefore unapt,
> All his senses he applied to vice.
>
> (1582–86)

Just as Paul in the Digby play characterized and condemned a use of
the senses—likely associated by Protestant reformers with a misuse
of the religious drama by Catholic performers and audiences—Discipline also defines and vilifies the domestic, female realm of childrearing as strongly affiliated with such misuse. At the same time,
Discipline appropriates the terms of performance in order to describe such inappropriate behavior.

Offering Moros as an explicit example of misconduct, God's
Judgment instructs the audience to attend to Moros's "false belief"
(1810), but then soon after distinguishes between "[i]nnocents . . . /
In whom discretion is geason" and those who "are the greatest fools
properly / Which disdain to learn sapience / To speak, to do, to
work all things orderly" (1873–77). Apparently interested in applying
the example of Moros to a larger context than the indulged youth of
the upper classes, God's Judgment indicates that what afflicts Moros
may be found throughout the nation. This claim is supported by Exercitation's assertion that

> Never will I believe that man good to be,
> Whether he be of the clergy or lay,
> Whom idle and not well-occupied I see,
> Which do nothing but eat, drink, and play.
>
> (1902–5)

The possibility that the message of the play may serve as a warning to those who might entertain any lingering allegiances to Catholic belief, ritual, or practice is further supported by Piety's subtle invocation to the Queen's Council and "all the Magistrates of this region" to "agree to maintain God's Gospel / Which is the most true and sincere religion. / To root out Anti-Christ, I pray God, they may take pain" (1975–79). More than a critique of young males playing at cards, visiting brothels, or spending money on clothes, *The Longer Thou Livest* offers an indictment of the nation's former religion as an infecting force capable of keeping the entire nation in an emasculated state of immaturity. Encouraged by indulgent females and characterized by behavior associated with the misguided audiences of the religious drama of the popish faith, the state of being that Moros represents must be revealed as more than just occasional mirth or youthful rebellion; the vices of the nation's youth demonstrate the infectious hold Catholicism potentially maintains over the entire populace, a body whom Discipline clearly invokes in the last lines of the play:

> Pray we for the clergy and whole spirituality,
> That they may teach and set forth God's truth alway;
> I beseech you, let us pray for the whole commonality,
> That upon us all God mercy take may,
> So that each one of us in the right way may stay.
>
> (1982–86)

To stay "the right way" indicates the necessity of a conscious effort to maintain a demeanor, a pattern of behavior, and a response clearly distinguishable from those that in the Renaissance came to characterize Catholic belief and worship. Emotionalism, physicality,

spectacle—all aspects of the older faith for which Protestant reformers found their most extreme examples in the religious drama—become further denigrated by association with femininity, sexuality,
seduction, and emasculation, and thus all of these were presented
as threats to "the most true and sincere religion" and to manhood
itself.

Afterword

AT THE END OF *The Killing of the Children of Israel,* the first of the two plays that comprise the Digby *Candlemas Day and the Killing of the Children of Israel,* Herod meets his end while describing to the audience his physical deterioration, including an apparent heart attack and the loss of his ability to stand.[1] Likewise, as Moros gets closer to his own damnation in *The Longer Thou Livest, the More Fool Thou Art,* he experiences a similar set of symptoms: something comes "over [his] heart" and he thinks he may have "the falling sickness" (1803, 1795). At the same time, Herod and Moros also parallel each other in their shared displays of manhood, which are in turn ultimately exposed as mere posturings. Lacking substance, longevity, and power, each doomed character is exposed as a mere actor whose tyrannical behaviors are destined for destruction. Yet the plays communicate startlingly different meanings for these examples of feigned manhood—meanings that reveal the significant role gender played in Protestant attempts to characterize response behaviors in order to define "true" religious belief. While in the Digby play Herod's destructive postering is answered with the redemptive power of an infant whose roots in the nurturing, maternal realm of female domesticity are consistently evoked, in *The Longer Thou Livest* that feminine

1. See Chapter Five.

realm is maligned as a primary cause of Moros's immaturity and emasculation: his inability to achieve true manhood as well as to recognize and join the true faith of England. In fact, *The Longer Thou Livest,* the *Marie Magdalene,* and other Protestant theater and polemical writings redraw the lines between a "masculine" and a "feminine" response, promoting Protestant behavior and belief while critiquing Catholicism. While the Digby *Candlemas Day and the Killing of the Children of Israel* attaches a salvific potential to feminine behavior, experience, and response, *The Longer Thou Livest* (along with the *Marie Magdalene*) associates the feminine with damnation, the diabolical, and Catholicism.

How, then, do we explain the possibility that, like the Digby *Conversion of Saint Paul* and the Digby *Mary Magdalene,* the Digby *Candlemas Day and the Killing of the Children of Israel* was one of the plays performed in Chelmsford in 1562?[2] While the two Digby saint plays certainly could have been adapted to suit Protestant sensibilities, surely *The Killing of the Children* encourages an aesthetic of devotional response, one grounded in a fundamentally different depiction of gender roles, which Protestant writers would have sought to erase rather than to publicize. Such a play could simply not be adapted to fit a Protestant agenda, especially one intent on using audience behavior and response as a means to determine religious belief. Or could it?

Clearly, Lewis Wager's *Marie Magdalene* can help us understand why a staging of the Digby *Mary Magdalene* may have been deemed appropriate in 1562. Indeed, Wager's play may offer a prophetic parallel to the righteous reform of religion enabled by Protestantism. Moreover, a similarly recursive approach, aided by William Wager's Protestant examination of manhood, gender, and religious performance in *The Longer Thou Livest,* alerts us to the possibilities of performance disclosed in the Digby *Killing of the Children.* Admittedly, the plays depart from one another in terms of the religion they espouse, the response roles they encourage, and the treatment of

2. See Chapter Two and Coldewey (1975).

gender they promote; nonetheless, I argue, they share a comparable indictment of feigned manhood. Moreover, in addition to the characteristics he shares with the Herod of *The Killing of the Children*, Moros and his swordplay mirror the other posturing, brutal Herods who populate the drama of the earlier faith (e.g., in the Chester cycle). Providing another example of how Protestant thinkers appropriated the Catholic religious drama even as they planned to malign it, the parallels between Moros and Herod suggest an expansion of the performance life of *The Killing of the Children* beyond its traditionally medieval, Catholic boundaries. If William Wager borrowed a theme regarding manhood from the earlier drama and reinterpreted it to suit (indeed, to support) his Protestant agenda, this adaptation would suggest that a similar reinterpretation (especially timely in 1562) was made of an example of the earlier drama, one containing the same theme.

Perhaps more practically, the manuscript of *The Killing of the Children* itself suggests the possibility for an alternative staging that would support such a reinterpretation of the religious meaning of feigned manhood. The primary force of the redemptive power of the infant Christ and of his domestic and maternal source, the Virgin Mary, resides primarily in the pairing of the episodes that the play contains. While the slaughter episode hints at this power, it is primarily the Candlemas episode, with its focus on women's bodies as well as divine bodies, that presents devotional practices and response roles as potentially gender-fluid experiences. Yet at the end of the slaughter episode, written in a hand clearly later than that of the text of the play itself, appears the marginal comment "Vacat ab hinc" ("From here, it is omitted"—or perhaps, "From here, it should be omitted")—an addition to the manuscript suggesting that the Candlemas pageant need not (or ought not to) be performed (Baker, Murphy, and Hall, 1982, 109).[3] Staged in isolation, without the woman-

---

3. See Baker, Murphy, and Hall (1982), 220, n. to l. 388f. for this translation, and lx–lxi for a brief discussion. See also the facsimile of the text, edited by Baker and Murphy (1976).

centered emphasis of the Candlemas pageant, the first half of the play shifts its focus to the display of manliness that Herod and his knights are so eager to maintain and that Watkyn, the emasculated messenger, wants so desperately to obtain. In combination with the Candlemas episode, Watkyn's fear of women and mothers (and, indeed, the ability of those women to resist him and Herod's knights) anticipates the redemptive and devotional power of Mary and her child. Yet without the Candlemas episode, these indications of such power seem employed instead as evidence of the false manhood Herod and his followers embody. Vocally and physically assailing the knights and Watkyn, the women question their opponents' manhood through a combination of actions, words, and attitudes that seems, instead, to forecast the combination of emasculation, immaturity, and reliance on "male" equipment (such as swords) that Moros illustrates.[4] Isolated from the Candlemas pageant, the women's activities and attitudes become, in turn, isolated from the devotional power of Mary and Christ. Lacking the spiritual power with which a combined staging of the Candlemas play would invest them, the women serve primarily to reveal men who are but imposters of men.

These imposters of men, trapped in an Old Testament world, thus add another dimension to the paradigm of reform that likened the change in England's old national religion to the faith of the New Testament ushered in by Christ. The restagings of the Digby *Conversion of Saint Paul* and the *Mary Magdalene* further evoke this paradigm of reform. The gender-attentive portraits of Herod and his men in *The Killing of the Children* represent, as in the *Saint Paul,* a form of behavior and response deemed inappropriate by Protestant thinkers that would engage an audience's own physical, emotional, and sense-driven involvement. These portraits serve as vehicles for vilifying the behavior and response these thinkers worked to asso-

4. These women mock the swords and armor and attack with their distaffs, they destabilize the supposedly manmaking process of knighting by "dubbing" the attackers with these distaffs, and they reduce the men to "prowde boyes" (297–337 and sd. after 349).

ciate with Catholicism: the threat, as in *The Longer Thou Livest*, of emasculation. Herod, as perhaps the chief representative of inappropriate response—upon hearing of Christ's birth, he expresses his intent to murder the redeemer of the world—is thus reduced to a nonman, whose death in *The Killing of the Children* is precipitated by the mothers' curse. Similarly, while Watkyn's delivery of that curse to Herod may be a sign of hope anticipating the blending of male and female voices and devotional experiences at the center of the Candlemas play, an isolated staging diminishes it to another example of nonmanly (and non-Christian) behavior, as Watkyn illustrates womanly emotions. Without the Candlemas play, that curse, as well as the women's voices and sorrow, is left in the same Old Testament world as Herod and his fellow impostures of power, religion, and manhood. Indeed, the women themselves become male impersonators—a disturbingly unnatural result of those who merely perform, rather than live, truly manly (and Protestant) lives.

Serving, then, as another example of a Protestant remaking of the earlier faith's drama, the Digby *Candlemas Day and the Killing of the Children of Israel* bears witness to the early stages of Protestant efforts to reform faith through a reform of response: these efforts become more apparent once an ostensibly medieval and Catholic drama is reexamined in relation to those Protestant plays sharing attentions to response, performance, drama, and gender. Continually investigating ways to distinguish the new faith from the old one, the attention of Protestant reformers to the role of response in religious belief and practice thus extended apparently to an attempt to establish (or even to reestablish) boundaries of gender portrayed as dangerously and unnaturally transcended by Catholicism itself.

The possible staging of *The Killing of the Children* in 1562 provides a particularly vivid example of one of the central assertions of this book: that a recursive approach to the early English religious drama, mindful of later incarnations of dramatic texts, can unveil a hidden history of performance life previously obscured in part by chronologically artificial boundaries. The gendering of response, then, is but one part of a larger politicizing of audience reception styles and devotional practices that establishes the role of the medieval English drama in shaping religious ideology well into the early modern period. Understanding this role requires an expansive notion of the performance capabilities and theological uses of this drama, and it also encourages us to reconsider what we mean by "medieval" and "Renaissance." Thus a main goal of this book has been to complicate the historical categories we apply to this genre of texts, whose own fluidity of performance possibilities seems to have been eagerly embraced and usefully politicized by various competing (and coexisting) forces with various allegiances: clergy and laity, artisans and merchants, Catholics and Protestants.[5] Examined recursively as factions eager to recycle for their own polemical purposes a popular genre that could be usefully reshaped, redirected, and reclaimed to endorse alternative theological beliefs, these forces disclose the fluid potential of this drama.

Yet this potential would not have been the message that the majority of these factions themselves would have emphasized. Rather, in laying claim to a proper understanding and use of the sacred drama, these factions often tried to establish clear boundaries between, for instance, the ignorance of Catholicism and the enlightenment of Protestantism; between clerical and laic claims to the Eucharist;

5. Referring to the work of Tessa Watt (1991, 325–27), Paul White (1999) has argued that "the sources most immediately accessible to historians" of the medieval and early modern drama—"city council minutes, church court records, polemical treatises—tend to highlight points of confrontation between Protestantism and the existing religious culture, and yet areas of cultural pratice characterized by consensus, accommodation, resolution of conflict, or simple contradiction (where, for example, traditional Catholic and emerging Protestant patterns of belief and practice coexist uneasily side by side) are often ignored" (122). At the same time, in his study of French confraternity drama, Robert Clark (1999) has worked to demonstrate how theater and ritual may allow for "a range of subject positions, including a resistant or antagonistic subject." As he argues, "Just as . . . medieval subjects were differentiated among themselves, it stands to reason that, even in such a shared experience, their participation in theatre and ritual may have been to a certain degree subjectively different" (45). In using the term "Protestant," I am aware of the fact that the word was probably not employed in England until the early 1550s. See, for example, MacCulloch (2002), 86–67.

between artisan and merchant; and between femininity and masculinity. Indeed, the establishment of boundaries could even include a historical categorization reminiscent of our own desires to rely upon chronological divisions. The desire of the post-Reformation Banns to distinguish a more ignorant (and past, Catholic) misuse of the Chester cycle from a more enlightened (and present, Protestant) proper use echoes the process by which the so-called primitive, unsophisticated, and didactic elements of the cycle are invoked to establish its essentially medieval quality.[6] However, even as they separate past from present, the old faith from the new one, the post-Reformation Banns, in crafting a claim to the meaning and power of the sacred drama, betray an attention to the role of audience response that challenges the very boundaries the Banns hope to define and impose. Placing an intrinsic responsibility upon current audiences to use the cycle properly, the Banns refer to former (supposed) misuses, but in so doing disclose the very flexibility of the form that they wished to define, control, and contain (through boundaries that invoked historical as well as other labels). In attempting to designate one form of response as correct (and all others as incorrect), the Banns thus ironically display the inherent fluidity of response, and the fluidity of the sacred drama itself.

A recursive approach thus uncovers an influential second life for the medieval religious drama in England. Various audience attentive figures throughout this drama serve as cultural barometers who model and shape alternative, often opposing, response roles for their audiences. Embedded in numerous elements of performance and theme, and fundamentally linked to theological beliefs and controversies, these mediating figures illustrate competing ideas regarding the role of the audience in relation to sacred performance. In the matrix of theology and performance, sponsor and player, authority and audience, these figures give voice to these conflicting ideas

6. See Chapter One and compare these additional lines from the post-Reformation Banns: "By craftesmen and meane men these pageaunts are playde, / and to commons and contry men accustomablye before. / If better men and finer heades now come, what canne be sayde?" (Lumiansky and Mills, 1983, 203–5).

within and *between* dramatic texts. They demonstrate in the late medieval and early modern periods a history of response consistently appropriated to shape religious ideology and its discourse. Indicative of larger ideological processes of religious doctrine in practice, these figures suggest that such processes were intricately linked to efforts to define and distinguish the proper use of one's receptive capacities. Shared by all those forces who sought ownership of the sacred drama as a form useful for authorizing and disseminating the proper role of a true Christian, an attention to audience response defines religious belief and practice. At the same time, an ongoing emphasis on distinguishing past from present modes of reception presents a revisionist, if politicized, history of the religious drama that attempts to inscribe contemporary ideas regarding the role of response upon a popular and useful form of worship.

Starting with the time period usually associated with the end of the Middle English religious drama, then, this book has provided a new way for examining the history and impact of a genre of performance and worship whose own innovative survival encourages such an approach. Indeed, the Chester post-Reformation Banns, by submitting both the cycle and its audience to a reinterpretation that tries to establish a correct response to the cycle, creates a recursive paradigm that urges us to consider a previous history of response that must necessarily be examined in hindsight. Making public such a reinterpretation points out the existence of a program, centered on the drama of the earlier faith, that privileged revision, recycling, and reform (rather than overt condemnation and destruction) to promote the new faith. At the same time, the acknowledgment of a previous form of audience response—if only to condemn and expunge it—suggests that the position of the audience in relation to the drama was a topic of consideration and concern prior to the Reformation.

"Response," of course, includes "use," and much of the shaping and reshaping of audience roles relates directly to the voicing of alternative beliefs regarding the appropriate employment of the sacred drama. Appropriating the drama of the earlier faith as a means for slandering Catholic belief and practice, Protestant reformers were nevertheless primarily concerned with the association of the drama with transubstantiation. While Catholic clerics perhaps sought to maintain authority over both the Eucharist and the eucharistic drama without draining it of its power—as we see in the Croxton *Play of the Sacrament*—Protestant authorities wished to reassign the transformative potential of the drama, replacing holy sacrament with holy word through a redefinition of response that replaced participation with revelation. Thus, faith in Lewis Wager's *Marie Magdalene* "is founded on God's promission":

> And most clerely to the mynde of man revealed,
> So that of God's will he hath an intuition,
> Which by the holy ghost to his heart is sealed.
>
>   (1992, ll. 1485–88)

The redeemed Magdalene of the play is "[t]o all the worlde an example / In whom the mercy of Christ is declared" (1768–69). Protestant audiences are not re-creative participants luxuriating in the communal space of performance; they are receptacles of divine revelation who must be prepared to receive the imprint of "the Lordes seale . . . [p]ryntynge in their hartes hys holy wourdes and covenauntes" (Bale, 1985, 98). The transformative power of the drama is thus apparently transferred from the communal space of performance and ritual participation to individual bodies who shall themselves be transformed by revelation, but only if they prepare themselves properly and do not misuse the drama as did the followers of the earlier faith.

Yet, even as Protestant forces defined a distinct audience role for followers of the new faith and characterized Catholic audiences as mere players (and Catholic ritual as mere exercises in duplicity), they paradoxically maintained a definition of the drama that invested it with a relevatory (and therefore divine) potential that maintains its connection to transubstantiation belief and practice. At the heart of this continual attention to audience reception and use of the sacred drama, then, lies the promise that the drama can indeed provide access to the divine. Thus, although various sponsors willingly embraced the flexibility of the genre for authorizing and communicating various belief systems, they also seized upon the drama as a divinely sanctioned activity whose intrinsically sacred nature predated later definitions of response and of the belief systems those definitions sought to empower. A shaping force of religious cultural discourse whose impact extended well beyond its medieval boundaries, the Middle English religious drama discloses a multiplicity of sacred players, themselves shifting incarnations of response, reception, and belief. Including those who "played at" the drama in various ways—as audiences, sponsors, actors, and worshippers—these sacred players inspire us to chart a history of response that may involve a more expansive approach to the performance capabilities and influence of a drama that can be both Catholic and Protestant, reformist and recusant, of the Middle Ages and of the Renaissance.

Bibliography

Aers, David, ed. 1986. *Medieval Literature: Criticism, Ideology, and History*. Brighton, Sussex, England: Harvester Press.

Anglo, Sidney. 1957. An Early Tudor Programme for Plays and Other Demonstrations against the Pope. *Journal of the Warburg and Courtauld Institutes* 20: 176–79.

Ashley, Kathleen. 1990. Image and Ideology: Saint Anne in Late Medieval Drama and Narrative. In *Interpreting Cultural Symbols: Saint Anne in Late Medieval Society*, ed. Kathleen Ashley and Pamela Sheingorn, 111–30. Athens: University of Georgia Press.

———. 1995 (for 1992). Contemporary Theories of Culture and Medieval Performances. In *Medieval and Early Renaissance Drama: Reconsiderations*, ed. Martin Stevens and Milla Riggio, special issue, *Mediaevalia* 18: 3–44.

Ashley, Kathleen, and Pamela Sheingorn, eds. 1990. *Interpreting Cultural Symbols: Saint Anne in Late Medieval Society*. Athens: University of Georgia Press.

Atkinson, Clarissa W. 1983. *Mystic and Pilgrim: The Book and the World of Margery Kempe*. Ithaca, N.Y.: Cornell University Press.

Aulén, Gustav. 1951. *Christus Victor*. Translated by A. G. Herbert. New York: Macmillan.

Axton, Richard. 1974. *European Drama of the Early Middle Ages*. London: Hutchinson.

Baker, Denise Nowakowski. 1994. *Julian of Norwich's Showings: From Vision to Book*. Princeton, N.J.: Princeton University Press.

Baker, Donald C. 1973. The Books of Myles Blomefylde. *The Library* 5: 75–87.

———. 1989. When Is a Text a Play? Reflections upon What Certain Late Medieval Dramatic Texts Can Tell Us. In *Contexts for Early English Drama*, ed. Marianne G. Briscoe and John C. Coldewey, 20–40. Bloomington: Indiana University Press.

Baker, Donald C., and John L. Murphy. 1967. The Late Medieval Plays of Ms.
    Digby 133: Scribes, Dates, and Early History. *Research Opportunities in Re-
    naissance Drama* 10: 3–44.
————, eds. 1976. *The Digby Plays: Facsimiles of the Plays in Bodley Mss. Digby 133
    and E Museo 160.* Leeds Texts and Monographs, Medieval Drama Facsimi-
    les, Vol. 3. Leeds, England: School of English, University of Leeds.
Baker, Donald C., John L. Murphy, and Louis B. Hall, eds. 1982. *The Late Medi-
    eval Religious Plays of Bodleian Mss. Digby 133 and E Museo 160.* Early English
    Text Society, Extra Series, Vol. 238. London: Oxford University Press.
Bale, John. 1849. Examinations of Anne Askew. In *Select Works of John Bale,* ed.
    Henry Christmas, 135–248. Cambridge, England: Cambridge University
    Press.
————. 1985a. *The Complete Plays of John Bale.* Vol. 1. Edited by Peter Happé.
    Cambridge, England: D. S. Brewer.
————. 1985b. King Johan. In *The Complete Plays of John Bale,* Vol. 1, ed. Peter
    Happé, 29–99. Cambridge, England: D. S. Brewer.
Barish, Jonas. 1981. *The Antitheatrical Prejudice.* Berkeley and Los Angeles: Uni-
    versity of California Press.
Beadle, Richard, ed. 1982. *The York Plays.* London: Edward Arnold.
————. 1991. The York Cycle: Texts, Performances, and the Bases for Critical
    Enquiry. In *Medieval Literature: Texts and Interpretations,* ed. Tim William
    Machan, 105–19. Binghampton, N.Y.: Centre for Medieval and Early Re-
    naissance Studies.
————, ed. 1994a. *The Cambridge Companion to Medieval English Theatre.* Cam-
    bridge, England: Cambridge University Press.
————. 1994b. The York Cycle. In *The Cambridge Companion to Medieval English
    Theatre,* 85–108. Cambridge, England: Cambridge University Press.
Beadle, Richard, and Pamela M. King, eds. 1984. *York Mystery Plays: A Selection
    in Modern Spelling.* Oxford, England: Clarendon Press.
Beadle, Richard, and Peter Meredith, eds. 1983. *The York Plays: A Facsimile of
    British Library Ms Additional 35290, Together with a Facsimile of the Ordo Pagi-
    narum Section of the A/Y Memorandum Book, and a Note on the Music by Rich-
    ard Rastall.* Leeds, England: School of English, University of Leeds.
Beckwith, Sarah. 1986a. Ritual, Church, and Theatre: Medieval Dramas of the
    Sacramental Body. In *Medieval Literature: Criticism, Ideology, and History,* ed.
    David Aers, 66–89. New York: St. Martin's Press.
————. 1986b. A Very Material Mysticism: The Medieval Mysticism of Mar-
    gery Kempe. In *Medieval Literature: Criticism, Ideology, and History,* ed. Da-
    vid Aers, 34–57. New York: St. Martin's Press.
————. 1993. *Christ's Body: Identity, Culture and Society in Late Medieval Writings.*
    New York: Routledge.
————. 1994. Making the World in York and the York Cycle. In *Framing Medi-
    eval Bodies,* ed. Sarah Kay and Miri Rubin, 254–76. New York: Manchester
    University Press.

———. 1996. Ritual, Theater, and Social Space in the York Corpus Christi Cycle. In *Bodies and Disciplines: Intersections of Literature and History in Fifteenth-Century England,* Medieval Cultures, Vol. 9, ed. Barbara A. Hanawalt and David Wallace, 63–86. Minneapolis: University of Minnesota Press.

———. 2001. *Signifying God: Sacred Relation and Symbolic Act in the York Corpus Christi Plays.* Chicago: University of Chicago Press.

Bevington, David. 1962. *From Mankind to Marlowe.* Cambridge, England: Cambridge University Press.

Brandenbarg, Ton. 1995. Saint Anne: A Holy Grandmother and Her Children. In *Sanctity and Motherhood: Essays on Holy Mothers in the Middle Ages,* ed. Anneke Mulder-Bakker, 31–65. New York: Garland.

Briscoe, Marianne G. 1985. Some Clerical Notions of Dramatic Decorum in Late Medieval England. *Comparative Drama* 19: 1–13.

Briscoe, Marianne G., and John C. Coldewey, eds. 1989. *Contexts for Early English Drama.* Bloomington: Indiana University Press.

Brown, Carleton, ed. 1913. Caiphas as Palm Sunday Prophet. In *Anniversary Papers by Colleagues and Pupils of George Lyman Kittredge,* 105–17. Boston: Ginn.

Butler, Judith. 1990. *Gender Trouble: Feminism and the Subversion of Identity.* New York: Routledge.

———. 1993. *Bodies That Matter: On the Discursive Limits of "Sex."* New York: Routledge.

Bynum, Caroline Walker. 1982. *Jesus as Mother: Studies in the Spirituality of the High Middle Ages.* Berkeley and Los Angeles: University of California Press.

———. 1987. *Holy Feast and Holy Fast: The Religious Significance of Food to Medieval Women.* Berkeley and Los Angeles: University of California Press.

———. 1989. The Female Body and Religious Practice in the Later Middle Ages. In *Fragments for a History of the Human Body,* Part 1, ed. M. Feher, Ramona Naddaff, and Nadia Tazi, 161–219. New York: Urzone.

———. 1991. *Fragmentation and Redemption: Essays on Gender and the Human Body in Medieval Religion.* New York: Zone Books.

———. 1995. *The Resurrection of the Body in Western Christianity, 200–1336.* New York: Columbia University Press.

Cartwright, Kent. 1999. *Theatre and Humanism: English Drama in the Sixteenth Century.* Cambridge, England: Cambridge University Press.

Cawley, A. C, ed. 1961. *Everyman.* Manchester, England: Manchester University Press.

Certeau, Michel de. 1992. *The Mystic Fable, Vol. 1: The Sixteenth and Seventeenth Centuries.* Translated by Michael B. Smith. Chicago: University of Chicago Press.

Chambers, E. K. 1903. *The Medieval Stage.* 2 vols. Oxford, England: Clarendon Press. Rpt. in 1996 as *The Medieval Stage,* 2 vols., Mineola, N.Y.: Dover Publications.

Clarke, R. Rainbird. 1960. *East Anglia*. London: Thames & Hudson.

Clark, Robert L. A. 1999. French Confraternity Drama and Ritual. In *Drama and Community: People and Plays in Medieval Europe*, ed. Alan Hindley, 3–44. Medieval Texts and Cultures in Northern Europe. Turnhout, Belgium: Brepols.

Clopper, Lawrence M. 1978. The History and Development of the Chester Cycle. *Modern Philology* 75: 219–46.

———, ed. 1979. *Records of Early English Drama: Chester*. Toronto: University of Toronto Press.

———. 1989. Lay and Clerical Impact on Civic Religious Drama and Ceremony. In *Contexts for Early English Drama*, ed. Marianne G. Briscoe and John C. Coldewey, 102–36. Bloomington: Indiana University Press.

———. 1990. "Miracula" and "The Tretise of Miraclis Pleyinge." *Speculum* 65: 878–905.

———. 2001. *Drama, Play, and Game: English Festive Culture in the Medieval and Early Modern Period*. Chicago: University of Chicago Press.

Cohen, Jeremy. 1983. The Jews as Killers of Christ in the Latin Tradition, from Augustine to the Friars. *Traditio* 34: 1–27.

Coldewey, John C. 1975a. The Digby Plays and the Chelmsford Records. *Research Opportunities in Renaissance Drama* 18: 103–21.

———. 1975b. The Last Rise and Final Demise of Essex Town Drama. *Modern Language Quarterly* 56: 239–60.

———. 1977. That Enterprising Property Player: Semi-Professional Drama in Sixteenth-Century England. *Theatre Notebook* 3: 5–12.

———. 1985. Plays and "Play" in Early English Drama. *Research Opportunities in Renaissance Drama* 28: 181–88.

———. 1989. Some Economic Aspects of the Late Medieval Drama. In *Contexts for Early English Drama*, ed. Marianne G. Briscoe and John C. Coldewey, 77–101. Bloomington: Indiana University Press.

———, ed. 1993. *Early English Drama*. Garland Reference Library of the Humanities, Vol. 1313. New York: Garland.

———. 1994. The Non-Cycle Plays and the East Anglian Tradition. In *The Cambridge Companion to Medieval English Theater*, ed. Richard Beadle, 189–210. Cambridge, England: Cambridge University Press.

Coletti, Theresa. 1979. The Design of the Digby Play of *Mary Magdalene*. *Studies in Philology* 76: 313–33.

———. 1990. Reading REED: History and the Records of Early English Drama. In *Literary Practice and Social Change in Britain, 1380–1530*, ed. Lee Patterson, 248–84. Berkeley and Los Angeles: University of California Press.

———. 1993. Purity and Danger: The Paradox of Mary's Body and the Engendering of the Infancy Narrative in the English Mystery Cycles. In *Feminist Approaches to the Body in Medieval Literature*, ed. L. Lomperis and S. Stanbury, 65–95. Philadelphia: University of Pennsylvania Press.

————. 1995. "Ther Be but Women": Gender, Conflict and Gender Identity in the Middle English Innocents Plays. *Mediaevalia* 18: 245–61.

————. 1999. Geneology, Sexuality, and Sacred Power: The Saint Anne Dedication of the Digby *Candlemas Day and The Killing of the Children of Israel. Journal of Medieval and Early Modern Studies*, 29.1: 25–59.

Collier, Richard. 1978. *Poetry and Drama in the York Corpus Christi Play.* Hamden, Conn.: Archon Books.

Collinson, Patrick. 1967. *The Elizabethan Puritan Movement.* Berkeley and Los Angeles: University of California Press.

Coster, William. 1990. Purity, Profanity, and Puritanism: The Churching of Women, 1500–1700. In *Women in the Church,* ed. W. J. Sheils and Diana Wood, 377–87. Oxford, England: Basil Blackwell.

Cox, John. 1994–95. The Devil and Society in the English Mystery Plays. *Comparative Drama* 28: 407–38.

Cox, John, and David Scott Kaston. 1998a. *A New History of Early English Drama.* New York: Columbia University Press.

————. 1998b. Introduction to *A New History of Early English Drama.* New York: Columbia University Press.

Craig, Hardin. 1955. *English Religious Drama of the Middle Ages.* Oxford, England: Clarendon Press.

————, ed. 1957. *Two Coventry Corpus Christi Plays.* Early English Text Society, Extra Series, Vol. 87. 2nd ed. Oxford, England: Oxford University Press.

Craik, T. W. 1962. *The Tudor Interlude.* Leicester, England: Leicester University Press.

Cressy, David. 1993. Purification, Thanksgiving and the Churching of Women in Post-Reformation England. *Past and Present* 141: 106–41.

Crouch, David. 1991. Paying to See the Play: The Stationholders on the Route of the York Corpus Christi Play in the Fifteenth Century. *Medieval English Theatre* 13: 64–111.

Cutts, Cecilia. 1944. The Croxton Play: An Anti-Lollard Piece. *Modern Language Quarterly* 5: 45–60.

Davidson, Clifford. 1984. *From Creation to Doom: The York Cycle of Mystery Plays.* New York: AMS Press.

————. 1986a. The Middle English Saint Play and Its Iconography. In *The Saint Play in Medieval Europe,* ed. Clifford Davidson, 31–122. Edam Monograph Series, No. 8. Kalamazoo: Medieval Institute Publications, Western Michigan University.

————, ed. 1986b. *The Saint Play in Medieval Europe.* Edam Monograph Series, No. 8. Kalamazoo: Medieval Institute Publications, Western Michigan University.

————, ed. 1997. *A Tretise of Miraclis Pleyinge.* Early Drama, Art, and Music Monograph Series, No. 19. Kalamazoo: Medieval Institute Publications, Western Michigan University.

Davis, Natalie Zemon. 1975. Women on Top. In *Society and Culture in Early Modern France*, ed. Natalie Zemon Davis, 124–51. London: Duckworth.

Davis, Nicholas. 1982. Another View of the *Tretise of Miraclis Pleyinge*. *Medieval English Theatre* 4: 48–85.

———. 1990. The *Tretise of Miraclis Pleyinge*: On Milieu and Authorship. *Medieval English Theatre* 12: 124–51.

Davis, Norman, ed. 1970. *Non-Cycle Plays and Fragments*. Early English Text Society, Supplementary Series, Vol. 1. New York: Oxford University Press.

———, ed. 1979. *Non-Cycle Plays and the Winchester Dialogues: Facsimiles of Plays and Fragments in Various Manuscripts*. Leeds, England: School of English, University of Leeds.

Davis, Ruth Brant. 1993. The Scheduling of the Chester Cycle Plays. In *The Chester Mystery Cycle: A Casebook*, ed. Kevin J. Harty, 231–57. New York: Garland.

del Villar, Mary. 1970–1971. The Staging of *The Conversion of Saint Paul*. *Theatre Notebook* 25: 64–68.

Diller, Hans-Jürgen. 1971. The Composition of the Chester *Adoration of the Shepherds*. *Anglia* 89: 179–98. Reprinted in Kevin J. Harty, ed., 1993, *The Chester Mystery Cycle: A Casebook*, 126–45. New York: Garland.

———. 1992. *The Middle English Mystery Play: A Study in Dramatic Speech and Form*. Cambridge, England: Cambridge University Press.

Dilthey, William, and Frederic Jameson. 1972. The Rise of Hermeneutics. Translated and with an Introduction by Frederic Jameson. *New Literary History: A Journal of History and Interpretation* 3: 229–44.

Doucet, A. 1956. Saint Joseph in Medieval Lyrics and Carols. *Cahiers de Josephologie* 4: 89–102.

———. 1957. Saint Joseph in Medieval Lyrics and Carols. *Cahiers de Josephologie* 5: 241–60.

Dox, Donnalee. 1997. Medieval Drama as Documentation: "Real Presence" in the Croxton *Conversion of Ser Jonathas the Jewe by the Myracle of the Blissed Sacrament*. *Theatre Survey* 38: 97–115.

Duffy, Eamon. 1992. *The Stripping of the Altars: Traditional Religion in England, 1400–1580*. New Haven, Conn.: Yale University Press.

Eccles, Mark, ed. 1969. *The Macro Plays*. Early English Text Society, Original Series, Vol. 262. London: Oxford University Press.

Elliott, Dylan. 1993. *Spiritual Marriage: Sexual Abstinence in Medieval Wedlock*. Princeton, N.J.: Princeton University Press.

Emmerson, Richard K. 1999. Contextualizing Performance: The Reception of the Chester *Antichrist*. *Journal of Medieval and Early Modern Studies* 29.1: 89–119.

Fichte, Jörg O. 1975. *Expository Voices: Essays on the Mode and Function of Dramatic Exposition*. Erlanger Beiträge zur Sprach- und Kunstwissenschaft 53. Nürnberg: Carl.

Filas, Francis. 1954. Introduction to the Theology of Saint Joseph. *Cahiers de Josephologie* 2: 207–20.

———. 1962. *Joseph: The Man Closest to Jesus*. Boston: St. Paul Editions.

Fish, Stanley. 1986. Is There A Text In This Class? In *Critical Theory since 1965*, ed. Hazard Adams and Leroy Searle, 524–33. Tallahassee: Florida State University Press.

Foster, Francis A., ed. 1926. *A Stanzaic Life of Christ*. Early English Text Society, Original Series, Vol. 106. London: Oxford University Press.

Garber, Marjorie B. 1992. *Vested Interests: Cross-Dressing and Cultural Anxiety*. New York: Routledge.

Gardiner, Harold C. 1946. *Mysteries' End: An Investigation of the Last Days of the Medieval Religious Stage*. New Haven, Conn.: Yale University Press.

Gash, Anthony. 1986. Carnival against Lent: The Ambivalence of Medieval Drama. In *Medieval Literature: Criticism, Ideology, and History*, ed. David Aers, 74–98. New York: St. Martin's Press.

Gibson, Gail MacMurray. 1985. The Play of *Wisdom* and the Abbey of St. Edmund. *Comparative Drama* 19: 117–35.

———. 1989. *The Theater of Devotion: East Anglian Drama and Society in the Late Middle Ages*. Chicago: University of Chicago Press.

———. 1995. Blessing from Sun and Moon: Churching as Women's Theater. In *Bodies and Disciplines: Intersections of Literature and History in Fifteenth-Century England*, ed. Barbara A. Hanawalt and D. Wallace, Medieval Cultures, Vol. 9, 139–54. Minneapolis: University of Minnesota Press.

The Golden Legend; or, Lives of the Saints as Englished by William Caxton. 1973. Vol. 3. New York: A.M.S. Press. [Originally issued as *The Golden Legend; or, Lives of the Saints as Englished by William Caxton*, ed. F. S. Ellis, Vol. 3. London: Temple Classics, 1900.]

Grantley, Darryll. 1984. The Source of the Digby *Mary Magdalene*. *Notes and Queries* 229: 457–59.

———. 1994. Saints Plays. In *The Cambridge Companion to Medieval English Theatre*, ed. Richard Beadle, 265–89. Cambridge, England: Cambridge University Press.

Graves, Pamela. 1989. Social Space in the English Medieval Parish Church. *Economy and Society* 18: 297–322.

Hahn, Cynthia. 1986. "Joseph Will Perfect, Mary Enlighten and Jesus Save Thee": The Holy Family as Marriage Model in the Mérode Triptych. *Art Bulletin* 68: 54–66.

Hale, Rosemary D. 1996. Joseph as Mother: Adaptation and Appropriation in the Construction of Male Virtue. In *Medieval Mothering*, ed. John Carmi Parsons and Bonnie Wheeler, 101–16. New York: Garland.

Happé, Peter. 1980. Properties and Costumes in the Plays of John Bale. *Medieval English Theatre* 2.2: 55–65.

———. 1982. *Conversion of Saint Paul. Research Opportunities in Renaissance Drama* 25: 3–44.

———. 1985. Introduction to *The Complete Plays of John Bale,* Vol. 1, ed. Peter Happé. Cambridge, England: D. S. Brewer.

———. 1986. The Protestant Adaptation of the Saint Play. In Davidson, ed., 1986b, 205–40.

———. 2004. "Erazed in the Booke": The Mystery Cycles and Reform. In *Tudor Drama before Shakespeare, 1485–1590: New Directions for Research, Criticism, and Pedagogy,* ed. Lloyd Edward Kermode, Jason Scott-Warren, and Martin van Elk, 15–33. New York: Palgrave Macmillan.

Harrington, Gary. 1995. The Dialogism of the Digby Mystery Play. *Mediaevalia* 18: 67–80.

Harty, Kevin J., ed. 1993. *The Chester Mystery Cycle: A Casebook.* New York: Garland.

Herlihy, David. 1983. The Making of the Medieval Family: Symmetry, Structure, and Sentiment. *Journal of Family History* 18: 116–30.

Hindley, Alan, ed. 1999. *Drama and Community: People and Plays in Medieval Europe.* Medieval Texts and Cultures in Northern Europe. Turnhout, Belgium: Brepols.

Hogg, James, and Lawrence F. Powell, eds. 1989. *Nicholas Love's "The Mirrour of the Blessyd Lyf of Jesu Christ."* 2 vols. Salzburg: Institut für Anglistik und Amerikanistik.

Homan, Richard L. 1984. Two Exempla: Analogues to the *Play of the Sacrament* and *Dux Moraud. Comparative Drama* 18: 241–51.

———. 1986. Devotional Themes in the Violence and Humor of the *Play of the Sacrament. Comparative Drama* 20: 327–40.

Hubert, Henri, and Marcel Mauss. 1964. *Essay on Sacrifice.* Translated by W. D. Halls. Chicago: University of Chicago Press.

Hudson, Anne. 1988. *The Premature Reformation: Wycliffite Texts and Lollard History.* Oxford, England: Oxford University Press.

Hughes, Paul L., and James F. Larkin, C.S.V, eds. 1964. *Tudor Royal Proclamations, Vol. 1: The Early Tudors (1485–53).* New Haven, Conn.: Yale University Press.

James, Mervyn. 1983. Ritual, Drama, and Social Body in the Late Medieval Town. *Past and Presence* 98: 3–29.

Jauss, Hans Robert. 1982. *Towards an Aesthetic of Reception.* Translated by Timothy Bahti. Theory and History of Literature, Vol. 2. Minneapolis: University of Minnesota Press.

———. 1988. Response to Paul de Man. In *Reading de Man Reading,* ed. Lindsay Waters and Wlad Gudzich, 202–8. Minneapolis: University of Minnesota Press.

———. 1990. The Theory of Reception: A Retrospective of Its Unrecognized Prehistory. In *Literary Theory Today,* ed. Peter Collier and Helga Geyer-Ryan, 53–73. Ithaca, N.Y.: Cornell University Press.

Jeffrey, David L. 1973. English Saints Plays. In *Medieval Drama,* ed. Neville Denny, 69–89. Stratford-upon-Avon Studies, Vol. 16. London: Edward Arnold.

————. 1975a. *The Early English Lyric and Franciscan Spirituality*. Lincoln: University of Nebraska Press.

————. 1975b. Franciscan Spirituality and the Rise of the Early English Drama. In *On the Rise of the Vernacular Literatures in the Middle Ages*, ed. R. G. Collins and John Wirthy. *Mosaic* 7.4: 17–45.

Jewel, John. 1846. *The Works of John Jewel*. 4 vols. Edited by John Ayre. Parker Society. Cambridge, England: Cambridge University Press.

Johnston, Alexandra F. 1973–1974. The Procession and Play of Corpus Christi in York after 1426. *Leeds Studies in English* 7: 55–62.

————. 1987. The *York Cycle* and the *Chester Cycle*: What Do the Records Tell Us? In *Editing Early English Drama: Special Problems and New Directions*, ed. Johnston, 121–43. New York: AMS Press.

————. 1989. What If No Texts Survived? External Evidence for Early English Drama. In *Contexts for Early English Drama*, ed. Marianne G. Briscoe and John C. Coldewey, 1–19. Bloomington: Indiana University Press.

Johnston, Alexandra F., and Margaret Rogerson, eds. 1979. *Records of Early English Drama: York*. 2 vols. Toronto: University of Toronto Press.

Johnston, Paul A. Jr. 1997. The Dialect of *A Tretise of Miraclis Pleyinge*. In Davidson, ed. (1997), 53–84.

Jones, Robert C. 1973. Dangerous Sport: The Audience's Engagement with Vice in the Moral Interludes. *Renaissance Drama* 6: 45–64.

Jordan, Constance. 1987. Women's Rule in Sixteenth-Century British Political Thought. *Renaissance Quarterly* 40.3: 421–51.

Kane, Harold, ed. 1983. *The Prickynge of Love*. Salzburg Studies in English Literature: Elizabethan and Renaissance Studies, Vol. 91. Salzburg, Austria: Institut für Anglistik und Amerikanistik, Universität Salzburg.

Kastan, David Scott, and Peter Stallybrass, eds. 1991. *Staging the Renaissance: Reinterpretations of Elizabethan and Jacobean Drama*. New York: Routledge.

King, Pamela. 1987. Spatial Semantics and the Medieval Theatre. In *Themes in Drama, Vol. 9: The Theatrical Space*, ed. James Redmond, 45–58. Cambridge, England: Cambridge University Press.

Kirchberger, Clare, ed. 1952. *The Goad of Love*. London: Faber & Faber.

Knox, John. 1878a. *The First Blast of the Trumpet against the Monstrous Regiment of Women*. Edited by Edward Arber. London: English Scholar's Library.

————. 1878b. *John Knox's Apologetical Defense of His First Blast, etc., to Queen Elizabeth*. In *The First Blast*, ed. Arber, 57–61.

Kolve, V. A. 1966. *The Play Called Corpus Christi*. Stanford, Calif.: Stanford University Press.

Le Goff, Jacques. 1980. *Time, Work, and Culture in the Middle Ages*. Translated by Arthur Goldhammer. Chicago: University of Chicago Press.

Lerer, Seth. 1996. "Representyd Now in Yower Syght": The Culture of Spectatorship in Late Fifteenth-Century England. In *Bodies and Disciplines: Intersections of Literature and History in Fifteenth-Century England*, ed. Barbara

Hanawalt and David Wallace, Medieval Cultures, Vol. 9, 29–62. Minneapolis: University of Minnesota Press.

Lewis, Flora. 1997. The Wound in Christ's Side and the Instruments of the Passion: Gendered Experience and Response. In *Women and the Book: Assessing the Visual Evidence,* ed. Jane H. M. Taylor and Lesley Smith, 204–29. Toronto: University of Toronto Press.

Lochrie, Karma. 1997. Mystical Acts, Queer Tendencies. In *Constructing Medieval Sexuality,* ed. Lochrie, Peggy McCracken, and James A. Schulte, Medieval Cultures, Vol. 11, 180–200. Minneapolis: University of Minnesota Press.

Lumiansky, R. M., and David Mills, eds. 1973. *The Chester Mystery Cycle: A Facsimile of Ms. Bodley 175.* Leeds, England: School of English, University of Leeds.

———, eds. 1974. *The Chester Mystery Cycle, Vol. 1: Text.* Early English Text Society, Supplementary Series, Vol. 3. New York: Oxford University Press.

———, eds. 1983. *The Chester Mystery Cycle: Essays and Documents.* Chapel Hill: University of North Carolina Press.

Luongo, Thomas. 1995. Catherine of Siena: Rewriting Female Holy Authority. In *Women, the Book, and the Godly,* ed. Lesley Smith and Jane H. M. Taylor, 189–203. Rochester, N.Y.: D. S. Brewer.

MacCulloch, Diarmaid. 2002. The Change of Religion. In *The Sixteenth Century: 1485–1603,* ed. Patrick Collinson, 84–111. Oxford, England: Oxford University Press.

Malvern, Marjorie M. 1975. *Venus in Sackcloth: The Magdalen's Origins and Metamorphoses.* Carbondale: Southern Illinois University Press.

Marshall, John. 1994. Modern Productions of Medieval English Plays. In *The Cambridge Companion to Medieval English Theatre,* ed. Richard Beadle, 290–311. Cambridge, England: Cambridge University Press.

———. 1995. "Her virgynes, as many as a man wyll": Dance and Provenance in Three Late Medieval Plays: *Wisdom / The Killing of the Children / The Conversion of Saint Paul. Leeds Studies in English,* n.s., 25: 111–46.

Meredith, Peter. 1981. John Clerke's Hand in the York Register. *Leeds Studies in English,* n.s., 12: 245–71.

———. 1982. *The Conversion of Saint Paul* at Winchester Cathedral. *Medieval English Theatre* 4: 3–44.

———. 1985. "Make the Asse to Speake" or Staging the Chester Plays. In *Staging the Chester Plays,* ed. David Mills, 49–76. Leeds Texts and Monographs, New Series, No. 9. Morley, Leeds, England: Moxon.

Mertes, G. R. K. A. 1987. The Household as a Religious Community. In *People, Politics and Community,* ed. Joel Rosenthal and Colin Richmond. New York: St. Martin's Press.

Mills, David, ed. 1980. *The Chester Mystery Cycle: A Facsimile of British Library Ms. Harley 2124.* Leeds, England: School of English, University of Leeds.

————. 1983a. Medieval and Modern Views of Drama. In *The Revels History of Drama in English, Vol. 1: Medieval Drama*, ed. L. Potter, 3–44. London: Methuen.

————. 1983b. Religious Drama and Civic Ceremonial. In *The Revels History of Drama in English, Vol. 1: Medieval Drama*, ed. L. Potter, 152–65. London: Methuen.

————, ed. 1985. *Staging the Chester Plays*. Leeds Texts and Monographs, New Series, No. 9. Morley, Leeds, England: Moxon.

————, ed. 1992. *The Chester Mystery Cycle: A New Edition with Modernized Spelling*. Medieval Texts and Studies, Vol. 9. East Lansing, Mich.: Colleagues Press.

————. 1993. The Two Versions of Chester Play V: *Balaam and Balaak*. In *The Chester Mystery Cycle: A Casebook*, ed. Kevin J. Harty, 119–25. New York: Garland.

————. 1994. The Chester Cycle. In *The Cambridge Companion to Medieval Drama*, ed. Richard Beadle, 109–33. Cambridge, England: Cambridge University Press.

Morison, Richard. 1957. A Discourse Touching the Reformation of the Lawes of England. [Quoted in Sidney Anglo, An Early Tudor Programme for Plays and Other Demonstrations against the Pope. *Journal of the Warburn and Courtauld Institutes* 20: 176–79.]

Morris, Richard. 1871. *Legends of the Holy Rood: Symbols of the Passion and Cross-Poems*. Early English Text Society, Original Series, Vol. 46. London: Trübner & Co.

Nelson, Alan H. 1974. *The Medieval English Stage: Corpus Christi Pageants and Plays*. Chicago: University of Chicago Press.

Neuss, Paula. 1973. Active and Idle Language: Dramatic Images in *Mankind*. In *Medieval Drama*, ed. Neville Denny, 41–68. Stratford-upon-Avon Studies Vol. 16. London: Edward Arnold.

Nichols, Ann Eljenholm. 1988. The Croxton *Play of the Sacrament*: A Re-Reading. *Comparative Drama* 22: 117–37.

Nisse, Ruth. 1997. Reversing Discipline: The *Tretise of Miraclis Pleyinge*, Lollard Exegesis, and the Failure of Representation. *Yearbook of Langland Studies* 11: 163–94.

Patterson, Lee. 1990. On the Margin: Postmodernism, Ironic History, and Medieval Studies. *Speculum* 65: 87–108.

Petroff, Elizabeth A., ed. 1986. *Medieval Women's Visionary Literature*. New York: Oxford University Press.

Phythian-Adams, Charles. 1979. *Desolation of a City: Coventry and the Urban Crisis of the Middle Ages*. Cambridge, England: Cambridge University Press.

Potter, Lois. 1980. The Reformation and the Moral Play. In *The Revels History of Drama in English, Vol. 2: 1500–1576*, ed. T. W. Craik, 177–206. London: Methuen.

Potter, Robert. 1975. *The English Morality Play*. London: Routledge & Kegan Paul.

Powlick, Leonard. 1993. The Staging of the Chester Cycle: An Alternate Theory. In *The Chester Mystery Cycle: A Casebook*, ed. Kevin J. Harty, 199–230. New York: Garland.

Prosser, Eleanor. 1961. *Drama and Religion in the English Mystery Plays. A Reevaluation*. Stanford Studies in Language and Literature, Vol. 23. Stanford, Calif.: Stanford University Press.

Ragusa, Isa, and Rosalie B. Green, eds. and trans. 1961. *Meditations on the Life of Christ*. Princeton, N.J.: Princeton University Press.

Riehle, Wolfgang. 1981. *The Middle English Mystics*. Translated by Bernard Strandring. Boston: Routledge & Kegan Paul.

Righter, Anne. 1962. *Shakespeare and the Idea of the Play*. Harmondsworth, Middlesex, England: Penguin Books.

Robinson, J. W. 1965. The Late Medieval Cult of Jesus and the Mystery Plays. *Publications of the Modern Language Association* 80: 508–14.

Rubin, Miri. 1986. The Eucharist and the Construction of Medieval Identities. In *Medieval Literature: Criticism, Ideology, and History*, ed. David Aers, 43–63. New York: St. Martin's Press.

———. 1991. *Corpus Christi: The Eucharist in Late Medieval Culture*. Cambridge, England: Cambridge University Press.

———. 1992. Desecration of the Host: The Birth of an Accusation. In *Christianity and Judaism: Papers Read at the 1991 Summer Meeting and the 1992 Winter Meeting of the Ecclesiastical History Society*, ed. Diana Wood, 169–86. Cambridge, Mass.: Blackwell.

———. 1996. The Body, Whole and Vulnerable, in Fifteenth-Century England. In *Bodies and Disciplines: Intersections of Literature and History in Fifteenth Century England*, ed. Barbara J. Hanawalt and David Wallace, 19–29. Medieval Cultures, Vol. 9. Minneapolis: University of Minnesota Press.

Rushton, Peter. 1983. Purification or Social Control? Ideologies of Reproduction and the Churching of Women after Childbirth. In *The Public and the Private*, ed. Eva Gamarnikow, David Morgan, Jane Purvis, and Daphne Taylorson, 106–17. London: Heinemann.

Salter, Elizabeth. 1974. *Nicholas Love's Mirrour of the Blessed Lyf of Jesus Christ*. Salzburg: Inst. fur eng. Sprache und Lit., University of Salzburg.

———. 1981. The Manuscripts of Nicholas Love's *Mirrour of the Blessed Lyf of Jesu Christ* and Related Texts. In *Middle English Prose: Essays on Biographical Problems*, ed. A. S. G. Edwards and Derek Pearsall, 115–27. New York: Garland.

Salter, F. M. 1955. *Medieval Drama in Chester*. Toronto: University of Toronto Press.

Sanders, Norman. 1980. Drama and Propaganda. In *The Revels History of Drama in English, Vol. 2: 1500–1576*, ed. T. W. Craik, 12–23. London: Methuen.

Sargent, Michael G., ed. 1992. *Nicholas Love's Mirror of the Blessed Life of Jesus Christ*. New York: Garland.

Sawyer Marsalek, Karen. "Doctrine Evangelicall" and Erasmus's *Paraphrases in The Resurrection of Our Lord*. In *Tudor Drama before Shakespeare, 1485–1590: New Directions for Research, Criticism, and Pedagogy*, ed. Lloyd Edward Kermode, Jason Scott-Warren, and Martine van Elk, 34–66. New York: Palgrave Macmillan.

Scherb, Victor. 2001. *Staging Faith: East Anglian Drama in the Later Middle Ages*. Cranbury, N.J.: Associated University Presses.

Seitz, Joseph. 1908. *Die Verehrung des hl. Joseph in ihrer geschichtlichen Entwicklung bis zum Konsil von Trient dargestellt*. Freiburg in Breisgau: Herder.

Severs, J. Burke. 1945. The Relationship between the Brome and Chester Plays of *Abraham and Isaac*. *Modern Philology* 42: 137–51.

Somerset, J. A. B. 1973. "Fair Is Foul and Foul Is Fair": Vice-Comedy's Development and Theatrical Effects. In *Elizabethan Theatre 5*, ed. G. R. Hibbard, 54–76. Hamden, Conn.: Archon Press.

Specter, Stephen, ed. 1991. *The N-Town Plays*. 2 vols. Early English Text Society, Supplementary Series, Vols. 11–12. Oxford, England: Oxford University Press.

Sponsler, Claire. 1997. *Drama and Resistance: Bodies, Goods, and Theatricality in Late Medieval England*. Minneapolis: University of Minnesota Press.

Staines, David. 1982. "To Out-Herod Herod": The Development of a Dramatic Character. In *Drama of the Middle Ages: Comparative and Critical Essays*, ed. Clifford Davidson and John H. Stroupe, 207–31. New York: AMS Press.

Stallybrass, Peter, and Allon White. 1986. *The Politics and Poetics of Transgression*. London: Methuen.

Stevens, Martin. 1972. The York Cycle: From Procession to Play. *Leeds Studies in English* 6: 37–61.

———. 1987. *Four Middle English Mystery Cycles*. Princeton, N.J.: Princeton University Press.

Stevens, Martin, and A. C. Cawley, eds. 1994. *The Towneley Plays*. Early English Text Society, Supplementary Series, Vol. 13. New York: Oxford University Press.

Swanson, Heather. 1989. *Medieval Artisans: An Urban Class in Late Medieval England*. Oxford, England: Blackwell.

Thrupp, Sylvia L. 1948. *The Merchant Class of Medieval London, 1300–1500*. Chicago: University of Chicago Press.

Travis, Peter. 1982. *Dramatic Design in the Chester Cycle*. Chicago: University of Chicago Press.

———. 1985. The Social Body of the Dramatic Christ in Medieval England. *Early Drama to 1600*, ed. Albert H. Tricomi, *Acta* 13: 17–36.

———. 1987. Affective Criticism, the Pilgrimage of Reading, and Middle English Literature. In *Medieval Texts and Contemporary Readers*, ed. Laurie Finke and Martin Shichtman, 201–15. Ithaca, N.Y.: Cornell University Press.

Turner, Victor. 1974. Social Dramas and Ritual Metaphors. In Turner, *Dramas, Fields, and Metaphors: Symbolic Action in Human Society,* 23–59. Ithaca, N.Y.: Cornell University Press.

———. 1984. Liminality and the Performative Genres. In *Rite, Drama, Festival, Spectacle: Rehearsals Toward a Theory of Cultural Performance,* ed. John J. MacAloon, 3–44. Philadelphia: Institute for the Study of Human Issues.

Twycross, Meg. 1978. "Places for Hearing the Play": Pageant Stations at York, 1398–1572. *Records of Early English Drama Newsletter* 2: 10–33.

Tydeman, William. 1978. *The Theatre in the Middle Ages: Western European Stage Conditions, c. 800–1576.* Cambridge, England: Cambridge University Press.

———. 1994. Introduction to *The Cambridge Companion to Medieval English Theatre,* ed. Richard Beadle, 1–36. Cambridge, England: Cambridge University Press.

Tyndale, William. 1848a. *Epistle to the Reader; Subjoined to His First Published Version of the New Testament.* In *Doctrinal Treatises and Introductions to Different Portions of Holy Scriptures,* ed. Henry Walter, 389–91. Cambridge, England: Cambridge University Press.

———. 1848b. *The Obedience of a Christian Man.* In *Doctrinal Treatises and Introductions to Different Portions of Holy Scriptures,* ed. Henry Walter, 127–344. Cambridge, England: Cambridge University Press.

———. 1848c. *The Parable of the Wicked Mammon.* In *Doctrinal Treatises and Introductions to Different Portions of Holy Scriptures,* ed. Henry Walter, 29–126. Cambridge, England: Cambridge University Press.

———. 1848d. *A Pathway into the Holy Scripture.* In *Doctrinal Treatises and Introductions to Different Portions of Holy Scriptures,* ed. Henry Walter, 1–28. Cambridge, England: Cambridge University Press.

———. 1848e. *Preface That He Made Before the Five Books of Moses.* In *Doctrinal Treatises and Introductions to Different Portions of Holy Scriptures,* ed. Henry Walter, 392–97.

———. 1848f. *A Prologue into the Second Book of Moses, Called Exodus.* In *Doctrinal Treatises and Introductions to Different Portions of Holy Scriptures,* ed. Henry Walter, 411–18. Cambridge, England: Cambridge University Press.

Vasvari, Louise O. 1995. Joseph on the Margin: The Mérode Triptych and Medieval Spectacle. *Mediaevalia* 18: 163–89.

Velz, John W. 1968. Sovereignty in the Digby *Mary Magdalene. Comparative Drama:* 32–43.

Wager, Lewis. 1992. *The Life and Repentaunce of Marie Magdalene.* In *Reformation Biblical Drama in England: The Life and Repentaunce of Mary Magdalene; The History of Iacob and Esau,* ed. Paul Whitfield White, 1–66. New York: Garland.

Wager, William. 1967. *The Longer Thou Livest the More Fool Thou Art.* Edited with *Enough Is as Good as a Feast* by R. Mark Benbow, 4–78. Lincoln: University of Nebraska Press.

Warner, Marina. 1976. *Alone of All Her Sex: The Myth and the Cult of the Virgin Mary.* New York: Vintage Books.

Wasson, John. 1979. The Morality Play: Ancestor of Elizabethan Drama? *Comparative Drama* 13: 210–21.

———. 1986. The Secular Saint Plays of the Elizabethan Era. In *The Saint Play in Medieval Europe*, ed. Clifford Davidson, 241–60. Edam Monograph Series, Vol. 8. Kalamazoo, Mich.: Medieval Institute Publications.

Watt, Tessa. 1991. *Cheap Print and Popular Piety, 1550–1640.* Cambridge, England: Cambridge University Press.

Weatherby, E. H., ed. 1935. *Speculum Sacerdotale.* Early English Text Society, Original Series, Vol. 200.

White, Eileen. 1987. Places for Hearing the Corpus Christi Play in York. *Medieval English Theatre* 9: 23–63.

White, Paul Whitfield, ed. 1992. *Reformation Biblical Drama in England: The Life and Repentaunce of Mary Magdalene; The History of Iacob and Esau.* New York: Garland..

———. 1993. *Theatre and Reformation: Protestantism, Patronage, and Playing in Tudor England.* Cambridge, England: Cambridge University Press.

———. 1999. Reforming Mysteries' End: A New Look at Protestant Intervention in English Provincial Drama. *Journal of Medieval and Early Modern Studies* 29.1: 121–47.

Winstead, Karen. 1997. *Virgin Martyrs: Legends of Sainthood in Late Medieval England.* New York: Vintage Books.

Woolf, Rosemary. 1962. The Theme of Christ the Lover-Knight in Medieval English Literature. *Review of English Studies*, n.s., 13: 1–16.

———. 1972. *The English Mystery Plays.* Berkeley and Los Angeles: University of California Press.

Wright, A. R. 1938. *British Calendar Customs: England, Vol. 2: Fixed Festivals.* Edited by T. E. Lones. London: William Glaisher.

Young, Abigail Ann. 1984. Plays and Players: The Latin Terms for Performance. *Records of Early English Drama Newsletter* 9: 56–62.

Young, Karl. 1933. *The Drama of the Medieval Church.* Vol. 2. Oxford, England: Oxford University Press.

Zita, Charles. 1988. Hosts, Processions and Pilgrimage: Controlling the Sacred in Fifteenth-Century Germany. *Past and Presence* 118: 38–66.

Index

Sacred Players: The Politics of Response in the Middle English Religious Drama was designed and typeset in Dante by Kachergis Book Design of Pittsboro, North Carolina. It was printed on 60-pound Natures Natural and bound by Thomson-Shore of Dexter, Michigan.